A Telic Theory of Trust

A Telic Theory of Trust

J. ADAM CARTER

OXFORD
UNIVERSITY PRESS

Great Clarendon Street, Oxford, OX2 6DP,
United Kingdom

Oxford University Press is a department of the University of Oxford.
It furthers the University's objective of excellence in research, scholarship,
and education by publishing worldwide. Oxford is a registered trade mark of
Oxford University Press in the UK and in certain other countries

© J. Adam Carter 2024

The moral rights of the author have been asserted

All rights reserved. No part of this publication may be reproduced, stored in
a retrieval system, or transmitted, in any form or by any means, without the
prior permission in writing of Oxford University Press, or as expressly permitted
by law, by licence or under terms agreed with the appropriate reprographics
rights organization. Enquiries concerning reproduction outside the scope of the
above should be sent to the Rights Department, Oxford University Press, at the
address above

You must not circulate this work in any other form
and you must impose this same condition on any acquirer

Published in the United States of America by Oxford University Press
198 Madison Avenue, New York, NY 10016, United States of America

British Library Cataloguing in Publication Data
Data available

Library of Congress Control Number: 2023950106

ISBN 9780192888969

DOI: 10.1093/9780191982460.001.0001

Printed and bound by
CPI Group (UK) Ltd, Croydon, CR0 4YY

Links to third party websites are provided by Oxford in good faith and
for information only. Oxford disclaims any responsibility for the materials
contained in any third party website referenced in this work.

For my parents, Wendy and Joe Carter, who have always been there for me.

Contents

Preface ix
1. What Is Good Trusting? 1
2. Trust as Performance 22
3. Forbearance and Distrust 36
4. Trust, Pistology, and the Ethics of Cooperation 46
5. Deliberative Trust and Convictively Apt Trust 55
6. Trust, Risk, and Negligence 77
7. Trust, Vulnerability, and Monitoring 100
8. Therapeutic Trust 119
9. Trust and Trustworthiness 142
10. Conclusions and a Research Agenda 163

References 185
Index 201

Preface

This book uses a telic normative framework in order to explain a range of phenomena related to *trust*, including its nature and varieties, the evaluative norms that govern good trusting and distrusting (both implicit and deliberative), how trust relates to vulnerability, risk, and monitoring, as well as to trustworthiness and, more generally, to our practices of cooperation.

The overarching theory of trust is centred around a simple idea: that trusting is a kind of *performance*—viz., an aimed attempt of an agent, and that the norms that govern what count as good and bad trusting are performance-theoretic, telic norms. Chapter 1 motivates the need for this kind of proposal by showing why traditional views of trust (e.g., doxastic, non-doxastic, and conative accounts of trust) lack the resources to satisfactorily explain what *good trusting* consists in.

Chapter 2 lays out the key elements of the 'trust as performance' view by (i) explaining the sense in which trusting is a constitutively aimed performance; and then (ii) showing how we can fruitfully assimilate the evaluative norms of trusting to telic norms of success, competence, and aptness which are applicable to aimed attempts as such. The core framework developed in this chapter—which will be extended further and precisified as we go on—supplies us with a fresh lens to view traditional philosophical problems about trust, and also to explore entirely new avenues that will be taken up in subsequent chapters.

Chapter 3 distinguishes between two fundamental species of mature human trust—*implicit trust* and *deliberative trust*—and then shows that both varieties have their own performative analogues in the case of *distrust*—viz., implicit and deliberative *distrust*. As we'll see, key to the theory of distrust that is then developed in this chapter is the distinction between wide-scope and narrow-scope (i.e., aimed) forbearance from trusting, with reference to which evaluative norms of success, competence, and aptness are applicable to narrow-scope (but not wide-scope) distrust.

Chapter 4 takes as a starting point the distinction between implicit and deliberative trust (from Chapter 3) and asks: Under what conditions is one kind of species of trust more appropriate than the other, and what kinds of considerations determine this? In answering this question, a broader normative distinction is drawn—one that delineates the kind of (telic) normativity applicable to trusting and distrusting and shows how it contrasts with a broader normativity applicable to the ethics of cooperation. In framing this distinction, an analogy is drawn to how norms that apply to believing stand in relation to norms that govern which inquiries to take up.

Chapter 5 zeroes in on deliberative trusting, which involves on the trustor's part (intentionally) aiming not just at trusting *successfully* (which is the constitutive aim of *implicit* trust, viz., that the trustee take care of things as entrusted), but at trusting *aptly*. The deliberative trustor's attainment of this more demanding aim may then itself be (or fail to be) successful, competent, and apt; when it *is* apt, the resulting trust is then *convictively apt*, of the highest telic quality. This chapter explores, in detail, what is involved on the part of the trustor in the *apt attainment* of apt trust. An answer is developed in two parts, through (i) the development of a substantive view of first- and second-order trusting *competences*, as well as a structural theory of how (when deliberative trust is apt) first-order and second-order aptness are 'connected', which will be, on the view proposed, only when the former is appropriately *based* on the latter.

Chapter 6 turns to the question of what kinds of risks of *inaptness* to trust the convictively apt trustor can *non-negligently* ignore. An initial answer to this question is suggested in Ernest Sosa's (2021) work on telic normativity, an answer to our question that would be framed in terms of what Sosa calls 'background conditions'. While prima facie promising, such a strategy is shown to come up short. A very different answer is then motivated and developed, one for which the irreducibly normative notion of '*de minimis risk*' plays a central role. The conclusion that is ultimately reached and then defended is that the convictively apt trustor can't non-negligently ignore what are termed *cooperative-relative risks* to the inaptness of trust, except when these risks count as *de minimis* with reference to cooperation-sustaining rules.

Chapter 7 takes up two foundational questions in the philosophy of trust: (i) in what sense does trusting essentially involve subjecting oneself to risk of betrayal?; and (ii) in what sense is monitoring for risks of betrayal incompatible with trusting? These questions have traditionally been pursued independently from one another. It will be shown that they are much more closely connected than has been appreciated. The central objective will be to demonstrate how the telic-normative approach to theorizing about trust (and its theoretical cognates) developed so far can be used to answer both questions in a principled way, one that reveals a deep connection between not just the questions themselves, but also between the concepts of vulnerability, monitoring, and *de minimis risk*.

Chapter 8 shows how *therapeutic trust*—roughly: trust that aims at *trust-building*—fits into the picture developed so far. Therapeutic trust is a vexed topic in the philosophy of trust, not least due to the fact that, in cases of therapeutic trust, the trustor's attitude towards the trustee's reliability is characteristically much *less* optimistic than in standard non-therapeutic cases, with risk of betrayal typically but not always higher. Several strategies that philosophers of trust have appealed to in order to make sense of therapeutic trust and its relationship with ordinary non-therapeutic trust are considered and shown to be problematic. A new way of thinking about therapeutic trust is then developed, one that avoids the problems facing the other three views while at the same time offering its own additional advantages (especially that of explaining why therapeutic trust is *good* when it is). Key to the positive proposal is a recognition of two very different species of therapeutic trust: what I call *default* therapeutic trust and the more philosophically interesting *overriding* therapeutic trust. In the latter case, one's trusting constitutively aims not at mere successful trust, nor at the mere building of trust, but at building trust *through* successful trust.

Chapter 9 reorients our view of the relationship between trust and trustworthiness by locating both within a broader picture that captures largely overlooked symmetries on both the trustor's and trustee's side of a cooperative exchange. The view I defend here takes good cooperation as a theoretical starting point; on the theory proposed, cooperation between trustor and trustee is working well when achievements in trust and responding to trust are matched on both sides of the trust exchange. In a bit more detail, the trustor 'matches' her achievement in trusting (an achievement in fitting reliance to reciprocity) with the trustee's achievement in responding to trust (an achievement in fitting reciprocity to reliance). From this starting point, we can then appreciate *symmetrical* ways that the trustor and trustee can (respectively) fall short, by violating what are shown to be symmetrical evaluative norms—of success, competence, and aptness—that regulate the attempts made by both trustor and trustee. The overall picture is shown to have important advantages over the received way of theorizing about how trust stands to trustworthiness, and it clears the way—by identifying key questions that have been obscured—to making further progress.

Chapter 10 concludes by briefly summarizing the key contours of the telic theory of trust as it has been developed across Chapters 1–9; a short list of research topics and questions (both theoretical and applied) is then outlined as an agenda for further work.

The book is written largely from scratch, although some chapters are expansions of ideas developed in some recent articles. Material from Chapters 1–3 draws in various places from my paper 'Trust as Performance' (2022, *Philosophical Issues: A Supplement to Noûs*), and Chapter 2 in particular is based around some ideas that I first developed in 'On Behalf of a Bi-Level Account of Trust', *Philosophical Studies* (2020). The account of the relationship between trust, risk, and negligence advanced in Chapter 6 relies on my general theory of *de minimis risk* that first appeared in a paper principally about virtue epistemology, 'De Minimis Normativism: A New Theory of Full Aptness', *The Philosophical Quarterly* (2021). Chapter 8 builds on (with some modifications) ideas developed initially in 'Therapeutic Trust', *Philosophical Psychology* (2022) and, finally, Chapter 9 draws from 'Trust and Trustworthiness', *Philosophy and Phenomenological Research* (2023).

This book was written as part of the Leverhulme-funded 'A Virtue Epistemology of Trust' (RPG-2019-302) project, which is hosted by the University of Glasgow's COGITO Epistemology Research Centre, and I'm grateful to the Leverhulme Trust for supporting this research.

I also want to thank my wonderful collaborators on this project, Christoph Kelp, Mona Simion, Emma C. Gordon, Angela O'Sullivan, and Ísak Andri Ólafsson, as well as my other friends and colleagues at COGITO and in Philosophy at the University of Glasgow.

Extra-special thanks are to two people: Angie O'Sullivan and Emma Gordon. Angie has been a fantastic research assistant on the 'Virtue Epistemology of Trust' project, and she gave me detailed feedback on every chapter during what turned out to be an intense period of revisions in August and September 2023. I can't say enough how thankful I am to Angie's diligence and hard work during this critical time, which have improved the book.

I am also incredibly grateful to have such a wonderful and loving partner, Emma Gordon, who not only gave me excellent feedback on all chapters (including many late-night thought-provoking counterexamples—especially to my cases on therapeutic trust!), but also was unwaveringly patient and supportive of me throughout—for which I am thankful and really very lucky.

1
What Is Good Trusting?

A good knife is a sharp knife. In virtue of what is trust good, *as such*, when it is? Standard accounts of the nature of trust suggest that good trusting ought to be assimilated in some way to good believing, or to good affect, or to good conation. This chapter raises doubts for all three of these main answer types, and the criticisms given then set the scene for motivating (in Chapter 2) a new *performance-theoretic* approach to trust and its evaluative normativity, which has the resources to do better.

1. Introduction

Trust is indispensable to the success of almost every kind of coordinated human activity, from politics and business to sport and scientific research. It is accordingly important that we know how to do it *well*—and how to avoid doing it badly.

But the question of what it is to trust well is not easily separable from the question of what kind of thing trust is. And the matter of what kind of thing trust is—viz., whether it is a belief,[1] or some non-doxastic attitude or stance (of one kind or another, perhaps *affective*,[2] perhaps *conative*[3]) is divisive.[4] It is also, as Jon Kvanvig (2016) puts it, somewhat 'stupefying' (2016, 8) given that the various distinct things trust has been identified with are also very different from *each other*. In response to considering the menu of disparate options about the nature of trust in the literature, Bernd Lahno (2004) writes, 'any adequate theory of trust must include behavioral, cognitive and affective dimensions or aspects' (2004, 30) by contrast, and more pessimistically, Thomas W. Simpson (2012) suggests that 'There is a strong *prima*

---
[1] See, e.g., Hardin (2002), Hieronymi (2008), and McMyler (2011). For a more moderate doxastic account, see Keren (2014, 2020).
[2] Some notable examples here include Baier (1986) and Jones (1996).
[3] See Holton (1994).
[4] For a representative picture of this divisiveness, see, e.g., Carter and Simion (2020) and Faulkner and Simpson (2017).

facie case for supposing that there is no single phenomenon that "trust" refers to, nor that our folk concept has determinate rules of use' (2012, 551).

Unsurprisingly, given the disparity of opinion about the ontology of trust, what we find in the philosophy of trust are various incompatible (and starkly different) pictures of the *evaluative normativity* of trust—viz., of what the relevant standards are that good trusting, *as such*, should be expected to meet.[5]

Generally speaking, evaluative norms—unlike prescriptive norms, which prescribe conduct—regulate what it takes for a token of a particular type of thing to be good or bad with regard to its type, where the 'goodness' here is *attributive* in Geach's (1956) sense—viz., the sense in which a sharp knife is a good knife, qua knife, regardless of whether it is good or bad *simpliciter*. (Likewise, in this sense, a known belief is a good belief, regardless of whether it would be good or bad *simpliciter*—viz., as it would be were the content of the knowledge instructions for igniting a terrible bomb.[6])

Without a defensible picture of plausible evaluative norms for trusting, we're not well positioned to say when trusting is good or skilled *as an instance of trusting*; we would need—at least in our evaluative theorizing—to seek out conditions under which trust is good or bad *simpliciter*—e.g., by investigating, like we might with anything else, when it paradigmatically leads to good (and bad) consequences, and if so what they happen to be.[7] It should be no surprise that philosophers of trust have attempted to go further than this—i.e., further than exploring (e.g., as social psychologists have[8]) how trust might be good because, e.g., it enhances cooperation[9]— typically by first taking some kind of stand on the ontology of trust—a stance on what kind of thing it is—which is then used as a kind of 'blueprint' for thinking about good trusting *as such*.

According to *doxastic accounts of trust*, trust is essentially a kind of *belief*, a belief about the object of trust, e.g., that the trustee will take care of things

---

[5] For overviews, see Carter and Simion (2020, sec. 2), McLeod (2023, sec. 3); see also Faulkner (2010, 2014), Frost-Arnold (2014), Hieronymi (2008), and Hinchman (2020).

[6] For a helpful overview of the prescriptive/evaluative norm distinction, with reference to attributive as opposed to predicative goodness, see McHugh (2012, 22) and, as this distinction applies to belief specifically, Simion, Kelp, and Ghijsen (2016, 384–86).

[7] We would be in poor shape philosophically if we asked only how belief is good *simpliciter* and not what makes something good qua belief (then there would be very little epistemology!). The same goes for emotion; it is of philosophical importance what makes an emotion good or bad as such, not merely good or bad *simpliciter*.

[8] See, for example, Berg, Dickhaut, and McCabe (1995) and Braynov and Sandholm (2002). For a philosophical incorporation of trust's importance to decision-theoretic cooperative behaviour, see Faulkner (2011, Ch. 1).

[9] See Hardin (2002). Cf., Cook, Hardin, and Levi (2005, Ch. 1).

as entrusted.[10] Good trusting, on simple doxastic accounts of trust on which belief of a particular sort is necessary and sufficient for trust, will just *be* a kind of good believing; that is, it will be an instance of the very thing—*belief*—whose attributive goodness it is always appropriate to assess by looking at its rationality, asking whether it's true or known, whether it coheres with other justified beliefs, whether its production manifested epistemic virtues, etc.[11] Rationality, reliability, truth, coherence, knowledge, etc.,— paradigmatic evaluative norms of belief, as such—are (on these views) also norms that would regulate what counts as good trusting, in so far as trusting is believing.[12] Moreover, if trusting is a kind of believing, then what the proponent of the doxastic account of trust tells us counts as good trusting will need to reflect any constraints on beliefs *as such*, including that we cannot bring them about via direct control.

According to *non-doxastic accounts of trust*, it's false that trust is a kind of belief, even if trusting sometimes accompanies belief. And by extension, it is false that some type of good believing is what it is that the evaluative normativity of trust should be thought of as regulating. But here things complicate quickly. Some non-doxastic accounts of trust maintain that trust is essentially an affective attitude, or an emotion—some even hold that whatever affective attitude it is, it *must not* be accompanied with belief. Other non-doxastic accounts of trust maintain that trust is a non-doxastic, non-affective conative attitude—e.g., a kind of moral stance—and so neither a belief nor a non-doxastic affective state.

In light of the above, it looks very much like the task of getting a clear grip on what *good trusting* involves threatens to fall into disarray; after all, *the evaluative norms of belief bear little to no resemblance to the evaluative norms of, e.g., hoping, being optimistic, adopting moral stances, etc.*[13] But perhaps all is not as bad as it seems.

---

[10] For a recent and helpful overview of doxastic accounts of trust, see Keren (2020).

[11] These are just some representative evaluative norms of belief. For related discussion, including of prescriptive norms of belief, see Simion, Kelp, and Ghijsen (2016), Whiting (2013), Benton (2014), McHugh (2012), Shah and Velleman (2005), and Gibbons (2013). For criticism, see Glüer and Wikforss (2009) and Papineau (2013).

[12] As Karen Jones (1996, 2–5) captures this idea, what we say about the nature of trust, viz., whether it is a belief, constrains what we say about the rationality of trust, given that belief already has clearly defined standards of rationality. See also Keren (2014) for related discussion.

[13] Consider, for example, some fundamental disanalogies that will bear on what the respective evaluative norms will look like. There is a disanalogy between belief and emotions on the one hand, and the adoption of a moral stance, on the other, when it comes to voluntariness (e.g., Alston 1989). However, adopting a moral stance lines up with emotion and other affective attitudes when it comes to direction of fit (see, e.g., Humberstone 1992).

Here is the plan for what follows. §2 demonstrates several insuperable problems for accounts of the evaluative normativity of trust that fall out of doxastic accounts of the nature of trust. §3 shows that different problems arise for attempts to extract an account of good trusting by looking at the attributive goodness of various non-doxastic attitudes (both affective and conative) that have been identified with trust. These criticisms then set the scene for an approach in Chapter 2 that can do better.

2. Good Trusting as Good Believing: The Doxastic Account

So *is* trust a kind of belief? Let's sharpen this initial question in two ways; first, by bracketing two-place trust (i.e., X trusts Y) and focusing on *three-place-trust*: schematically (S trusts X to ϕ).[14] Second, for simplicity, let's consider just cases of *interpersonal* three-place trust, which have been a central focal point in the philosophy of trust, and which involve one person trusting another person to—in a broad sense—take care of something, ϕ, as entrusted,[15] and which further involves (unlike in cases of *mere* reliance) subjecting oneself to the possibility of betrayal.[16]

In the specific case of *testimonial trust*—of special interest in social epistemology—when a hearer forms a testimony-based belief on a speaker's say-so,[17] the something she trusts the speaker for is the truth, or perhaps knowledge,[18] of what she says. On a simple way of thinking of the relationship between testimonial trust and three-place interpersonal trust generally, the former is just an instance of the latter, an instance where 'the truth' is

---

[14] The distinction between two- and three-place trust was drawn initially by Horsburgh (1960). According to one popular way of thinking about relationship between two- and three-place trust, three-place trust is fundamental in the sense that two-place trust is explained in terms of it. For some representative examples of three-place fundamentalism, see, e.g., Baier (1986), Holton (1994), Jones (1996), Faulkner (2007), Hieronymi (2008), and Hawley (2014). Cf., Faulkner (2015).

[15] The locution 'as entrusted' is meant to encompass views on which the trustee counts as taking care of things as entrusted only if doing so in a particular way, including, e.g., out of goodwill (Baier 1986; Jones 1996) or in conjunction with a belief that one is so committed (e.g., Hawley 2014). The present proposal—which is theoretically neutral on this point—is compatible with opting for any such kind of gloss.

[16] As Annette Baier (1986) puts it, interpersonal trust involves subjecting oneself 'necessarily to the limits' of another's goodwill (1986, 235) and in a way that differs from the kind of reliance we place in mere objects. For related discussion, see McMyler (2011, 124).

[17] For an overview of what qualifies as a testimony-based belief, see, e.g., Graham (2016, 172–73).

[18] See, e.g., Kelp (2018) for a view friendly to this suggestion.

plugged in for ϕ in the schema, and where betraying the hearer's trust involves misinforming her.

With these caveats aside, let's now consider the *strong doxastic account* of three-place interpersonal trust (hereafter, trust) according to which trust is essentially a belief, viz., a belief that the trustee will take care of things as entrusted.[19]

This kind of proposal—variations of which have been defended by Russell Hardin (2002), Pamela Hieronymi (2008), and Benjamin McMyler (2011)—is strong because it takes believing something about the object of trust to be type-identical with trusting.[20] And there are some marks in its favour. For one thing, in paradigmatic cases of testimonial trust, the hearer trusts what the speaker says only if the hearer *believes* that the speaker has told the truth. And, more generally, as Hieronymi (2008) notes, if you entrust any kind of task to someone while believing they won't do the thing, it seems you're not *really* trusting them to do it.[21]

Unfortunately, regardless of whatever else we might say for or against a strong doxastic account of trust, there are serious problems for the idea that trusting *well* is principally a matter of believing well, viz., of holding rational, reliable,[22] true, coherent, etc., beliefs about the object of trust—and regardless of what features in the content of that belief (i.e., that the trustee

---

[19] Although the examples of interpersonal trust I use as illustrative throughout the book will typically involve trust placed between adult persons, this is just for simplicity in presentation; the positive view developed from Chapter 2 onwards is meant to be applicable to, e.g., trusting children. Note, though, that some special issues arise in Chapter 8, when we'll look specifically at *therapeutic trust* as illustrated by an adult trustor and (often, in my example cases) teenage children.

[20] I also consider, later in this section, a more sophisticated kind of doxastic account in this chapter due to Keren (2014; 2019).

[21] In support of this line of thought—viz., that one's trust tracks one's belief that the trustee will prove trustworthy—Hieronymi offers the following case-pair involving the betrayal of a secret. 'SECRETS: Consider two cases. In one, I fully believe you are trustworthy; in the other, I have doubts about your trustworthiness, but, for other reasons (perhaps to build trust in our relationship, perhaps because I think friends should trust one another, or perhaps simply because I have no better alternative), I decide to tell you my secret. Suppose that, in both cases, you spill the beans, and that you do so in the same circumstances, for the same reasons (2008, 230)'. According to Hieronymi, once we hold fixed both (i) the 'importance of the good entrusted'; and (ii) 'the wrongness of the violation,' then: '[...] it seems plausible that one's degree of vulnerability to betrayal tracks one's degree of trusting belief...further, this seems to be because, in the second case, there was less trust to betray (2008, 230-31)'. If the degree of one's trust is, as Hieronymi thinks, positively correlated with the degree of one's belief the trustee will prove trustworthy, then this counts in favour of the strong doxastic account, which would straightforwardly explain this correlation. See Chapter 6 for additional discussion of this case.

[22] Of course, a norm of reliability will be an example of an 'externalist' norm on good trusting just as reliability is a paradigmatically externalist norm on good believing, in that that in virtue of which one satisfies the norm needn't be reflectively accessible to the trustor. See McLeod (2002, 91–100) for discussion.

will encapsulate the trustor's interests,[23] or prove trustworthy out of goodwill,[24] etc.). To appreciate this point, consider that any belief, as such, is better than it would be otherwise if it complies with the paradigmatic evaluative epistemic norms of belief, e.g., norms that hold that beliefs ought to be supported by evidence and known.[25]

However, (a) complying with a standard evidence norm[26] (i.e., on which evidential support improves a belief's quality) fails to improve trust for the reason that there is a constitutive tension between trusting and complying with evidential norms; and (b) complying with the knowledge norm, specifically, undermines (or: moots) trust (rather than improves it) because it eliminates vulnerability.

On the first point, consider the following case due to Jeremy Wanderer and Leo Townsend (2013):

> PARANOID PARENT. A paranoid parent [...] organises a babysitter for their child, and then proceeds to spend the evening out monitoring their babysitter's antics remotely, via a 'nanny-cam'. The paranoid parent is not only a lousy date, but also a lousy trustor; in performing the seemingly rational act of broadening the evidential base relevant to her judgments of trustworthiness, she is, precisely, failing to trust the babysitter (2013, 1).

The kind of belief that the proponent of a strong doxastic account identifies with trusting is such that the paranoid parent improves its quality qua belief—by strengthening the evidence basis for the belief—only by *at the same time* doing something that apparently undermines her trust. As Wanderer and Townsend put it, cases like PARANOID PARENT indicate that part of 'what it is to trust' is to *refrain* from complying with evidence

---

[23] (Hardin 2002).   [24] (Jones 1996; Baier 1986).
[25] Because we are discussing evaluative rather than prescriptive norms here, the 'ought' should be read as a kind of 'ought to be' rather than an 'ought to do'—viz., in the sense that a good knife ought to be sharp. For some useful discussion of the difference here, see, along with McHugh (2012, 22) and Simion, Kelp, and Ghijsen (2016, 384–86) and Schroeder (2011, 5–8) for evaluative norms featuring 'ought' claims specifically.
[26] As Wanderer and Townsend (2013) put it, 'No matter how the norms of Evidentialism are construed, trust invariably seems to stand in tension with them' (2013, 7). See also Booth (2007). For a simple expression of an evaluative evidence norm on belief, take the following from Jonathan Adler (1999): 'One's believing that p is proper (i.e. in accord with the concept of belief) if and only if one's evidence establishes that p is true' (1999, 51). Alternatively, see Richard Feldman (2000): 'When adopting (or maintaining) an attitude towards a proposition, p, a person maximises epistemic value by adopting (or maintaining) a rational attitude towards p' (2000, 685).

norms on belief (2013, 2).[27] So, you can't by complying with such norms thereby trust *better*.[28]

Likewise, consider knowledge as a norm governing what counts as good belief—a position embraced by, e.g., 'knowledge-firsters'.[29] If the kind of belief that the proponent of a strong doxastic account identifies with trusting satisfies the knowledge norm, it arguably ceases *thereby* to qualify as trust. But this is not because of anything to do with trust's relationship to evidence. Rather, it is to do with a constitutive tension between trusting and *securing* an outcome. If you have—put roughly—some kind of 'guarantee' that it is impossible for X to betray your trust, then as the thought goes, you are thereby no longer trusting them to do anything.

This idea, viz., that trusting essentially involves subjecting oneself willingly to non-negligible vulnerability—at the very least, as Baier (1986, 244) notes, to the limits of another's goodwill, though also to the limits of her competence[30]—is mostly uncontroversial.[31] As Hardin (1992) summarizes:

---

[27] This idea is sometimes captured in terms of a prima facie incompatibility between trusting and monitoring. As Baier (1986) vividly expresses the idea, 'Trust is a fragile plant [...] which may not endure inspection of its roots, even when they were, before inspection, quite healthy' (1986, 260). Belief, by contrast, not only withstands but also *improves* through inspection of its roots.

[28] It's worth noting that, in cases like PARANOID PARENT, we needn't assume there is any epistemic norm that plausibly *obligates* the gathering of additional evidence (by the parent) in this case. For all I've said, epistemic norms are strictly norms of permission (though, cf., Simion (2023) and Ichikawa (2024) for recent work challenging this idea). As I take it, the example's efficacy against the doxastic account depends not on anything to do with *prescriptive* epistemic normativity but entirely with *evaluative* epistemic normativity. That is: the case relies on the parent's belief being such that it would increase in its quality qua belief by being supported by additional evidence supplied by the nanny cam, and this is so *even if* there is not a norm *prescribing* such additional evidence gathering that would include, e.g., monitoring the babysitter. Thanks to an anonymous referee at OUP for prompting further clarification here.

[29] See, e.g., Williamson (2013, 5). A typical way that this view is defended by knowledge-first philosophers involves two steps: first, there is a defence of the view that justification is the primary norm governing belief; and then, there is the further and crucial step that involves a defence of the thesis that a belief is justified if and only if it is known. See Williamson (2016) and Sutton (2007) for representative statements of this idea. For an overview, see Benton (2014).

[30] Perhaps also: to the trustee's capacity to remain in conditions conducive to her cooperation, even if we hold fixed *both* goodwill and competence. For example, you might entrust someone to repay a debt. They are capable and willing, but fail to repay the debt due to an unexpected natural catastrophe.

[31] For various expressions of this idea, see, along with Hardin (1992), e.g., Baier (1986, 244), McLeod (2023, sec. 1), Nickel and Vaesen (2012, 861–62), Carter (2020b, 2301, 2318–19), Carter and Simion (2020, sec. 1.a), Becker (1996, 45, 49), Dasgupta (1988, 67–68), Dormandy (2020, 241–42), Kirton (2020), O'Neil (2017, 70–72), Potter (2020, 244), and Hinchman (2017). Cf., Pettit (1995, 208).

As virtually all writers on the subject agree, trust involves giving discretion to another to affect one's interests. This move is inherently subject to the risk that the other will abuse the power of discretion (1992, 507).

But then if trust essentially involves rendering oneself vulnerable to betrayal (this is a point we'll delve into more deeply in Chapter 7), it is hard to see how—by coming to *know* that the trustee has taken care of things as entrusted—the trustor has improved any trust she might have had prior to acquiring this knowledge as opposed to having simply rendered her trust moot.

That said, here is another problem for the idea that we can—as the proponent of the strong doxastic account must permit—profitably defend an account of what it is to trust well that is constrained by facts about what it is to believe well. The reasoning behind this second problem, which concerns *voluntariness*, goes as follows. Belief is never subject to arbitrary voluntary control. And that means that norms of believing never regulate what it takes for something subject to arbitrary control to be good or bad with regard to belief. If trust is a species of belief, then norms of good believing are *always* applicable to trust. Some cases of trust are subject to arbitrary voluntary control. So, norms of belief sometimes do not regulate trust.

The idea that belief is not subject to arbitrary voluntary control is platitudinous, and is central to marking the difference between 'belief' and 'make belief'.[32] However, the idea that trust is, at least sometimes, subject to arbitrary voluntary control[33] is something we could give up only on pain of failing to countenance *therapeutic trust*—viz., where one trusts (e.g., a teenager with no established track record of reliability) with the intended aim

---

[32] For a classic defence of this position, see Williams (1970). See also Scott-Kakures (1994) and, for an overview, Vitz (2008). It is worth noting, as Heil (1983, 355–56) points out, that we often use language to talk about belief—such as duty-based language—that seems to imply a kind of voluntariness. Such language is found in Descartes—who seems in the *Fourth Meditation* to speak of belief through the will (see Cottingham 2002, 352–55) but it is also used widely by contemporary writers (e.g., BonJour 1980, 60–61) who say (in various ways) that affirmation about whether something is so without suitable 'inspection' of what one is affirming violates an epistemic duty, perhaps a duty to be epistemically responsible in one's belief formation (Kornblith 1983, 34–37). It is a mistake though to think that this kind of talk implicates the idea Williams challenges of having direct arbitrary control over belief (though, cf., Vitz 2010). One helpful way to see why is to consider how *judging* whether something is so is both an intentional action but not subject to arbitrary control. For a detailed discussion on this point, see Sosa (2021, 32, 105 n. 59) and Sosa (2017, 88–91).

[33] This is a point raised in work by Holton (1994).

of bringing about (or increasing) trustworthiness.[34] To the extent that therapeutic trust is voluntary in exactly the sense in which belief is not, as the worry goes, good believing does not provide us any kind of blueprint for good trusting.[35]

A third argument against the assimilation of good trusting to good believing focuses on cases of *trusting through doxastic suspension*. For example, suppose you see your friend holding a bloody knife, standing next to a body, after which you accuse your friend of the murder. Your friend, appreciating how overwhelming their guilt looks in light of the evidence, implores you to not rush to judgement until you hear the full story. They ask you to *trust them*—and wait until you hear the full explanation before drawing any conclusions whatsoever about what you've just seen.

Suppose you do then trust your friend. In doing so you are explicitly *not* forming a belief about whether they will prove trustworthy in this case, nor are you forming a belief that they will or will not betray your trust in any way. You trust through doxastic suspension, such that the suspension from belief *constitutes* your trusting. Belief, as a kind of affirming, categorically precludes suspension.[36] Thus, the trust you place in your friend here isn't something we could account for as good or bad trust in terms of norms governing belief, e.g., by asking if the belief counts as knowledge, or if it is rational.[37]

A recent and more sophisticated variation on the doxastic account is defended in work by Arnon Keren (2014; 2019), who holds that trusting

---

[34] The first notable discussion of therapeutic trust as a species of trust is due to Horsburgh (1960, 5, 7–8, 12). See also Jones (2004, 5–7) and Frost-Arnold (2014, 1960–3).

[35] Therapeutic trust cases (see Chapter 8) also raise another problem for strong doxastic accounts, which concerns the relationship between trust and expectation. As Peter Railton (2014) puts it, 'Belief that p is a degree of confidence [...] in a representation, p, that gives rise to and regulates a degree of expectation that things are or will be as p portrays them' (2014, 145). Therapeutic trust, however, often does not involve any such expectation. What this means then, in addition to the strong doxastic account being problematic in its own right, is that an account of good trusting can't be an account of something that *essentially* involves an expectation. Granted, some proponents of doxastic accounts have sidestepped entirely issues to do with therapeutic trust by biting the bullet (Hieronymi 2008) and simply denying that therapeutic trust is genuine trust. See, however, Frost-Arnold (2014) for criticism of this strategy.

[36] For discussion, see Turri (2012) and Carter (2018). For an extended treatment of forbearance, see Sosa (2021, Ch. 3).

[37] It is contentious in recent literature on epistemic partiality in friendship (e.g., Stroud 2006 and Goldberg 2019) whether suspending judgement in this case is not good epistemic practice. I want to emphasize that I'm not taking any stand on this point; the example here is simply meant to have the structure of good trust *in the absence of belief*, regardless of whether the absence of the belief consisting in one's suspension is justified or not.

someone with something requires belief that they will come through, but that this belief (when one trusts) *pre-empts* (i.e., obviates the need for) any other evidence about whether she will come through.[38] So, for example, if you trust someone to pick you up from the airport, you'll decline to bring cash for a bus ticket, etc., but also, since the belief you have that they'll come through pre-empts any other evidence, you don't look out for defeaters, additional confirmation, etc. Notice that, at least if epistemic norms on *belief* permit such evidential pre-emption, thinking about trust along Keren's lines seems to have better resources than standard doxastic accounts do for ruling out cases like PARANOID PARENT as cases of good trusting; after all, the seeking out of additional information via monitoring (as takes place) seems incompatible with genuine trusting (much less good trusting), as well as with pre-emptive believing, even though not with more standard believing.

So might good trusting then be a matter of good *pre-emptive believing* in the sense Keren identifies with trusting? It should be granted at the outset that there are cases where a belief looks like it becomes better qua belief on account of having (or acquiring) the property of being pre-emptive. For example, suppose Stephen Hawking tells me a true proposition 'p' about black holes, and I believe 'p'. By the lights of reliability, rationality, truth, and knowledge norms etc. is my belief going to get better or worse if (after getting testimony from Hawking) I check with my (non-theoretical physics) friends whether they also think 'p'? Here (and likewise in cases of expert testimony) it seems plausible my belief will be better by being a pre-emptive belief than otherwise. But, importantly, it's not clear how we'd get from here to the idea that trusting well lines up with *pre-emptively believing well*. Consider that either the evaluative normativity of pre-emptive believing should be understood as reducing to the evaluative normativity of believing (more generally) or not. If so, then objections to the more standard doxastic accounts (which are committed to assimilating good trusting to good believing) apply. If not, which I think is the more faithful interpretation of Keren's view, then the evaluative normativity of *pre-emptive believing* will presumably track not the reliability or rationality of the pre-emptive belief, but rather, it will track, specifically, how well one's belief *pre-empts* other evidence. *That* (rather than whether a belief is rational, reliable, etc.) will be what matters for whether a *pre-emptive belief* is a good instance of *its* kind.[39] However, and here's the problem, one could be an excellent 'pre-empter'

---

[38] For a related pre-emptive approach to epistemic normativity, see Zagzebski (2012).
[39] For example, one might take every precaution to acquire and weigh evidence that would bear on the target belief.

when believing the trustee will prove trustworthy (she screens off relevant evidence and pre-empts unimpeachably), while nonetheless *not trusting well* on account of, e.g., trusting recklessly. In sum, the 'pre-emption quality' metrics of a belief (e.g., did the believer really screen off or bracket other relevant evidence?) track features of a belief that are compatible with the belief taking on too much risk of betrayal to qualify as an instance of good trusting.

It's looking like trusting well simply doesn't line up very well with believing well. Would it be of any use to weaken the account—such that trusting well might be understood as a function of satisfying *at least* (some) norm of belief along with perhaps some other norms? An initial hurdle, of course, is that we've already seen that there are reasons to think good belief (or any kind of belief for that matter) may not be necessary for trusting, well or otherwise. But, even if those problems could be overcome, we'd need to know exactly what those other norms are. After all, the good cracking of an egg, even if necessary for a good cake, provides us little clue for what the standard is for a good cake.[40] Let's now look at some non-doxastic norms, norms on trust whose motivation is sourced in very different, *non-doxastic* approaches to the ontology of trust.[41]

3. Alternative Norms on Good Trusting: Non-Doxastic Accounts

3.1 Good Trusting as Good Affect

Non-doxastic accounts of the nature of trust embrace a negative and a positive thesis. The negative thesis, common to all non-doxastic accounts, is just the

---

[40] Granted, if belief is necessary for trust, then we will know that when a norm on good believing is not complied with when one trusts, then the quality of that trust is to that extent defective. This is information about the evaluative normativity of trust, but it is not a useful guide to what good trusting involves, unless we know *in addition* what other norms, beyond norms of belief, would need to be complied with to trust well.

[41] Might it be worth one final push for the line that norms of good trusting are doxastic norms—by pointing out that (i) trusting testimony is a paradigmatic form of trust; and (ii) that trusting testimony is something you do if and only if you actually uptake what the speaker says? The answer here is 'no'. The reason is that it might just be that testimonial trust incidentally involves belief because of what testimony demands but that such belief isn't essential to trust *as such*. Compare: trusting someone with a secret involves sharing the secret with them; but trust doesn't essentially involve anything like this. We should thus be wary about generalizing norms of trust, as such, from the testimonial case where believing the word of another is the standard shape that trusting takes.

denial of the claim that belief (i.e., that the trustee will prove trustworthy) is central to trust of the three-place interpersonal variety.

What distinguish non-doxastic accounts from each other are the positive theses they maintain about the nature of trust. Perhaps the most common non-doxastic proposal-type maintains that trust is, rather than a belief, an *affective attitude*.[42]

On Karen Jones's (1996) influential account, that affective attitude is *optimism* 'that the goodwill and competence of another will extend to cover the domain of our interaction with her' (1996, 4).[43] For Lawrence Becker (1996), the relevant affective attitude is, instead, 'a sense of security about other people's benevolence, conscientiousness, and reciprocity' (1996, 43). For Victoria McGeer (2008), it is a kind of 'hope'; for Guido Möllering (2001), it is a 'leap of faith'.

Despite their (in some cases, subtle) differences, each of these affective attitude accounts of trust implies that any standard for good trust—a standard often captured by our talk of 'justified trust'—will take a different shape from the standards we expect good or justified *belief* to meet. According to McGeer (2008):

> The question of whether our trust can be justified, then, becomes a question of *whether certain feelings towards others can be justified*, which is not to say they can't be, but rather that their justification conditions are different from, and perhaps not as stringent as, those on belief or on belief-based predictions of reliability (2008, 241, my italics).

Likewise, as Jones (1996) puts it:

> we can be justified in trusting even when we would not be justified in predicting a favourable action on the part of the one trusted. Our evidence for trusting need not be as great as the evidence required for a corresponding justified prediction. In this respect trusting is *more like hoping than like predicting* (1996, 15, my italics).

---

[42] For some representative defences of this kind of view, see de Sousa (1987), Calhoun (1984), Rorty (1980), and Lahno (2001).

[43] Jones clarifies that this kind of optimism she takes to be central to trust needn't involve any tendency to—as optimism is often taken to imply one would do—'look on the bright side', given that, in the context of a very difficult joint task, you could trust someone, through your optimism directed at their goodwill, without any optimism about the success of the task (Jones 1996, 6).

Let's think now about the plausibility of the thesis that trusting well is a matter of good affect by examining whether trusting well might be a matter of *hoping* well. There is at least some initial intuitive pull behind this idea. Just consider the structural similarities between the conditions under which the *opportunity* to both trust someone and hope for something arise. These are, in short, conditions of limited agency in conjunction with some desire for an intended outcome. Here's McGeer (2004) on conditions for hoping, specifically:

> Hope arises in situations where we understand our own agency to be limited with respect to the things or conditions that we desire [...] If our own agencies were not so limited, we would not hope for what we desire; we would simply plan or act so as to achieve it. Hope signifies our recognition that what we desire is beyond our current (or sole) capacity to bring about (2004, 103).[44]

Trust arises in broadly similar situations, e.g., situations when we want some result through cooperation, but our own agency isn't sufficient for guaranteeing that outcome, and we recognize this insufficiency, and thus the need for reliance. Perhaps, as the thought might go, such similarities in hoping and trusting conditions should lead us to expect that good trusting is just a kind or species of good hoping, in that it is (like hoping well) fundamentally a matter of doing well by way of navigating limited agency in the pursuit of our goals.[45]

As it turns out, there are problems for the above kind of assimilation of good trusting to good hoping. And the reasons why this is so, we'll see, turn out to plausibly generalize to other positively valenced affective attitudes about others' actions and intentions—including (along with hope) optimism and a sense of security (about those actions and intentions).

First, consider cases of *hoping against the odds* for some outcome O, when one's agency is limited, and where 'the odds' is to be understood as the likelihood that O will come about. Some cases of hoping for an outcome are clearly *not* against the odds—e.g., suppose a student has applied for an international student visa, fills out the many complicated forms properly,

---

[44] See also Shade (2000) for a similar view about the relationship between hoping and having limited agency.
[45] I set aside here questions about whether hope is *ever* worth taking up (see, e.g., Bovens 1999) for a negative line here.

waits and hopes it is approved. If she gets what she's hoped for here, she's not hoped against the odds, *despite* there being some chance in play (e.g., there could be a glitch in the system, or an unsympathetic visa administrator, or other kinds of bad luck, etc.). Let's now set these cases aside, and think about cases where one hopes (even significantly) *against* the odds: these will be different from the above case; they will be cases where, given the extent to which the obtaining of the successful outcome would be down to luck, one's actional contribution to bringing that outcome about would (clearly) fail to qualify as intentional. It is debatable just 'how much' luck acting intentionally requires,[46] but for simplicity, let's give an easy case: suppose you play the lottery (a large lottery), hope to win, and (by fluke luck) win. The level of risk of failure in succeeding in what you intended to do here was extremely high: but it's hardly the case that the hope here is *defective* (as a case of hope) when you hope to win. Compare: suppose one played the lottery and *did not* hope to win: the omission of hope here would if anything seem comparatively more defective than playing the lottery (even a large one) and positively hoping to win. And this point is compatible with assuming one at the same time does not believe (indeed, even strongly disbelieves) they'll get what they hope for. Your 'hoping' isn't cheapened when you've bought a ticket on a wing and a prayer.

The moral of lottery-style cases, and the seeming appropriateness or fittingness of hoping here, is this: when we shift from hoping 'with the odds' to hoping 'against the odds' it's really not at all clear that we should expect a corresponding downgrade in the quality of hope as such—viz., that our hope would become worse qua hope when we transition from the visa application case to the lottery case. However, and here is the important disanalogy, *there is* an important sense in which the transition from trusting with the odds to trusting against the odds is something we can expect will mark a downgrade in quality.[47] For example, there is a clear downgrade in quality from trusting a doctor for medical information to trusting a known crank.

Here is one explanation for this disanalogy. Although there is a sense in which both hoping and trusting essentially involve subjecting oneself to risk

---

[46] Some notable views, following in a tradition due to Anscombe (1963), hold that acting intentionally is luck-precluding in that it requires *knowledge* that one is doing what they are doing (intentionally). Other versions of knowledge conditions on intentional action are defended by, e.g., Pavese (2022) and Beddor and Pavese (2022). For some more relaxed approaches to actional control meant to be suitably luck precluding, see, e.g., Shepherd and Carter (2023), Carter and Shepherd (2023), and Carter and Kearl (2023).

[47] This, at least, is what we should expect in paradigmatic cases of three-place interpersonal trust that are non-therapeutic. Therapeutic trust cases are more complicated and discussed in Chapter 8.

in a broad sense (in the case of interpersonal trust, risk of betrayal, in the case of hoping, that what is hoped for doesn't come about), we take good trusting to be incompatible with 'poorly navigating' these risks implied by trusting[48] (e.g., as trusting a quack for medical advice is illustrative of this point), where—in contrast—we relax *significantly* in the case of hope any expectation at all that hoping well involves our having 'navigated well' the risk that the particular thing hoped for doesn't come about. The lottery case is illustrative of this point.

In sum, then, reflection on the contrast between hoping against the odds and trusting against the odds reveals an important disanalogy between hoping well and trusting well, and this disanalogy is grounds for some scepticism that good trusting is a kind of good hoping.

It's worth considering one line of rejoinder. Perhaps the previous discussion has overlooked an important element of the value of good hoping, and that this further element is one shared with good trusting. It's worth considering the following passage from McGeer (2004) concerning the relationship between hoping well and being reflectively creative and determined:

> It is often remarked that those who hope well become even more determined when obstacles are put in their way: they adapt more easily to real world constraints without sacrificing their creative energy; they explore more pathways toward reaching their goals; and they often discover reserves of untapped power in the process. In explanation of this, I want to suggest that hope is the energy and direction we are able to give, not just toward making the world as we want it to be but also toward the regulation and development of our own agency. In hoping, we create a kind of imaginative scaffolding that calls for the creative exercise of our capacities and so, often, for their development. To hope well is thus to do more than focus on hoped-for ends; it is crucial to take a reflective and developmental stance toward our own capacities as agents—hence, it is to experience ourselves as agents of potential as well as agents in fact (2004, 105).

I don't object to any of this.[49] Let's grant the point that good hoping involves a kind of resilient attitude in the face of obstacles, becoming

---

[48] For discussion on this point, see Carter (2020b) and Coleman (1990).
[49] And, first, I take it that granting the above positive remarks is compatible with the previous remarks that suggest non-defective hoping can line up with hoping (significantly) against the odds. Note, however, that if McGeer is right about this, then this gives us some reason to resist a notable dominance-theoretic argument against the value of *ever* hoping (period) which has been advanced by Bovens (1999). Here is a summary of that argument. Just suppose that,

(through reflection) more adaptable and creative in our stance 'towards our own capacities'. As I read McGeer above, I imagine a case where one is stranded and hoping someone will come along and help. Hoping well, as she sees it, is more than just 'focusing' on the hoped-for end, but, say, being creative in thinking about ways one might try to flag down help. The person hoping for help might (e.g., perhaps by undergoing various kinds of imaginative rehearsal[50]) simulate ways of effectively shouting, waving, making a sign, etc. And, as I think McGeer observes correctly, taking this 'reflective and developmental stance toward our own capacities as agents' is more befitting of hoping well than merely, say, focusing even harder on the desired outcome's obtaining (e.g., fantasizing about a car coming by to save you).

That said, these very kinds of reflections on our agency not *only* don't obviously improve the quality of trust, but they are in some important respects (which we'll explore later in this book) antithetical to it. Consider again PARANOID PARENT from Section 2. Let's run a twist on that case. Suppose you *actually trust* the babysitter, and so are not simply monitoring their every movement through the nanny cam—where such monitoring would be incompatible with genuinely trusting.[51] Now, add to the case that, on your evening out, you don't ever actually look at the nanny cam, but you spend most of your time creatively reflecting on ways you *could* exercise your agency to get a peek at it, and you fantasize about how you could speed home immediately to try to catch the nanny in a possible act of babysitting betrayal (e.g., sleeping). Such creative reflections on our own agency don't

---

for some projected state of the world σ you have a choice between (i) hoping for it or (ii) not hoping for it. The projected state σ will either come about or it will not. If it does not come about, then you would have been worse off having hoped than not having hoped, given that you will then be left with a greater sense of frustration after hoping than after not hoping. But suppose that σ does come about. Are you thereby better off having hoped? Bovens thinks not: '[...] is there anything to be gained from having hoped for it? In hoping for something, I tend to fill in the contours in the brightest colors. Suppose that my hopes come true, but not precisely in the bright colors that I had pictured. Had I not hoped for anything, I would have been delighted. But having hoped as I have, I experience a sense of frustration rather than satisfaction' (1999, 670). But then the idea is that, whether the state of the world does or does not come about, I am always better off not having hoped for it rather than having hoped for it. Hence, by dominance, I should not hope. That is, at any rate, the reasoning which (in previous work—e.g., Carter 2022, and in an early draft of this manuscript) I had raised mostly uncritically in connection with thinking about the evaluative normativity of hoping (in connection with trusting). I now take it, including after helpful comments from a referee at OUP, that McGeer's point (in the quoted passage from her 2004, 105) suggests a value in hoping that isn't captured by Bovens's dominance reasoning.

[50] For some helpful discussion on how such imaginative rehearsal, or mental simulation, can be effective, see Aronowitz, and Lombrozo (2020).

[51] This assumption is one we'll explore in detail in Chapter 7.

obviously, in any way, *improve* the quality of trusting, or are reflective of good trusting, in the way such reflections on agency (and corresponding imaginative rehearsal/simulation) might stand to improve (as per McGeer) hoping, or be reflective of good hoping. Even more, there is—again as we'll think about in more detail later in Chapter 7—some cause to question whether, after significant enough focus and time reflecting on how your agency could intervene, you might *cease* to be trusting at all.

We've seen now two reasons to be sceptical that good trusting is a kind of good hoping, illustrated by (i) cases of trusting vs hoping against the odds, and (ii) by cases where what seems (by way of reflecting creatively on our agential powers) to be expressive of good hoping isn't reflective (or even obviously, in extreme cases, compatible with) good trusting. And note the general lines of thinking in (i) and (ii) look applicable to other kinds of positive affect distinct from hope. Take mere optimism. Non-criticizable optimism seems (per i) risk-tolerant (e.g., take cases of remaining optimistic against the odds) in ways that good trusting isn't; or, put another way: we shouldn't expect that a shift from optimism 'with the odds' to optimism 'against the odds' is going to track any downgrade in the quality of one's taking an optimistic attitude (much as was the case with hope, but *not* with trust). Regarding (ii): it is plausible that (as per McGeer) creative reflections on our own agency (e.g., for the sort described in the passage above from her 2004, p. 105) might improve the quality of optimism for reasons that are similar to how doing so would improve the quality of hoping, but as we've seen, not the quality of trust.[52]

In sum, the evaluative normativity of trusting simply does not line up with the evaluative normativity of paradigmatic kinds of positively valenced

---

[52] Note that, as an aside, there is also some reason to think that tendencies to hope might over time make us *worse* at the sort of risk assessment good trusting plausibly demands of us. This is for two reasons, which are related. First, and as Bovens notes, the very act of hoping for something inclines us to a predictable error in reasoning, which is to 'overestimate the subjective probability that the [hoped for] state of the world will come about' (1999, 680). A well-studied way in social psychology in which this kind of overestimation occurs is via the mechanisms of the availability heuristic. But perhaps even worse, rationally speaking, is that hoping for an outcome has been demonstrated to encourage—as McGeer puts it—'superstitious ideas of our own agential powers' such that we are led, via hoping, to overestimate the sense in which our hoping *itself* raises the likelihood that the hoped for event will come about—and this is *two* rational mistakes bundled into one. That hoping is, psychologically, a kind of invitation to misperceive the causal efficacy of our own agency (in connection with the hoped-for event) is a common view in the psychology of hope (e.g., Charles R. Snyder et al. 1991) and it reveals an important way in which hoping of any sort stands to throw a spanner in our capacities for risk assessment (*vis-à-vis* the hoped-for event) that good trusting can't plausibly afford for us to compromise.

affect (e.g., hope, optimism) of the sort that trust has variously been identified in the literature.

3.2 Good Trusting as Good Conation

The standards that regulate what counts as good trusting must be other than those that regulate good belief *or* good affect. What about good *conation*—viz., goodness with respect to some motivational state or states that one has?[53]

Within the category of non-doxastic accounts of the nature of trust, affect-based theories like Jones's are but one type of proposal. A different albeit prominent non-doxastic account is the 'participant stance' account, due to Richard Holton (1994), and which takes trust not to consist in the manifesting of any affective attitude, per se, but rather in a kind of 'normatively laden stance' that implies a readiness to react in certain fitting ways to the trustee's e.g., betrayal or cooperation;[54] as Holton puts it:

> [...] you have a readiness to feel betrayal should it be disappointed, and gratitude should it be upheld (1994, 67).

Is trusting perhaps a matter of doing *this* in a good way—viz., is it a matter of good readiness to feel (certain kinds of) reactive attitudes? We can envision at least two dimensions of conative quality here. One dimension concerns *how* ready one is to feel betrayal if trust is disappointed, gratitude should it be upheld. Along this dimension, presumably, the readier, the better. A separate dimension of quality concerns not the extent of the readiness, but *what* one is ready to feel. Here, the gold standard would seem to be a matter of *fittingness*: what one is ready to feel is betrayal (rather than something else) if and only if trust is betrayed; gratitude[55] (rather than something else) if and only if trust is upheld.

---

[53] For relevant discussion on conative states and (some representative views about) how they are taken to be motivating, see, e.g., Rosati (2016, sec. 3), Björklund et al. (2012), and Mele (2003).

[54] A recent participant stance view that is difficult to taxonomize straightforwardly is due to Berislav Marušić (2017) and which is strictly a kind of doxastic account, though one that incorporates elements of a participant-stance account, in the sense that the account maintains that trust is a belief held from the participant stance. From the perspective of assessing what it is to trust well, this kind of doxastic participant stance proposal will be committed to the position that norms of good trusting must incorporate norms of good believing. However, as I argued in Section 2, this commitment turns out to be problematic.

[55] Or, perhaps, some similar kind of positive affect, like 'relief' or 'affirmation'.

Bearing in mind these two dimensions of conative quality implied by the participant stance view—in short, 'readiness quality' and 'fittingness quality'—consider now the following case:

THREE EASY MARKS: X, Y, and Z share a common flaw: deep-seated naivety. Too easily and often, each trusts unreliable websites, used car dealers, and people peddling get-rich-quick schemes. For simplicity, suppose all three are betrayed 90% of the time when they trust, and that they trust to the exact same extent—viz., none distrusts more than any other. But each trusts differently with reference to the two key quality dimensions of trusting that are implied by the participant stance view. X is consistently ready, when X trusts, to feel disappointment at perceived betrayal and gratitude at perceived trustee cooperation; however, X's perceptions are not well calibrated with reality. X too often misjudges when the trustee has in fact betrayed versus cooperated; consequently, X too often, though very readily, fits disappointment with cooperation, gratitude with betrayal. Put simply: X scores high in 'readiness quality', poor in 'fittingness quality'. Y is in the opposite position. Y's perceptions (of betrayal and cooperation) are, unlike X's, well calibrated with reality; but Y is *inconsistently ready*, whenever Y trusts, to actually feel disappointment at betrayal when Y (accurately) perceives it and gratitude at cooperation when Y (accurately) perceives it. Put simply: Y scores high in fittingness quality, but low in readiness quality. Z shares, *ex hypothesi*, the common flaw of naivety with X and Y; however, Z scores as high as X in readiness quality and as high in Y in fittingness quality.

Here are two observations about the THREE EASY MARKS case. First, all three are—in an obvious sense—bad trusters! All three, we are assuming, trust in ways that lead to betrayal more often than not.[56] This, crucially, includes Z, whose overall conative score is impeccable—that is, Z does great, and clearly better than either X or Y, by those combined metrics that would seem to matter for good trusting on the participant stance view—viz., readiness to feel certain fitting attitudes in response to betrayal and cooperation on the part of the trustee.

---

[56] Note that we are assuming the social-epistemic environment for trust here is a normal one and so is not unusually epistemically hostile. What best explains their poor reliability is thus not going to be any abnormal features of their environment.

The proponent of the participant stance view has a few moves available in reply, but none looks very promising. One move is to simply bite the bullet and say that Z represents good trusting in virtue of the dimensions of trusting quality that distinguish Z favourably from X and Y. This move, though, looks like a non-starter, given what we've already stipulated about Z's betrayal ratio. A more sophisticated move would be to insist that Z's goodness as a trustor as represented by Z's admirable readiness to feel certain appropriate attitudes to the trustee, given different ways the trustee might behave, distinguishes some important dimensions of good trusting, even if good conation doesn't capture all good ways in which one might trust.

I think we should regard this more sophisticated reply with some suspicion, however. The reason why can be put in terms of an additional *ex ante* desideratum we should expect any account of good trusting to satisfy: namely, that an explanation of what makes for good trusting can't be orthogonal to the value of a trust's being successful—i.e., the trustee's taking care of things as entrusted.

Here a brief analogy to epistemic norms will be of use. Evaluative norms of belief are obviously *not* orthogonal to successful belief—viz., true belief and knowledge. Consider, for example, the evaluative epistemic norms that aim to capture *justified belief*—e.g., these norms tell us that justified beliefs are 'reliably produced' beliefs, 'beliefs that fit the evidence', etc. Both of these are, as Sanford Goldberg (2015) notes, 'standards of success in connection with our pursuit of truth (and avoidance of error)', or perhaps in connection with our pursuit of knowledge (and avoidance of ignorance).[57] Put differently: it is because in believing we aim at truth and knowledge that the evaluative norms of belief capture (in different ways) standards of success in connection with *these* rather than some other aims. The norms are not orthogonal to, but rather importantly constrained by, what counts as successful attainment of the aim of the kind of attempt one makes by believing.

But, as THREE EASY MARKS illustrates, the norms of good conation—of which the norms of good trusting will be a proper subset on the participant stance view—are *entirely* orthogonal to successful trusting; this is because the satisfaction of conative norms (i.e., readiness to feel certain attitudes in response to trusting outcomes) floats entirely freely of the aim, in trusting, that the trustee take care of things as entrusted. 'Z' in our example case illustrates this, maximally satisfying conative norms while

---

[57] For a recent function-driven defence of this view, see Simion (2019).

trusting in ways that rarely ever result in the attainment of the aim Z makes an attempt at attaining in trusting.

4. Concluding Remarks

This chapter took as a starting point a question that an account of trust ought to be able to answer: what is *good* trusting? At the very least, what we say about the nature of trust ought to be compatible with a plausible view of the evaluative normativity of trust.

What we've seen, however, is that getting this right is easier said than done. If the leading contenders on offer are right, then we should expect good trusting to be principally a matter of good believing (e.g., Hieronymi 2008; McMyler 2011), or good affect (e.g., Jones 1996; Baier 1986), or good conation (e.g., Holton 1994). What this chapter has attempted to show is that good trusting doesn't plausibly line up with any of these things.

Rather than to simply try to select and then make do with the lesser of the known evils, I will—in the next chapter—suggest a different way forward, one that involves the identification of trust as a *performative kind*. As we will see, if we think of trust as a performative kind, we avoid the problems that face accounts of the evaluative normativity of trust that are restricted to theorizing about good trusting as a species of good believing, good hoping, good emoting, good conation, etc. And this is the case even if trust sometimes or even usually involves combinations of these attitudes (both doxastic as well as non-doxastic) or stances.

2
Trust as Performance

It is argued that the evaluative normativity of trust is a special case of the evaluative normativity of aimed performances generally. The view is shown to have advantages over competitor views.

1. Introduction

As we saw in Chapter 1, good trusting is not something we can capture in terms of good believing, good affect, or good conation. So where do we go from here?

Attempting to salvage any of these views, with some special pleading, does not look especially promising. Neither does opting for some kind of disjunctive (or conjunctive) proposal. But the good news is that we needn't resort to such strategies. This is because there is a simple view that gets us everything we could want—and more—out of a view of the evaluative normativity of trust, and with none of the baggage that comes with any of the other views.

Here is the key thesis I will defend and further develop in what follows:[1]

(†) Trusting is a performance—viz., an aimed attempt of an agent; the evaluative normativity of trust is a special case of the evaluative normativity of performances generally.

Several key ideas here need some unpacking. In this chapter, I will:

- briefly outline the normative structure of performances, construed as *aimed attempts*, giving special attention to the three central evaluative

---

[1] This chapter expands significantly on §4 of Carter (2022), 'Trust as Performance', *Philosophical Issues*, 32 (1), 120–47; the initial ideas in §3 of this chapter were first developed as part of Carter (2020b), 'On Behalf of a Bi-Level Account of Trust', *Philosophical Studies*, 177 (8), 2299–322.

norms that apply to any performance type: *success, competence,* and *aptness*;
- characterize the three central evaluative norms that apply to trusting: *successful trust, competent trust,* and *apt trust*;
- show how the key thesis (†) satisfies key desiderata on any account of good trusting which other proposals canvased in Chapter 1 (i.e., good trusting as good believing, good affect, good conation) failed to meet.

Let's take these in turn.

2. Telic Normativity

A certain kind of normativity—*telic normativity*—is applicable to *all* performances—viz., aimed attempts of agents.[2] A theory of telic normativity explains what makes performances better or worse in connection with those aims. A simple example, familiar from virtue epistemology, is that of the archer's performance of shooting an arrow at a target. This performance is an attempt with an aim (hitting the target) constitutive of that attempt-type, and an idea we'll begin exploring is that *trusting* someone with something is like this as well. That is, we'll explore the idea that what makes archery shots (and other aimed attempts) good instances of the kinds of things they are are *structural features of these attempts* that, when shared by trust, are features that can help us account in a principled way for good (and bad) trust quality along several theoretically distinct and important dimensions.

But before getting knee-deep in the *telic normativity framework* (and in archery talk often used to illustrate it), I want to address what, for some readers, might look like a point of puzzlement. On the one hand, some readers will be (perhaps all too!) familiar with archery analogies precisely *because* these examples are often used as an illustrative way of understanding what makes beliefs count as justified and known in *virtue epistemology*—e.g., especially the spirit of Ernest Sosa's work. On Sosa's

---

[2] The key ideas of telic normativity originated from Ernest Sosa's (2005) John Locke lectures, which were later published as *A Virtue Epistemology* (2007, 2009) and refined in Sosa (2015) and, in more recent work, redescribed as *telic normativity* (previously: *performance normativity*) in Sosa (2021). For overviews of recent work on performance normativity, see Kelp (2020) and Fernández Vargas (2016). For critiques and developments of performance normativity, see, e.g., Chrisman (2012), Kelp et al. (2017), and Carter (2021a).

view, beliefs are aimed performances like archery shots, and 'knowledge' is reserved for those (doxastic) shots that hit their target (truth)[3] through competence or intellectual virtue.

But haven't we just (in the previous chapter) argued *against* the idea that good trusting is a kind of good *believing*? So: why are we headed in this direction at all—a direction that seems tailor-made for application to *beliefs*?

The fact is that the *general* telic normativity framework, which has been given its most notable development in virtue epistemology, has applicability *well beyond epistemology*. The general theory, after all, is not a theory about belief norms per se, but a theory that specifies a suite of evaluative norms that are meant to apply to any kind of aimed attempt. The fact that the framework has got results in epistemology is a reason to see what it can do elsewhere.

To take just one example,[4] Mona Simion (2021) has recently attempted to apply the general telic normativity framework to *blame*: for Simion, *blaming* is like firing an archery shot—and the normativity of the former a special case of the normativity of performances, of which the latter is also a case. This view does *not* require, for Simion, any commitment to thinking that blaming is a kind of believing, *nor* for that matter that *beliefs* are like archery shots.[5]

This offers a reference point now for thinking about what's about to happen in what follows. I'm going to talk *not about virtue epistemology* (though I would at a push[6]) but about the normativity of *attempts* as *attempts*.

On the general (attempt-neutral) telic normativity framework, there are three central ways we can evaluative *any* given (aimed) attempt. First, we can evaluate the attempt against the norm of *success*. An attempt is a 'better' attempt if it succeeds in attaining the aim internal to the kind of attempt it is

---

[3] This is somewhat a simplification; 'truth' is the constitutive aim of the kinds of traditional beliefs that were the focus of Sosa's initial presentation of performance-theoretic epistemology in his 2007. From 2015 onwards, multiple belief types are distinguished, where *judgemental* beliefs are better understood as aiming constitutively at *apt alethic affirmation* (or knowledge). We'll get into these details in later chapters while developing our telic account of trust in more detail.

[4] See also, e.g., Carter and Willard-Kyle (2023) for a recent application of the telic framework to interrogative attitudes.

[5] For Simion, beliefs are less like archery shots than they are like blood pumped by working hearts. See, e.g., Simion (2019).

[6] The key ideas of my favoured version of virtue epistemology are developed in my (forthcoming) *Stratified Virtue Epistemology: A Defence*.

than if it fails—viz., a shot that hits the target is better than one that misses.[7] A free throw in basketball is better *qua the kind of thing it is* (a basketball-goal-directed attempt) if it goes in than if it doesn't, if it *succeeds* in attaining its internal aim than if it doesn't. The underlying idea here is that there is at least one kind of dimension of performance or attempt quality, 'success' quality, which tracks just one thing about an attempt: whether (or not) its constitutive aim is (or isn't) attained.

Granted, the archer's shot might very well hit the target even if the archer doesn't *realize* this (maybe it got suddenly dark), and so she can't appreciate or know that it was successful. A basketball shot might go in only due to a fluke gust of wind etc. None of this matters, at least for whether these performances meet specifically the *success* norm. And neither does it matter if the shot was in other ways very good, nor whether it would have succeeded if not for bad luck. It doesn't matter, at least, when it comes to evaluating *whether* the attempt was *successful*.

But, you might think, some of these things *do* matter when we evaluate a performance. A performance unsuccessful only because of bad luck might still be good, even excellent (qua the kind of performance it is) in other ways, *despite* not succeeding. (Or: there might be ways in which a performance is *bad* even if successful if too risky or lucky—consider a reckless attempt that succeeds *through* dumb luck.)

The telic normativity framework can make sense of this kind of thinking by introducing a totally different evaluation dimension of performances: whether they are *competent*. Regardless of whether an attempt actually succeeds in attaining its aim—that is, regardless of how a given attempt stacks up against the *success norm* (i.e., did it attain its internal aim or not?)—the attempt is going to be better if competent than if incompetent. A competent attempt—to a first approximation, for now[8]—will issue from a disposition to succeed (at attaining the aim internal to the performance-type) reliably enough when one tries in normal conditions, where what counts as 'normal conditions' is going to just be those conditions under which good performance (for that attempt-type) is valued or otherwise matters.

For example, take the attempt to play an F♯ note on the clarinet. A total beginner lacks a disposition to play an F♯ note reliably when they try

---

[7] See Sosa (2020) for the most recent presentation of the evaluative normativity of attempts as attempts.
[8] This is an initial characterization, which will be superseded by a more developed view in Chapter 5.

because, perhaps, they simply lack any idea which holes of the clarinet to cover to make that particular sound come out. They're not *disposed to reliably* succeed in playing an F♯ in any but the most unusually favourable conditions (e.g., conditions where someone is willing to help them by guiding their fingers on the correct holes). But good performance at the clarinet is valued in conditions that extend beyond those where one is lucky enough to get finger-guiding assistance. Our beginner (without knowledge of what the holes even mean) simply lacks a disposition to succeed cross-situationally within those 'normal' situations we care about when it comes to playing on the clarinet an F♯.

Crucially, though, note that there are important *limits* to how far these situations plausibly extend. If you put a professional clarinet player, for instance, under water, no sound is going to come out of the instrument when they put their fingers in the right spot and blow like they usually would. The same goes for circumstances of unusually high wind or velocity which would distort the sound's pitch (maybe causing it to come out as a G♯.) and the same goes for cases where the professional clarinet player is simply drugged with a facial muscle relaxer and/or nearly asleep. The excellent player, who ordinarily plays competently, will *retain* a disposition to succeed when they try in normal conditions (for that performance-type), even if (right now) they're for whatever reason *not* in the right shape or situation.

The above clarinet example is meant to illustrate the kinds of things that matter for *having a disposition* to reliably succeed (at doing something when you try) in normal circumstances. Let's now return to thinking about *performance quality* specifically, which is principally what the telic normativity framework is designed to help us evaluate in a rigorous way. When an aimed attempt is *competent*, it has this status *regardless* of whether it succeeds, and *if and only if* that attempt issues from the exercise of the kind of agential disposition we've just been talking about. That is, a disposition to succeed when one tries while in normal shape and normally situated (for doing that kind of thing), and where this disposition manifests (through the agent's exercising it) when the agent *is in fact in the right shape and situation to do so*. Performances like *that* are *competent performances*. That's an evaluative status of a performance that we pre-theoretically do care about (we might talk of this colloquially as a 'skilled' performance, or as an 'adroit' performance—indicating that it 'exhibits good form' for the kind of thing it is).

It's pre-theoretically obvious how an aimed performance could be successful without being competent—we might talk about this in ordinary language as 'beginner's luck!' It's perhaps a bit less obvious, though, how a performance would attain the status of being competent while nonetheless missing its mark. You might think: if, in attempting to do something, ϕ, you exercise a disposition you have to ϕ (in certain shape and in certain situations), and you *in fact are* in those very conditions, then doesn't that just mean that when you exercise that disposition, you simply *will* ϕ? The answer is 'no'; the kinds of dispositions of agents that are needed for performing competently are almost always *fallible* dispositions.[9] This is why, for example, there's something *good* about Steph Curry's free throw shot even when it misses. Steph's shot is competent. And it's competent *because* he exercises a disposition that he has to shoot not *infallibly*, but *reliably*, in normal conditions (which he's in). This is just one of those times it misses.

Our telic normativity framework has now described two distinct evaluative norms governing any kind of aimed attempt, and we've seen further that the conditions for satisfying these two norms (success and competence) are logically independent.

Let's now look at a *third* kind of evaluative norm our general framework gives us, one the satisfaction of which requires that you also satisfy the two others, but importantly, isn't *secured* through their satisfaction. The third norm is called *aptness*. The easiest way to understand the aptness norm (and what it takes to satisfy it) is to think about a case that has a kind of 'Gettier structure'[10]—viz., such that a given performance is *successful* and also *competent* but not *successful because competent*. How might this come about? Let's go back to archery: suppose a *competent shot* is fired at the target. While it's in the air, an unexpected gust of wind blows it off course, so now it's headed just away from the target. Luckily, though, a second gust of wind then 'cancels out' the first gust, bringing the arrow back on track, and it hits the target. The shot is competent, and it's also successful; but the shot isn't successful because competent—the second lucky gust of wind is what accounted for why it hit the target rather than missed; even though the shot manifested competence here, its *success* didn't. *Aptness*, within the telic

---

[9] For relevant discussion here, see, along with Sosa (2010), Carter (2022) and Heering (2023).
[10] For discussion, see Sosa (2007, Ch. 2; 2010, 467, 474–75) and Greco (2009, 19–21; 2010, 73–76, 94–99). Cf., Pritchard (2012, 251, 264–68).

normativity framework, is a technical term that is meant to pick out performance quality that 'shores up' what's missing in cases of Gettier structure. A performance is *apt* if and only if it's accurate because competent; when it comes to evaluating performance quality, the aptness norm says a performance is of a higher quality if it is not just successful and competent, but *apt*, viz., successful *through* competence rather than luck.

These three evaluative norms—*success, competence,* and *aptness*—point to *three distinct ways that any performance might be good*. The 'goodness' here is attributive goodness; it applies to performances qua the kind of aimed attempt they are. (The executioner's skilled movements might be successful, competent as well as apt, while at the same time reprehensible.) There are, within the telic framework, even further norms, but we needn't worry about any of these for now.

With the above three in mind, let's now return to *trust*, and think about how our working telic normativity framework might apply to it.

3. Trust as Performance

Suppose you trust your friend with a secret, and you find out later that your friend spilled the beans. There is a clear sense in which your trusting your friend with that secret *did not succeed* in attaining *what it was* at which, by trusting them with that secret, you thereby aimed. They did *not*—put generally—*take care of things as entrusted*. Their having done so would have involved, in this case, their *not* repeating what you had told them.

The above case of spilling an entrusted secret is a simple case of three-place interpersonal trust which is betrayed. There are various ways we might be inclined to *evaluate* what's going on here. For example, you might think the trustee has done something at least prima facie *wrong*. You might think whether it's wrong depends perhaps on what was gained from spilling the secret (maybe it saved a life). Or, we could ask whether there are any false or irrational beliefs in play etc.

Regardless of what verdicts we reach when asking the above kind of questions (including questions of substantive morality),[11] there is a clear sense in which this case of three-place trust, *evaluated as an aimed attempt*, comes up short. Recast in the language of performance normativity: your trusting here didn't do very well by the lights of the evaluative norm of *success*

---

[11] In Chapter 4, we'll think about how telic assessments of trust interface with broader kinds of assessments.

(as applicable to any performance-type), and in a way that is broadly analogous to how an archer's shot would be better if it hit the target than not, a belief better if it is accurate (true) rather than inaccurate (false). In the case of three-place interpersonal trust, we can accordingly capture the applicable evaluative *success* norm as follows:

> **The Evaluative Success Norm of Trust (ESNT):** S's trusting X with ϕ is better if X takes care of ϕ as entrusted than if X does not.

Remember: the 'better', in ESNT, is just the 'better' of attributive goodness:[12] three-place trust where the trustee *in fact takes care of things as entrusted* is better than otherwise as an instance of the kind of aimed attempt it is—that is, an attempt on the part of the trustor, by means of reliance, *that the trustee take care of things as entrusted.*

The reader can now see how our discussion of telic normativity in §2 offers a roadmap for extracting our other two main norms of interest, competence, and aptness, which will be derivative in their formulations of the way we've formulated the success norm ESNT.

Let's think now about trust that is *competent*. Just as missed shots and false beliefs can be *competent* despite failing to secure the relevant aim, likewise, trust can be competent even when it is not successful. Suppose, to continue our initial example, that when your friend you entrusted with the secret spills the beans, this is only *due to a fluke accident* (never mind how) and that the friend is really very trustworthy. By trusting your friend and getting betrayed in this case, you are more akin to Steph Curry missing a free throw (where the shot is competent, but not successful—this is just one of those times it misses) than you are to a shooter who just heaves up a ball with wild form and misses. The fact that competent trust can be betrayed is just a special case of the more general idea, discussed in the previous section, that the agential dispositions or skills underwriting almost any kind of human performance are not infallible dispositions.

When trust is competent, it will derive from the exercise of reliable trusting disposition (for simplicity, call this a *skill*[13]), which one possesses only if

---

[12] See Chapter 1. This is the kind of 'good' that features in: 'A good knife is a sharp knife'.
[13] Note that Sosa's own terminology has shifted over the years when it comes to skill, in connection with shape and situation. For one thing, earlier discussions (Sosa 2010, 465, 470) use the term 'seat' rather than 'skill'. For another, Sosa sometimes describes what one has, when one has the skill (i.e., what one retains even when in improper shape and while improperly situated) as an *innermost competence* (2015, 83) distinct from the complete competence one has when one's skill is conjoined with proper shape and situation. By contrast, the term *inner*

is one _____? How should we fill in that blank? Fortunately, we've got a recipe for this: we've seen in §2 that, on the telic normativity framework, for any aimed attempt, A, where 'X' is the constitutive aim of that attempt, the kind of reliable (cf., not infallible) disposition one needs to possess to be in the market for A-ing *competently* is a disposition to *reliably attain A's aim (X)* (when one tries while in the kind of shape and situation that are pertinent to A-ing). When trust is competent, it will accordingly derive from exercise of a reliable trusting skill which one possesses only if is one is *disposed to trust successfully reliably enough when one trusts in proper shape and properly situated.*

Let's think about that last bit. Trusting skill is indexed to a 'proper shape and situation' just like any other skill. Compare: it does not count against your having the skill to drive a car if you would fail to perform reliably behind the wheel when attempting to drive *if* drugged and placed on slick roads. Likewise, it doesn't count against your skill to trust well if under highly abnormal circumstances (e.g., a surprise birthday party) you'd be betrayed more often than not. In a bit more detail: it doesn't count against someone's having a skill to trust well if the trustor would not trust successfully reliably enough in conditions where, for example, risk to the trustor is excessively high and gains of betrayal are enormous; or where the level of effort that would be required by the trustee to take care of things as entrusted is abnormally high.[14]

When a skilled trustor *is* in proper shape and properly situated—we will look at these conditions in more detail in Chapter 5—the trustor then has the (complete) *competence* to trust well, and not *merely* the skill to do so. Trusting that issues (non-deviantly) from such a competence is good, qua trust, in an important respect—viz., the very same respect in which other kinds of competent performances are good (qua their performance-type) *even if* it is one of those times where the performance does not succeed. This is implied by the more general performance-theoretic idea that a given attempt is better if it issues from a disposition to reliably attain its aim in normal conditions than otherwise.[15] Accordingly, we can now add the following evaluative competence norm on trusting (ECNT) to our picture:

competence (2017, 191) is meant to pick out what one possesses when they possess both skill and shape, but not the situational element of the complete competence. For general discussion on these points, see Sosa (2015, Ch. 3; 2017, Ch. 12).

[14] For related discussion on normal boundaries within which good trusting is valued, see Carter (2020b, sec. 6).

[15] This is a first approximation, to be superseded with more detailed discussion in Chapter 4.

The Evaluative Competence Norm of Trust (ECNT): *S*'s trusting *X* with ϕ is better if *S* trusts *X* with ϕ competently than if *S* does not.

Because (as noted in §2) *any* performance could be both successful and competent without being *apt*—which is of a higher quality qua performance than either successful or competent performance, or a conjunction of them—the same goes for trust. For example, suppose you competently trust a reliable colleague to pay back a loan on a particular date (say, 1 January). On 31 December, your colleague is in an accident which causes total amnesia. Struggling to regain memory, your colleague begins to remember who you are and then simply fabricates a specific memory (which luckily happens to be veridical) that they owe you money which must be repaid by 1 January. Because the friend is of a good and trustworthy character, they are on the basis of this fabricated but veridical memory moved to repay the loan, which they do. Your trusting them is thus successful. They *have* taken care of things as entrusted. The trust is also competent; but qua performance it nonetheless falls short in that it is not successful through competence, but successful just by dumb luck (i.e., that the trustee fabricated a veridical memory rather than a fictitious one).[16] Thus, in addition to ESNT and ECNT, trust is also evaluable with respect to the following norm of *aptness*:

The Evaluative Aptness Norm of Trust (EANT): *S*'s trusting *X* with ϕ is better if *S* trusts *X* with ϕ aptly than if *S* does not.

Apt trust is a kind of *achievement*, a success through competence. A common view in the axiology of achievements is that the value of an achievement does not reduce to the value of attaining the relevant success any old way (including through luck *even when* the attempt was a competent attempt—as in the 'lucky success' case above).[17] And this idea is captured nicely by EANT, according to which the attributive goodness of apt trust

---

[16] Another variation on this kind of case, with the same results, will appeal not to amnesia but to what Sven Bernecker (2010, 137–38) calls 'trace creation' and 'trace implantation'— where memory traces are created *in vitro* and implanted. While this is perhaps less plausible than amnesia, it makes for a cleaner case given that there is no worry that the amnesia would undermine one's trustworthy character.

[17] For discussion, see, e.g., Greco (2010, Ch. 6), Sosa (2010), Pritchard (2009, 2009), and Bradford (2013, 2015, 2015).

asymmetrically entails the attributive goodness of successful, competent trust—just as we should expect it would.[18]

In sum, then, (i) the evaluative normativity of trust can be straightforwardly modelled as a special case of the evaluative normativity of performances generally; and (ii) ESNT, ECNT, and EANT capture (for now) three distinct evaluative norms against which any instance of (three-place interpersonal) trust can be evaluated as better or worse *as an instance of trusting*—with EANT representing a higher standard of good trusting than ESNT and ECNT. When we trust someone with something, our working view tells us that EANT is the gold standard. Trust that satisfies *merely* both ESNT and ECNT is (in two different ways) good trusting; but it could be better.

4. Taking Stock

Before adding anything further to the picture just developed, let's step back for a moment. We began Chapter 1 by asking 'What is good trusting?' We saw the usual suspect answers weren't great. So how does the view we've got to now answer the question we began with? It answers it by saying, in effect, 'Well, good trusting is trusting that satisfies evaluative norms that govern good trusting as such—these are evaluative norms that govern trust *as performance* or aimed attempt—and they are ESNT, ECNT, and EANT.' On this view, then, good trusting isn't to be assimilated to good believing, good affect, or good conation, per se, but *good performance* in the sense that good trust is (in the best case) apt trust, trust whose success manifests the trustor's trusting competence. Let's see now how this way of thinking about good holds up against the problems (from Chapter 1, §§2–3) facing the competing views surveyed.

4.1 vs. the Doxastic Account

There were problems with the idea—implied by doxastic accounts of trust— that the evaluative norms of trust are (a subset of) the evaluative norms of belief. In short, we saw that there is a constitutive tension between trusting

---

[18] Put another way: the idea that apt trust is better than inapt trust implies that apt trust is better (qua trust) than either mere successful trust or mere competent trust, or (as the veridical memory case above suggests) mere successful *and* competent but inapt trust.

and complying with evidence and knowledge norms of belief. But these problems are not applicable to the performance-theoretic account, which *does not assimilate good trusting to good believing in the first place*. To be clear, the idea that trusting someone X with ϕ is an aimed attempt, by means of reliance, that the trustee take care of ϕ as entrusted, is entirely compatible with tokenings of trust involving in some and even many cases ϕ-related beliefs on the part of the trustor. On the proposal here, it's just not the case that the attributive goodness of trusting simply boils down to how good those beliefs are.[19]

Moreover, note that the proposal is not committed—problematically, as the doxastic account is—to predicting that good trusting will be a function of doing something well *involuntarily* to the same extent that belief is involuntary. In later chapters, we'll discuss how trust, qua performance, can admit of multiple theoretically interesting types, one of which (which I'll call *deliberative trust*) is both voluntary and intentional.

Finally, the proposal is not challenged by cases—distinctively problematic for doxastic accounts—where good trust is achieved by suspending belief rather than by believing anything about the object of trust well. This point will be a central focus of Chapter 3, which distinguishes wide-scope and narrow-scope forbearing from trust, where the latter (even though not the former) admits of telic assessment.

4.2 vs. the Affective Account

A key problem for the would-be assimilation of good trusting to good affect is that we should expect that good trusting, as such, will be incompatible

---

[19] It's worth noting that apt trust, as well as successful and competent trust, will very often require not only beliefs but also (often) combinations of affective and conative attitudes. This is because we can expect trusting will often, like other performances (and especially performances linked to cooperative activities), require the good execution of a range of other subsidiary activities. Even so, by way of emphasis, the performance *itself* is evaluated with reference to the standards of success, competence, and aptness, *qua* the performance-type it is, and *not* with reference to the standards that regulate what make the subsidiary activities that are often necessary for good trust good as the kind of things they are. While the performance-theoretic account doesn't make the mistake of assimilating good trusting to good ϕ-ing for some ϕ (or any set of ϕ-ings) the execution of which is among the subsidiary activities that good trusting usually involves, it *does* accommodate the data point that good trusting will plausibly often, as Bernd Lahno (2004) puts it, 'include behavioral, cognitive and affective dimensions or aspects' (2004, 30). Other proposals are comparatively more restricted in how this data point could be accommodated—as each predicts the goodness of good trusting will primarily be a matter of the goodness of one of these things but to the exclusion of others. In this respect, the performance-theoretical account can claim a kind of ecumenical edge.

with poorly navigating risks that, by trusting, one thereby incurs. However, as we saw in Chapter 1, the prospects here aren't promising. On the performance-theoretic view, *successful* trust is of course compatible with poor risk assessment (in the sense that, analogously, e.g., hitting the bullseye and guessing correctly are compatible with using poor form and getting lucky), but—crucially—competent trust and apt trust are *not*. And in fact, this is a result that is effectively 'built in' to the content of the competence norm and (by extension) the aptness norm.[20]

4.3 vs. the Conative Account

As the THREE EASY MARKS case illustrated, the norms of good conation—of which the norms of good trusting will be a proper subset on the participant stance view—are *entirely* orthogonal to successful trusting, given that the satisfaction of conative norms (i.e., readiness to feel certain attitudes in response to trusting outcomes) floats entirely freely of the aim, in trusting, that the trustee actually take care of things as entrusted. The performance-theoretic account, by contrast, takes that aim as the normative starting point—in that it is with reference to this aim that we understand not only the evaluative norm of successful trust but also by extension competent and apt trust.

5. Concluding Remarks

This chapter has laid out the key contours of a core idea that will now be developed in more detail, extended, and applied in various ways throughout the book. The idea can be summed up, in slogan form, as 'trust *as* performance'; the norms that govern what count as good and bad trusting are performance-theoretic 'telic' norms of success, competence, and aptness. And these are norms that apply to trust construed as a performance

---

[20] If a given instance of three-place trust at least satisfies the competence norm, we can explain in a principled way why that particular instance of trusting didn't poorly navigate the risk at play. We do that by first pointing out that the norm will be satisfied only if the agent possesses a certain kind of dispositional skill to navigate such risks reliably in appropriate circumstances, and then emphasize that one must in fact be in those circumstances to satisfy the competence norm. This is a principled reason to associate competent trust with trust that properly navigates risk of betrayal (even if not infallibly so).

constitutively aimed at the trustee taking care of things as entrusted; when the trustee does take care of things as entrusted, that's what it is for trust to succeed. But just as there's more to believing than getting true beliefs, there's more to trusting than trusting (merely) successfully. Thus, we can evaluate trusting for competence (did the trust issue from a disposition on the part of the trustor to reliably enough trust successfully?) and also for *aptness* (was trust not only successful and competent, but successful *because* competent?).

As we've seen (in §4), the above simple picture of trust and its constituent normativity is built with resources to sidestep a range of key problems that faced (respectively) accounts of trust that would have us assimilate good and bad trusting to good and bad believing, affect, and conation. This is an initially promising start, though plenty of questions remain.

For one thing, it seems that, sometimes, the trust we place in others is merely implicit, below the surface of conscious reflection. Consider the trust you might place in a family member without giving a moment's consideration as to whether to trust them. Other times, trust seems much more deliberative and calculating.

Can such a distinction in the *way* we place our trust be reconciled with our core evaluative norms ESNT, ECNT, and EANT? Relatedly, just as a skilled inquirer will in some circumstances skilfully forbear from belief (e.g., by withholding judgement), presumably something closely analogous will go for trusting. But how might the view presented so far account for this—viz., for cases where it seems as though the good trustor skilfully *refrains* from trusting in a way that is to her credit as a trustor? Is this even something we can make sense of when we take, as we have, as a starting point the guiding idea that trusting is aimed performance?

With these questions in mind, the next chapter takes up the task of developing further the account sketched thus far, with a particular focus on distrust and forbearance.

A Telic Theory of Trust. J. Adam Carter, Oxford University Press. © J. Adam Carter 2024.
DOI: 10.1093/9780191982460.003.0002

3
Forbearance and Distrust

This chapter adds to the framework developed so far in two ways. We begin by distinguishing two core species of trust—*implicit* and *deliberative*, which differ in their constitutive aims. The implicit/deliberative distinction (which we return to in later chapters) offers us a useful vantage point from which we may extend our framework from trust to *distrust*, and in doing so, to recognize both (i) how distrust, like trust, may be implicit or deliberative; and (ii) how the distinction between wide-scope distrust—what I call Pyrrhonian *mistrust*—and narrow-scope distrust allows us to appreciate how the latter (in both its implicit and deliberative varieties), though *not* the former kind of distrust, is answerable to telic norms of success, competence, and aptness.

1. Varieties of Trust qua Performance: Some Distinctions

Let's now pick up on a thread of argument from the end of the previous chapter (in connection with doxastic accounts). It was suggested that a prima facie advantage of the performance-theoretic approach to trust and its evaluative normativity is that it is not committed (in taking trusting to be a kind of aimed attempt) to predicting that good trusting will be a function of doing something well *involuntarily*. At least, it is not committed to trusting being involuntary to the same extent that believing is (or is generally taken to be). And that point was offered as one of the advantages the proposal had over doxastic accounts.

But you might think a problem lurks in the opposite direction: archery shots, on which the account models trust, are paradigmatically voluntary, but surely trust isn't always so? Put another way, even if on the performance-theoretic approach trust isn't always involuntary (as it might be on a doxastic account) it might equally seem problematic if trust is always *voluntary* or intentional (as we might expect it to be on the view that trusting always involves an aimed, archery-style attempt). After all, some of our interpersonal trust seems entirely *implicit*, arising spontaneously or automatically, and without any prior deliberation or reflection. This point calls out now for more elaboration.

In order to organize our thinking here, let's zero in on our 'high quality' evaluative norm from Chapter 2—the *evaluative aptness norm of trust* (EANT). According to EANT, S's trusting X with ϕ is better if S trusts X with ϕ aptly than if S does not, and S's trust is apt just in case it is successful (satisfying ESNT) because competent (satisfying ECNT).

Let's explore now the idea that trust can be apt even when trust is *implicit*. We of course very often trust others with small things without ever consciously deliberating about *whether* to have trusted them in the first place; can we do *this* better or worse—in ways that are successful, competent, and apt? Consider, by way of comparison: we *believe* many things *are particular ways* around us, implicitly, which guide action despite our having never attempted, through any conscious deliberation, to 'settle the question' for which a stance (i.e., on whether *p*—e.g., that the table is an arm's length away) would constitute an answer.[1] It seems then that, at least in so far as we aren't objecting to the virtue epistemologist's idea that beliefs are like archery shots assessable for success, competence, and aptness in virtue of both being (constitutively) aimed attempts (even if beliefs and archery shots differ in their paradigmatic voluntariness), we've got no particular reason to think implicit trust would not be evaluable for success, competence, and aptness unless, e.g., voluntary and/or intentional in ways beliefs are not. Another way of getting at the above point is to draw attention to the fact that a given attempt's *constitutive aim* (of the sort that would suffice for telic assessment) needn't always be determined by *intentional aiming*.

Within a performance-theoretic framework, the aim that implicit trust constitutively attempts to secure is best understood as (following here Sosa's terminology) merely *teleological*, not intentional.[2] And it is the teleological aim of implicit trust with reference to which we assess implicit trust for success, competence, and aptness. No full-blown intentional aim is needed for

---

[1] For an extended discussion on this point in connection with performance epistemology, see Sosa (2015, Ch. 3, n. 5).

[2] On this point, it is useful to consider Sosa's (2015) remarks on what is needed for performative assessment as follows: 'functional states can have teleological aims. Thus a state of alertness in a crouching cat may be aimed at detecting vulnerable prey. Whether as a state it can count as a "performance" in any ordinary sense is hence irrelevant to our focus on "performances" that have an aim and to which we may then apply our AAA aim-involving normative account. All that really matters for this latter is that the entity have a constitutive aim, whatever may be its ontological status or the label appropriately applicable to it in ordinary parlance' (2015, Ch. 5, n. 5). For other discussions of functional and teleological assessment, see Sosa (2017, 71–72, 129–30, 152; 2021, 24–31, 52–58, 64, 110, 118).

such performance-theoretic assessment. By way of comparison, and as Sosa (2021, 25, fn. 12) notes, we can assess our implicit or 'functional' beliefs for success, competence, and aptness—those that guide behaviour below the surface of conscious reflection—not because a thinker intentionally aims at anything but just because teleologically our perceptual systems aim at correctly representing our surroundings. And they can do this better or worse *vis-à-vis* the teleological aim of correct or true representation.

On many more substantial matters, however, our trust is not merely implicit but *deliberative*, and it is deliberative in a way that is broadly analogous to how some of our considered inquiries (i.e., inquiries into 'whether p' questions) are deliberative. In such cases, we *do* consciously consider whether to judge or suspend (intentionally omitting judgement). Likewise, when one faces a salient choice whether or not to trust someone X with something ϕ one deliberates on *whether* to trust X with ϕ or whether instead to forbear (intentionally omit trusting).

Let us continue this analogy further. Following Sosa (2015, Ch. 3; 2020, 2021), it is plausible that when we *deliberately judge* whether p, we intentionally aim not just at getting it right any way but at getting it right *aptly* (for performance-theoretic virtue epistemologists: aiming to get it right aptly is tantamount to aiming at apt belief—*knowledge*[3]—rather than at truth any old way).[4]

This is, by way of an athletic comparison, just as a basketball player aims by shooting not *merely* to make the shot any old way (e.g., to chuck it and hope[5]) but to make it competently, to make a well-selected shot.[6] And, plausibly, *mutatis mutandis*, for deliberative—rather than mere implicit—trust: in deliberately trusting, we intentionally aim, in trusting, not *merely* at successful trust (like a basketball player chucking from half court, or an inquirer who aims at truth through a guess) but at *aptness*—viz., at apt trust.

The relevant performance-theoretic analogies (which I'll flesh out further in this book) are thus, and to a first approximation for now:

- implicit belief aims (teleologically) at truth, deliberative belief (judgement) aims (intentionally) at apt belief (knowledge).

---

[3] For a recent defence of the idea that inquiry is knowledge-aimed, within a wider knowledge-first virtue epistemology, see Kelp (2021).
[4] Cf., Schechter (2019) for criticism.   [5] Unless, of course, time is expiring.
[6] The coach will berate a player who chucks it from half court, even if it goes in. For discussion, see Sosa (2015, Ch. 3) and Carter (2016).

- implicit trust aims (teleologically) at successful trust, deliberative trust aims (intentionally) at apt trust.
- implicit belief, when apt, is knowledge; judgemental belief, when apt, is apt belief (knowledge) of a *higher quality* (i.e., *fully apt* belief, or *knowing full well*[7])—what results when one aptly attains the aim (aptness) of judgemental belief.
- implicit trust, when apt, is apt trust; deliberative trust, when apt, is apt trust of a *higher quality* (i.e., *fully apt* trust)—when one aptly attains the aim (apt trust) of deliberative trust (we will explore deliberative trust, and apt deliberative trust (i.e., *convictively apt trust*) in detail in Chapters 5 and 6).

In sum, what our performance-theoretic analogies suggest is following working picture (which Chapters 5 and 6 will develop in more detail): (i) trust comes in two varieties (implicit and deliberative); (ii) both are evaluable for success, competence, and aptness; but (iii) deliberative trust is (when apt), and on account of its constitutive aim, trust of a higher quality.

2. From Trusting to Distrusting

Here is how all of the above connects with the question of *good distrust*. As a first point of note: the right way to characterize the *way* we aim at aptness, *when we deliberate about whether to make the relevant attempt (or not) in the first place*, is in terms of a *biconditional aim*: to ϕ iff one's ϕ-ing would be apt. For example, with reference to this biconditional aim, we can make sense of why a skilled basketball player, *outside her threshold for sufficient reliability*, might be smart—indeed, in a way creditable to her skill and acumen—to 'hold fire' (and perhaps pass instead) rather than shoot. Or to wait out the clock rather than shoot.

Just as we can actually *make some attempt*, X, in the endeavour to attain that biconditional aim, we can also *forbear* from X-ing in the endeavour to attain that *very same* biconditional aim—viz., to ϕ iff one's ϕ-ing would be apt. For example, the inquirer pursues the 'positive' Jamesian aim (attaining aptness) by (positively) affirming whether p in the endeavour to affirm if and only if doing so would be apt; but the inquirer can also contribute to the

---
[7] This term is coined in Sosa (2021).

biconditional aim by contributing to its subsidiary (negative Jamesian) aim, *avoiding inaptness*, by *forbearing* on whether *p*, and doing so *also* in the endeavour to affirm if and only if doing so would be apt.[8]

We are getting close now to seeing how *distrust* is itself something we can evaluate for success, competence, and aptness—given that (put generally) forbearances, like the performances of which they are omissions, can be *aimed*. But first, there an ambiguity that needs to be addressed.[9]

The following locution <*forbear from X-ing in the endeavour to attain aim A*> is crucially ambiguous between a narrow-scope and a wide-scope reading. *Narrow-scope forbearance* should be read as: '(Forbearing from *X*-ing) in the endeavour to attain a given aim *A*.' By contrast, *wide-scope forbearance* should be read as: 'Forbearing from (*X*-ing in the endeavour to attain a given aim *A*).'

Wide-scope forbearance from trusting is something akin to the Pyrrhonian analogue in the case of human cooperation as opposed to inquiry. It is a wide-scope abstaining from trusting simpliciter, thus, including from *trusting in the endeavour to attain any aim*. Call this Pyrrhonian mistrust, an omission from trust—though not an omission to trust specifically in the endeavour to trust if and only if that trust would be apt.[10]

By contrast, *narrow-scope forbearance* from trusting, but not wide-scope forbearance, is constitutively *aimed* forbearance from trusting.[11] Take a simple case of three-place interpersonal narrow-scope forbearance from trusting: when I consciously deliberate whether to trust the stranger with

---

[8] See Sosa (2021) for a detailed discussion of this idea within telic virtue epistemology.

[9] See Sosa (2021, 49) for discussion.

[10] This is just a simplification of the Pyrrhonian view in epistemology—which prescribes suspension in many cases where this suspension is a kind of forbearance from affirming. Saddling the Pyrrhonian as a 'suspender' or 'omitter' of belief is a simplification because a more charitable interpretation of the Pyrrhonian is one where, e.g., Sextus permits acquiescing to the appearances, or perhaps even affirming on matters of how things seem or appear, while withholding beyond that. For discussion, see Sextus (PH 1.13 and 1.19–20) and Fine (2000, 208).

[11] It is worth noting a connection between, on the one hand, the distinction between widescope/narrow-scope forbearance from trusting, and, on the other, Jane Friedman's (2013) remarks on how to characterize a certain kind of agnosticism of interest in epistemology. As Friedman puts it: '[…] the sort of neutrality or indecision that is at the heart of agnosticism is not mere non-belief and can only be captured with an attitude. This means that the attitude will have to be one that represents (or expresses or just is) a subject's neutrality or indecision with respect to the truth of some proposition. This will have to be either a sui generis attitude of indecision, or some other more familiar attitude' (2013, 167). On the present proposal it is worth noting that while wide-scope forbearance from trusting, mere omission, needn't involve any positive characteristics, narrow-scope forbearance—much like the kind of positive attitude of indecision that Friedman associates with agnosticism—will often have (some combinations of) attitudes, affect, and/or conation. In this respect, narrow-scope distrust is like both the agnosticism that Friedman describes, as well as trust itself (see Section 4.3 for discussion).

my keys, and intentionally forbear, my forbearance is aimed; I forbear in the endeavour to, *by forbearing*, avoid trusting inaptly. Call this narrow-scope kind of aimed forbearance from trust *deliberative distrust*; it is

- (forbearing from trusting) in the endeavour to avoid inapt trust, and *not*
- forbearing from (trusting in the endeavour to avoid inapt trust).

Deliberative distrust is subject to the evaluative norms of *success, competence*, and *aptness*. The success norm on deliberative distrust says: S's (deliberative) distrusting X with ϕ is better if S's forbearing from trusting X with ϕ avoids inaptness than if S doesn't. (Deliberative distrust *fails* if, (i) one deliberatively distrusts X with ϕ; and (ii) *were* one to have trusted (X with ϕ), one's trusting (X with ϕ) would have been *apt*.) That would have been bad distrust along the success dimension. This is so *even if* that distrust was *competent*.

The competence norm on deliberative distrust says: S's (deliberative) distrusting X with ϕ is better if S forbears from trusting X with ϕ competently than if S doesn't; this will require that S's deliberative distrusting X with ϕ manifests S's competence to (narrow-scope) forbear in ways that reliably lead to avoiding inaptness, when the truster is in proper shape and properly situated. The *overly cynical* person might forbear from trusting a reliable trustee successfully (and avoid inaptness given that the reliable would-be trustee would have failed to prove trustworthy on this occasion) but would still fail to do so competently. Finally, the aptness norm on deliberative distrust says: S's deliberative distrusting X with ϕ is better if S deliberatively distrusts X with ϕ aptly than if S does not.

Question: judgemental belief is to deliberative trust as implicit belief is to implicit trust. But what about *this* analogy: Deliberative trust is to implicit trust as deliberative distrust is to _____?

The answer, of course, is *implicit distrust*, which rounds out our picture. Implicit distrust, like implicit trust, is teleological rather than intentionally aimed forbearance from trusting. *Wide-scope* forbearance from implicit trusting differs from Pyrrhonian mistrust (wide-scope forbearance from deliberative trust) not necessarily in respect of involving some different policy or stance, per se, but simply with respect to what kind of trust is, in fact, omitted.[12] *Narrow-scope* implicit distrust is constitutively aimed,

---

[12] Possibly, an individual could wide-scope forbear from one kind of trusting without wide-scope forbearing from the other.

teleologically, not (as is narrow-scope deliberative distrust) at *avoiding inaptness*, but at avoiding *unsuccessful trust*—viz., trust where the trustee fails to take care of things as entrusted. As such, implicit distrust is evaluable as successful, competent, and apt in connection with the aim of avoiding *unsuccessful* trust, trust that fails ESNT: implicit distrust is better if successful (i.e., if *not* forbearing would have resulted in unsuccessful trust) than if not, competent than if not (i.e., if one's forbearance manifested a competence to not too easily forbear when, had one refrained from forbearing, one would have trusted successfully), apt than if not.

In sum, by modelling the evaluative normativity of distrust performance-theoretically as norms of forbearance, we get the following picture:

(i) *wide-scope forbearance from trusting* (of any kind) is not performance-theoretically evaluable;
(ii) narrow-scope forbearance from trusting (just like trusting itself) comes in two varieties, *deliberative distrust* and *implicit distrust*, each of which is performance-theoretically evaluable, for success, competence, and aptness in connection with
  (a) the intentional aim of avoiding inapt trust (in the case of deliberative distrust); and
  (b) the functional/teleological aim of avoiding unsuccessful trust (in the case of implicit distrust).

In order to make these distinctions in distrust quality more concrete, I'll conclude with an example case illustrating each—beginning with the wide-scope varieties of forbearance (i.e., from deliberative and implicit trust) that lie *outside* performance-theoretic evaluation.

2.1 Wide-Scope Forbearance from Trust (Pyrrhonian Mistrust and Non-Pyrrhonian Mistrust)

What I've termed 'Pyrrhonian mistrust', i.e., forbearance from (deliberative trusting in the endeavour to trust iff one would do so aptly), is simply an *omission from deliberative trusting*. In the three-place case of interest, it is an omission from deliberatively trusting X with ϕ. I'm using the term 'Pyrrhonian' only because *what it omits* is the taking of an intentional stance—(broadly) analogous to the kind of omission from intentional judgement that characterizes a Pyrrhonian withdrawal from intentional judgement (viz., of whether something is so). What one omits is *not* necessarily implicit trust (though omissions from deliberative trust are compatible with omissions from implicit trust). For an example featuring an omission from mere deliberative trust but not implicit trust, suppose a misanthrope's plan is to withdraw from all cooperation; the plan is, however, flawed, as the misanthrope implicitly trusts a neighbour *N* with a small task, *T*, though she would not have done so had she deliberated. Even though the misanthrope omits deliberative trust in the case of *N* with *T*, she (despite herself) fails to omit implicit trust of *N* with *T*. While her *implicit* trust in this case is performance-theoretically assessable for success, competence, and aptness, her non-Pyrrhonian mistrust, viz., her forbearing from (deliberative trust in the endeavour to attain apt trust), is not.

Contrary to the situation of the misanthrope, who exhibits Pyrrhonian mistrust,[13] we can imagine a *recovering misanthrope* in the inverse position: she wide-scope forbears from implicit trust *but not* from deliberative trust. Her misanthropic tendencies are so deeply ingrained that she—assume *ex hypothesi*—is simply *incapable* of implicit trust. She trusts, if ever, only with a strong will to do so, to overcome these tendencies. Suppose, then, that with such will to overcoming her tendencies, she intentionally, deliberately, trusts her neighbour *N* with *T*. Omitted here is implicit trust, not deliberative trust. While her *deliberative trust* of *N* with *T* in this case is performance-theoretically assessable for success, competence, and aptness, her non-Pyrrhonian mistrust is not.

2.2 Narrow-Scope Intentionally Aimed Forbearance from Trusting: Deliberative Distrust (Successful, Competent, and Apt)

Suppose *A* is deciding whether to trust a friend, *B*, to watch *A*'s very young children, *C*, for the weekend. The choice is complicated, but after deliberation on such things as risk of betrayed trust, difficulty of task, trustee goodwill and competence, etc., *A* decides *not* to trust *B* with *C*, and does so in the endeavour to trust if and only if that trust would be (not merely successful but) apt.

---

[13] I am using 'mistrust' in the case of wide-scope forbearance (compared to mere distrust) to indicate the wholesale character of the relevant omission from trusting—in that wide-scope cases omit not only trusting but also omit (omission in the endeavour to trust iff doing so would be apt).

This intentional forbearance from trusting *succeeds* even if *B would* have succeeded in taking care of the children for the weekend, and so long as *B* would very easily have failed. This is because, if *B* very easily would have failed, then had *A* trusted, she would not have *avoided inapt trust*, even though B so happened to take care of C just fine. However, *A*'s deliberative distrust of *B* with *C fails* if *were A* to have trusted *B* with *C*, her trusting would have been *apt*. Likewise, *A*'s deliberative distrust of *B* with *C* is competent if that distrust reliably enough would have avoided inaptness, and apt iff *A*'s successful deliberative distrust of *B* with *C* manifests this competence.

2.3 Narrow-Scope Functionally Aimed Forbearance from Trusting: Implicit Distrust (Successful, Competent, and Apt)

One simple example case that can be used to illustrate narrow-scope (teleologically) functionally aimed forbearance from trusting involves bias-driven *testimonial injustice*.[14] Suppose a member of a marginalized group, *M*, testifies that *p* in an open trial, in which *A* is a racist juror.[15] Due to racism, *A* implicitly distrusts *M*'s testimony, including *M*'s assertion that *p*, despite never intentionally determining whether to trust *p* (any more than, say, *A* is reflecting on whether to believe *that* the testifier is speaking, something *A* believes implicitly). In addition, were *A* to deliberate about whether to trust *p* specifically, *A* would have been triggered to reflect on racism in a way that would have offset the racist and implicit tendency to forbear.

In such a case, *A*'s implicit distrust is successful if, had *A* trusted *M*'s testimony that *p*, *A would* have ended up believing falsely whether *p*. Likewise, the implicit distrust is *not* successful if, had *A* trusted *M*'s testimony that *p*, *A* would have ended up believing truly whether *p*. Likewise, *A*'s implicit distrust of *B* that *p* is competent if that distrust reliably enough would have avoided unsuccessful trust, and apt iff *A*'s implicit distrust of *M* with *p* manifests this competence. If we assume, *ex hypothesi*, that *M did testify*

---

[14] See Fricker (2007) for the canonical presentation. It is worth noting that an alternative kind of example that might be used to illustrate this species of implicit distrust involves implicit distrust of *experts*. For discussion of this phenomenon, and some of the biases that lead to it, see Baghramian and Croce (2021, sec. 4).

[15] Note that the details of this case are importantly different from a more familiar case of a racist juror in social epistemology, due to Lackey (2007, 598), the latter of which is meant to illustrate the phenomenon of 'selfless assertion'.

truthfully that p in trial, *A*'s implicit distrust will be inapt because unsuccessful. Because racially driven implicit bias is unreliable,[16] *A*'s implicit distrust of *M* whether *p* will, in addition, fail to be competent.

3. Concluding Remarks

This chapter has taken some initial steps to expand our working telic theory of trust, the core ideas of which were outlined in Chapter 2. We began by registering a distinction that will be important in much of the rest of the book—between *implicit* and *deliberative* trust. This distinction was then used to illuminate the wider point that just as trusting can be implicit or deliberative, so can *distrusting*. The focus of the chapter then lay squarely on distrust itself, its nature and normativity. It was shown that—and here was the second key expansion of the view—at least one kind of distrust, what we called *narrow-scope distrust*—is plausibly an aimed performance in its own right no less than trusting is, and that it is thus answerable (in both its implicit and deliberative modes) to norms of success, competence, and aptness of *forbearance* from trusting.

Stepping back for a moment, our framework is now much richer than what we began with. But it also invites new questions, particularly in light of the implicit/deliberative distinction.

Given that implicit and deliberative trusting are distinct *performances*, distinguished by their constitutive aims, one might wonder what kinds of considerations would ever make one variety more appropriate than the other. For example, is an implicit trustor in any way worse off generally speaking than a deliberative trustor? And more to the point—what would determine such a thing?

Answering *this* question requires that we look beyond trust itself as an aimed performance, but also at the wider kind of cooperative practice within which trusting (and distrusting) of both varieties constitute performative moves. This is the task that the next chapter will take up.

---

[16] See, for instance, Saul (2017), Munroe (2016), and Díaz and Almagro (2019).

4
Trust, Pistology, and the Ethics of Cooperation

Implicit and deliberative trust differ, but under what conditions is one kind of trust more appropriate than the other, and what kinds of considerations determine this? This chapter takes up this question, and in doing so, distinguishes between two distinct though complementary domains of normativity of interest in the philosophy of trust. The guiding analogy this chapter develops is that telic assessment of beliefs stands to intellectual ethics as the telic assessment of trust stands to the ethics of cooperation.

1. Introduction

On the picture developed so far, implicit trust is to be distinguished from deliberative trust. Implicit trust is not the result of conscious deliberation any more than are (for example) your beliefs that guide your behaviour, but which aren't a response to any 'whether' question. For example: 'My phone is ringing', 'A dog is barking', 'My leg hurts'. Even though these beliefs don't 'settle questions', such beliefs can be still be successful (if true), competent (if reliably enough true), and apt (if true because competent).[1]

Likewise, on the view advanced so far, we might trust someone with something, ϕ, implicitly, and not as a result of ever having deliberated about whether to trust them with ϕ.[2] But *even so*, this implicit trust—which aims

---

[1] See Chapter 3, sec. 1. For discussion in the context of performance-theoretic virtue epistemology, see Sosa (2015, Ch. 3, n. 5; Sosa 2017, 71–72, 129–30, 152; 2021, 24–31, 52–58, 64, 110, 118).

[2] Granted, we might *also* take implicit attitudes of trust towards individuals themselves; you might implicitly trust your partner, and in such a way that this implicit trust then carries over to particular tasks. As I noted in previous chapters, I am taking three-place trust as a theoretical focus. This does *not* mean however that what is said about implicit three-place trust does not have potential ramifications for what we say about implicit two-place trust. On the contrary, it might be that implicit two-place trust is to be explained in terms of implicit three-place trust. On this point, I'm remaining neutral. See Hardwig (1991) and Domenicucci and Holton (2017) for discussion. Thanks to Emma Gordon for discussion on this point.

constitutively just at the trustee's taking care of things *as entrusted*—is subject, like implicit belief is, to evaluative norms of *success* (i.e., *did* the trustee take care of things as entrusted or did they not?), *competence*, and *aptness*. ESNT, ECNT, and EANT detailed in Chapter 2, straightforwardly characterize the evaluative normativity of implicit trust.[3]

But do ESNT, ECNT, and EANT also satisfactorily capture the evaluative normativity of *deliberative trust*? Recall that in deliberately trusting, we intentionally aim, in trusting, not *merely* at successful trust (like a basketball player chucking from half court, or an inquirer who aims at truth through a guess), but at *aptness*—viz., at *apt trust*.[4]

This means that, in deliberatively trusting someone to ϕ, (e.g., as one might do when assessing whether to agree to a particular business proposition), one is making a kind of attempt that will be competent just in case the trustor manifests *not merely* a disposition to trust in ways that don't too often lead to betrayal (this is what competent *implicit* trust requires), but in ways that *don't too often issue in inapt trust*.[5]

The achievement of *apt deliberative trust* is more impressive, as a trusting performance, than the achievement of mere apt trust. It demands more, namely, the *apt attainment of apt trust*. One fails to attain *this* aim even if one trusts aptly but might too easily have not done so.

When deliberative trust (which aims at apt trust) is *itself* apt, then trust is *convictively apt* (the choice of terms will be clearer in Chapter 5). Convictively apt trust is, qua performance, analogous in important respects with what is called *fully apt judgement* in performance-theoretic virtue epistemology.[6] In particular, whereas a fully apt judgement is the highest grade of achievement-type in the theory of knowledge, likewise, convictively apt trust is the highest grade of achievement-type in the theory of trust.

However, there is quite a bit to be said about convictively apt trust that takes us beyond its structural analogies with fully apt judgement.

---

[3] That is: (i) *S*'s trusting *X* with ϕ is better if *X* takes care of ϕ as entrusted than if *X* does not (from ESNT), (ii) *S*'s trusting *X* with ϕ is better if *S* trusts *X* with ϕ competently than if *S* does not (from ECNT); and (iii) *S*'s trusting *X* with ϕ is better if *S* trusts *X* with ϕ aptly than if *S* does not.

[4] Note that it is the constitutive aim of any given performance-type that determines what counts as 'success' for that performance-type and, by extension, competence and aptness (see Chapter 2).

[5] For a detailed discussion of the distinction between these competences in the case of belief, see Sosa (2019).

[6] See, e.g., Sosa (2015, 2021); cf., Carter (2021).

This chapter and the next will be organized around two central questions about deliberative (and convictively apt) trust. In the course of answering these questions, the aim will be to understand this kind of trust more deeply, how it relates to implicit trust more broadly in the philosophy of trust, what kind of specific skills it demands of us, and (in Chapter 6) what kinds of things this high-grade trust permits us to non-negligently take for granted.

Our guiding questions in this chapter and the next are as follows:

Appropriateness Question: Implicit and deliberative trust differ, but under what conditions is one kind of trust more appropriate than the other, and what kinds of considerations determine this?

Substance and Structure Question: How should we think about what is involved—not just structurally, but also substantively—in the *apt attainment* of apt trust?

The remainder of this chapter will answer the Appropriateness Question, and Chapter 5 will answer the Substance and Structure Question.

2. Implicit and Deliberative Trust

Consider the following two characters, Fidel and Misty, who navigate their respective potential trusting relationships very differently, in one key respect. Fidel almost never trusts deliberatively, almost always only implicitly.[7] Misty almost never trusts implicitly, almost always only deliberatively.

Is either doing better than the other? We of course don't know without more details. But before supplying them—and in order to get a better grip on what details *matter*—it will be instructive to consider by way of analogy their *zetetic* counterparts,[8] Fidel-I and Misty-I, who are inquirers who navigate *inquiry* very differently.

---

[7] It is worth noting that there is some overlap between the kind of default implicit trustor imagined here and what Jones (2004) calls a 'basal' trustor. For discussion, see Nickel (2015). Further, note that a performance of implicit trust, in the here and now, might be causally related to past deliberation. In fact, that will be the most plausible construal of many cases of implicit trust—as with friendships developed over time. The point remains though that trust, in the here and now (in a given occasion of three-place trust) is not deliberative when the trustor does not deliberate *on this occasion* whether to trust the trustee. Thanks to Emma Gordon for discussion here.

[8] I am using 'zetetic' in the sense of Friedman (2020), and as pertaining to *inquiry*.

Fidel-I almost never inquires into any question of whether *p*; he forms his beliefs unreflectively; they guide his actions despite never constituting the answer to any deliberate inquiry into whether *p*. Misty-I is, by default, unusually sceptical—her inquiries are guided by constant wonder, and she almost always affirms whether something is so only after careful scrutiny.[9]

Let's consider what we should say about Fidel-I and Misty-I, and then how this might organize what we should say about Fidel and Misty. The first thing we might wonder about Fidel-I and Misty-I is what kind of *epistemic environment* each is in, whether it is a cooperative and friendly one (few deceptions and liars about), or whether it is a risky environment to navigate, full of easy error possibilities. If they are both in a friendly environment, then, as one line of thought would go, Fidel-I is—*all else equal*—using a better strategy than Misty-I, one that results in *far more true beliefs and knowledge*. If they are both in an epistemically *unfriendly* environment, however, then—on this same line of thought, Misty-I is—*all else equal*—using a better strategy than Fidel-I, one that results in *far fewer false beliefs and less ignorance*. This kind of diagnosis lines up with John Greco's (2013, 2020) recent work in the epistemology of testimony: according to Greco, the optimal strategy among close-knit communities is *not* to scrutinize testimony at all; whereas the better strategy when testimony is being introduced into a community for the first time is not to accept it *without* careful scrutiny. Greco's rationale is that different strategies align better with different epistemic environments.[10]

But if we stipulate that both Fidel-I and Misty-I are in the very *same* epistemic environment—and further, that this epistemic environment is

---

[9] This is, by stipulation, that she does so. Granted, such a character might be highly unrealistic, given that various assumptions we must make that guide action. For the sake of this thought experiment, let's assume Misty is on the extreme end of what is psychologically possible.

[10] In a bit more detail, Greco's tack is to reject the widely held assumption that either all testimonial knowledge requires inductive evidence on the part of the hearer, or none does. His rationale for rejecting this presumption draws from what he takes to be two distinct kinds of activities governed by the concept of knowledge: knowledge *origination* (e.g., uptake) and knowledge *distribution*. As Greco sees it, it's reasonable to suppose that the norms (e.g., quality control) governing originating activities differ from norms (e.g., easy access) governing distributing activities. Greco's key move at this point is to claim that 'testimonial knowledge *itself* comes in two kinds' (2013, 20), in so far as it is sometimes serving the distributing function, sometimes the originating function. Accordingly, some knowledge-generating intellectual virtues will be apposite to one kind of testimonial knowledge, some to the other, given that 'what is required for reliable distribution is different from what is required for reliable origination' (2013, 23).

equally friendly and unfriendly—then should we say then that their strategies break even?

When evaluating a thinker's beliefs and judgements as the kinds of things that are truth- and knowledge-directed, the answer is probably that we simply don't have enough information. For example, how *good* is Misty-I at the scrutiny that she subjects her beliefs to prior to affirming when she does? At any rate, when assessing their strategies from *this* point of view, the main information that we need to evaluate their strategies is information that helps us work out the extent to which the beliefs they form via these strategies *succeed* in the kind of attempts that they are. Ernest Sosa (2021) calls this kind of telic assessment of beliefs qua attempts *gnoseological* or 'knowledge-related' assessment. This is the *kind of assessment* that tells us that (all things equal) Fidel-I will do better than Misty in a good epistemic environment, Misty-I better than Fidel-I in a bad epistemic environment, and 'it's unclear' in a middling environment.

However, gnoseological assessment—e.g., where evaluative norms of success, competence, and aptness are central—has its limits. It doesn't tell us other things we might care about when comparing Fidel-I and Misty-I more broadly, as inquirers. Gnoseological assessment is silent about *what questions one should or should not take up and sustain.*[11] These kinds of considerations are proper to the *ethics of inquiry*, viz., to zetetic ethics.[12]

The norms of zetetic ethics forbid (unlike the gnoseological norms, e.g., of success, competence, and aptness) for example, spending one's time inquiring into trivial or pointless truths (e.g., truths about grains of sand on a beach, blades of grass, etc.[13]), *even when* one inquires into such truths in ways that pass scrutiny in terms of success, competence, and aptness. Norms of zetetic ethics (e.g., Alston's 2006, 32, 'maximise true beliefs on matters of importance') unlike gnoseological norms—can help us to explain why there is something defective about an inquirer with a wealth of trivial knowledge and no false beliefs. And, in the particular case of Fidel-I and Misty-I, norms of zetetic ethics (e.g., 'Pure moral deference is prohibited'[14]) can help

---

[11] For a presentation of the difference—in the context of performance-theoretic virtue epistemology—between gnoseology and 'intellectual ethics', see Sosa (2021, Ch. 2).

[12] Though, cf., Kelp (2020) for resistance to drawing such a clear distinction between these domains.

[13] For discussions of pointless and trivial truths and the problems they pose for theories of zetetic ethics (as well as, relatedly, theories of epistemic value), see, Kvanvig (2008), Treanor (2014), and Carter (2011).

[14] For some defences of this idea, see, e.g., McGrath (2011, 2011), Hills (2009), Crisp (2014); cf., Enoch (2014).

us answer questions like the following: Is Fidel-I inquiring well if he accepts—even if *knowledgeably so*—all of his philosophical and ethical views second-hand, without seeking first-hand insight into why they are true?[15] Relatedly, is it permissible for Fidel-I to *terminate* his inquiry into whether democracy is better than autocracy by sheer deference to a reliable authority? (Conversely, is Misty-I making some kind of mistake when she fails to simply defer to what the CDC says about the transmissibility of Covid-19, seeking additional first-hand confirmation?)

Capturing what are the correct zetetic norms is a big task,[16] not one I'm going to take up here. The point of the foregoing discussion of Fidel-I and Misty-I is to highlight that there are two importantly different ways—viz., with respect to telic gnoseological norms and the norms of zetetic ethics—by which we might *answer* the question '*under what conditions is implicit belief more appropriate than judgemental belief?*' Certain kinds of things matter for gnoseological assessment of these strategies, other things matter for zetetic assessment.

3. A Structural Analogy

What goes for Fidel-I and Misty-I, I want to now suggest, goes for what we should say, *mutatis mutandis*, about Fidel (the more instinctively cooperative, implicit trustor) and Misty (the less instinctively cooperative, deliberative trustor) in our original case. The guiding analogy here is that **gnoseology is to zetetic ethics as pistology is to the ethics of cooperation**.

Just as zetetic ethics concerns which inquiries to take up and sustain, and gnoseology concerns good and bad thinking *once an inquiry has been taken up* (and here norms of success, competence, and aptness are pertinent), likewise, we can think of the ethics of cooperation as concerning which kinds of people and tasks we should develop cooperative relationships with and place our interest in *initially*, such that holding fixed these relationships and interests, we are then positioned to place our trust (or not) to further

---

[15] For discussion, see Sosa (2021, Ch. 1).
[16] For a 'knowledge-first' approach to zetetic norms, see Kelp (2021). However, it is worth clarifying that, on Kelp's view, epistemology itself—all included—is best understood as the theory of inquiry. With this in mind, norms governing inquiry will for Kelp be a larger class of norms than those that I am calling zetetic norms here (as distinct from gnoseological norms). For another more expansive conception of the zetetic, see Friedman (2020).

these interests.[17] And pistology[18] (and norms such as EANT, ESCT, and EAPT, as well as the performance-theoretic norms governing distrust in Chapter 3) concerns good and bad trusting (and distrusting) *given* the kinds of relationships and interests we are working with. Just as gnoseology and zetetic ethics are two kinds of complementary projects in epistemology (where the norms we are looking to uncover are distinctive to each kind of project), pistology—the philosophy of good trusting as such—and the ethics of cooperation are best understood as two separate and analogously complementary projects in the wider philosophy of trust.

With this broad picture of the philosophy of trust in view, we can now, in a principled way, answer the Appropriateness Question: 'Implicit and deliberative trust differ, but under what conditions is one kind of trust more *appropriate* than the other, and what kinds of considerations determine this?'

When we restrict ourselves to a purely *pistological* assessment, it looks like the 'conditions most appropriate' for implicit and deliberative trust are just those more likely to facilitate success, competence, and aptness in each case. Broadly analogously with Greco's 'two-pronged' approach in the epistemology of testimony, we might then say that in close-knit environments—where there is a shared history of trust[19]—implicit trust has advantages (all else equal) over deliberative trust, and that the opposite is the case in environments where risks of betrayal are higher.[20]

---

[17] What is the *scope* of the ethics of cooperation? We should think of it as, in principle, very wide. The analogy *gnoseology is to zetetic ethics as pistology is to the ethics of cooperation* invites us to think of the ethics of cooperation as standing to trust as zetetic ethics stands to gnoseology, viz., as encompassing norms on trusting that (like zetetic norms on belief) are not restricted to whether the relevant attempt is successful, competent, or apt. For the purposes of the analogy, the ethics of cooperation will at least include norms about how we build and sustain relationships that can serve as preconditions for trusting. However, this is compatible with recognizing that the ethics of cooperation has other dimensions to it where the importance of trust lies alongside other ethical values in connection with cooperation, including justice. To make one example, a substantial part of Plato's *Republic* (especially book VIII) can be understood as a project in the ethics of cooperation, in so far as the ideal state is conceived of in terms of whether the state is organized in a way that would facilitate harmonious cooperation between individual members.

[18] The term 'pistology' derives from the Greek 'pistis' (Πίστις), which means trust or faith. Philosophical pistology (the theory of good trusting as such) should not be confused with theological 'pistology', as this term has been used by Niebuhr (1991), which is concerned to a greater extent with faith than trust.

[19] Within environments where trust has been established, Greco thinks not only that scrutiny is not necessary but also that we should think of trust (and reciprocity on the part of the trustee) as a product of 'joint agency'. For discussion, see, e.g., Greco (2019, 2020).

[20] And given that cooperative activities often take place across the spectrum of such environments, from the perspective where we want our trust to be successful, competent, and apt, it is of course going to be best to traffic in both varieties of trust rather than to have any one as a default.

However, we get a completely different answer when we approach the same question from the 'other side' of the philosophy of trust—viz., from the ethics of cooperation. Here the kind of normativity involved is not restricted to good trusting as such, and includes more broadly how to orient ourselves so as to establish conditions conducive to cooperation.

With this much broader kind of normativity in play, it becomes relevant (for instance) that deliberative as opposed to implicit trust can be positively *counterproductive* in close-knit relationships. For example, as Fay Niker and Laura Sullivan (2018) have recently argued, deviations from implicit trust can lead to ruptures in trust in cases of 'thick' interpersonal relationships, e.g., when there is a shared history of trust.[21] Imagine, for example, the effects on a trust relationship that might arise from a romantic partner *explicitly* and deliberately weighing up whether to trust you on a particular occasion, rather than to simply do so implicitly. Niker and Sullivan take it that suitably close relationships are often predicated upon such deliberation being moot.

Likewise, just as plausible norms of zetetic ethics forbid intellectual apathy as a general tendency, plausible norms governing the ethics of cooperation will be violated by an individual who never (or too rarely) establishes and sustains the relevant kinds of relationships that are themselves the very *preconditions* for successful, competent, and apt trust. Crucially, part of sustaining such relationships will involve being *trustworthy* and cooperative oneself. (Trustworthiness will be a central focus of Chapter 9).

The theory being developed here is in the main a theory of *pistology* (more akin by way of analogy to the theory of knowledge, in epistemology, than to zetetic ethics), one that is developed further in the remaining chapters.

4. Concluding Remarks

The key 'takeaway' from this chapter is the contrast between two distinct though complementary domains of normativity of interest in the philosophy of trust. There is the kind of telic normativity that applies to trust qua aimed attempt. Telic evaluation of trust (and distrust) for success, competence,

---

[21] As Niker and Sullivan (2018) note, this category 'most often will refer to committed romantic relationships, close friendships, familial relationships such as that between a parent and his/her (adult) child, and so on' (2018, 2). For related discussion, see Tsai (2018).

and aptness is *pistological* assessment, in the very same sense that telic evaluation of beliefs (and disbelief) for success, competence, and aptness is—in Ernest Sosa's terminology—gnoseological assessment.

Moreover, just as Sosa distinguishes between gnoseology and intellectual ethics, where the norms of the latter pertain to what kinds of inquiries to take up and sustain, by way of analogy, we should distinguish between *pistology* and the ethics of cooperation, where the norms governing the latter pertain to which cooperative relationships we should pursue and sustain.

Distinguishing between telic pistological assessment and the kind of assessment that is applicable more widely in the ethics of cooperations was needed in order to answer the Appropriateness Question that we began with. As we've seen, the question gets entirely different answers depending on whether the kind of assessment at issue is purely pistological or not.

The telic theory of trust that I'll continue to develop in more detail in further chapters is concerned primarily with pistological assessment and the telic norms that go hand in hand with such assessments. That said, this is not the last we'll hear of the ethics of cooperation, or of cooperative practices. As it will be later shown, the fact that trusting is a kind of performative move within our wider practices of cooperation turns out to be essential to understanding how trust relates to risk, negligence, vulnerability, and monitoring—the topics of Chapters 6 and 7.

A Telic Theory of Trust. J. Adam Carter, Oxford University Press. © J. Adam Carter 2024.
DOI: 10.1093/9780191982460.003.0004

5
Deliberative Trust and Convictively Apt Trust

This chapter aims to bring the achievement of apt deliberative trust—i.e., *convictively apt* trust—into sharper view by exploring its *substance* and *structure*. Important to understanding its *substance* will be to clearly distinguish between *first-order trusting competence* and *second-order trusting competence* and especially how the latter is paired with a different skill/shape/situation profile than the former. Key to understanding its *structure* will be to appreciate, by way of analogy with fully apt judgement, the relationship in cases of apt deliberative trust, between (i) the exercise of second-order trusting competence, and (ii) the kind of attempt one makes in deliberatively trusting.

1. Introduction

On the telic theory of trust developed so far, deliberative trust that is *itself* apt is convictively apt trust—trust of the highest grade. The structure of this kind of trust is more sophisticated than the structure of (mere) apt trust, given that apt trust is *that at which we (intentionally) aim* in deliberatively trusting, and so deliberative trust is itself apt only if *that* aim, the aim of apt trust, is itself aptly attained.

Apt deliberative trust is of special interest because it is what we very often aspire to in trusting,[1] much like, in inquiring, we want our deliberative judgements (viz., of whether *p*) to be not just *successful* in attaining their aim (i.e., of the aim apt belief, viz., knowledge) but *apt* in attaining that aim.

In order to bring the achievement of apt deliberative trust—viz., convictively apt trust—into sharper view, let's zero in on the following question:

---

[1] We are, after all, only rarely in the fortunate position of Fidel from Chapter 4.

Substance and Structure Question: How should we think about what is involved—not just structurally, but also substantively—in the *apt attainment* of apt trust?

The answer given to this (two-component) question—over the rest of this chapter—will be organized in two parts, which focus (i) first (in §2) on *substance*, and (ii) second (in §3) on *structure*.

Important to understanding the *substance* of apt deliberative trust will be to clearly distinguish between *first-order trusting competence* and *second-order trusting competence* and especially how the latter is paired with a different skill/shape/situation profile than the former; likewise, key to understanding the *structure* of apt deliberative trust—and where *conviction* enters into the story—will be to appreciate, by way of analogy with fully apt judgement, the relationship in cases of apt deliberative trust between (i) the exercise of second-order trusting competence, and (ii) the attempt one makes in deliberatively trusting.

2. The Substance of Apt Deliberative Trust

2.1 First-Order Trusting Competence

Apt deliberative trust involves two kinds of trusting competence, *first-order trusting competence* and *second-order trusting competence.*

We've already introduced the first variety in Chapter 2. It is (in short, and to be developed further) a disposition to trust in ways that don't too often lead to betrayal. As such, one could possess and exercise this disposition without realizing they have it and thus without appreciating its limits (and what situations lie beyond those limits).

As was noted in passing in Chapter 2, *all* competences—viz., dispositions of an agent to perform well—are indexed to both *shape* and *situation* conditions that are appropriate for their exercise. Understanding these aspects of competence is important to appreciating the *substance* of any particular competence—viz., *what a given competence is a competence to do and in what conditions*. Here, it will be helpful to recall Sosa's (e.g., 2017) handy way to flesh out this point—within the wider theory of performance normativity—in terms of the 'SSS' acronym: *skill, shape, and situation*.[2]

---

[2] See, along with Chapter 2 (Section 2), also Sosa (2015, 2017, 2021, 2020), Kelp (2020), Fernández Vargas (2016), Turri (2011), and Carter (2021a).

To possess the *skill* to do something, ϕ, is to possess a disposition to succeed reliably enough at ϕ-ing *when you try and are in proper shape and situation for ϕ-ing*. For example, it simply doesn't matter—when it comes to assessing whether you possess the skill to land a plane—whether you can always land a plane safely via emergency water landing, if that's *all* you can do. What we are interested in, implicitly (when attributing or withholding the skill to land a plane to you), is whether you can land the plane reliably enough in situations that feature normal runways; that is, after all, the kind of situation where reliable performance at landing a plane is principally valued.[3] By the same token, it *doesn't* count against your skill to land a plane if, even when approaching a normal runway, you almost always get in a crash when you attempt to land the plane *after* someone has covertly drugged you with Dimethyltryptamine. The *skill* to land a plane is accordingly best unpacked as the disposition to land a plane reliably enough when sober/awake/alert (i.e., *proper shape*), while behind the cockpit of a working plane, approaching a suitably flat runway, with plenty of pressurized ambient oxygen (i.e., *properly situated*).[4]

Of course, what counts as 'proper' shape and situation for any kind of performance with an aim varies from domain to domain, as the conditions where good performance is valued differ across domains; the same goes for the threshold for 'reliable enough' performance.[5] On the former point, consider that although a pilot *does* need to be able to land a plane in the dark to count as having the skill to land a plane, it isn't, by contrast, a mark against an *archer*'s skill to hit the target if the archer (as opposed to the pilot) would perform unreliably in the dark.[6]

---

[3] Because our competence-discerning judgements need to keep track of who would perform well in situations where (as Sosa puts it) 'human accomplishment is prized (or otherwise of special interest)', it is our *own human interests and needs* that—as we should expect—play a role in fixing the limits of proper shape and proper situation that circumscribe a given competence-type.

[4] See Chapter 2 (and, in particular, Section 2) for discussion on these points, when the telic normativity framework was introduced.

[5] Consider, for example, that we don't test for one's driving competence by asking: would the driver perform reliably enough (make it to the destination safely, avoid accidents, etc.) if deprived of oxygen and placed on abnormally slick roads; driving poorly in those conditions doesn't count against one's possessing a competence to drive reliably enough when in proper shape and properly situated—viz., in normal driving conditions. The same goes for more mundane competences, like visual-perceptual competences: one possesses the (innermost) visual-perceptual competence if one's visual-perceptual beliefs are reliably enough correct when one is in proper shape (i.e., awake, alert) and properly situated (not in the dark, in thick fog, etc.).

[6] Darkness lies outside the bounds of the situations in which reliable performance matters for good archery. Even the best archer might be terrible in the dark.

A final point of clarificatory groundwork before we return to the substance of first-order trust: one can have the *skill* to do something without having the *complete competence* to do that thing; possessing the complete competence to ϕ requires not only possessing the skill to ϕ (i.e., which one might retain while drugged or poorly situated) but also that one possess this skill while being in proper shape and properly situated.[7] When one exercises one's skill *in those conditions*—viz., when one possesses the complete competence—one's *performance* is competent.

The above offers us a useful vantage point from which to revisit the Evaluative Competence Norm of Trust (ECNT) (and by extension, the Evaluative Aptness Norm of Trust, EANT) from Chapter 2. According to ECNT, S's trusting X with ϕ is better if S trusts X with ϕ competently than if S does not. Because any performance is competent just in case it issues from a skill exercised in appropriate shape and situation for the exercise of that skill, the performance of *first-order trust* is competent just in case it issues from a trustor's (first-order) trust skill *exercised in appropriate shape and situation*. The *substance* of a *first-order trusting competence* is just a specification of those conditions (in substantive detail), along with an indication of what counts as sufficient reliability in those conditions.

So what exactly are the *shape and situation* conditions pertinent to first-order trusting competence? Consider first the *shape* of first-order trusting competence. Presumably, this will involve at least certain healthy levels of cognitive functioning (e.g., the sort by which we might spot obvious *betrayal indicators*[8]) and which preclude various kinds of mental incapacitation (e.g., being drugged, sleep deprived, and unusually pliant, etc.).

Moreover, it is plausible that one is not in proper shape for first-order trust if one is cognitively compromised due to *ex ante* manipulation or coercion. Here, a distinction is needed between (i) *manipulation ex ante* into trusting (e.g., manipulation prior to one's placing one's trust[9]), and (ii)

---

[7] The idea that one can retain one's innermost competence to (for example) drive a car even while drunk or on slick roads comports well with the familiar idea—defended variously by Tony Honoré (1964), Anthony Kenny (1976), and Mele (2003, 447–70)—that one can retain a general ability to do something, ϕ, even when one lacks a specific ability to ϕ.

[8] Granted, empirical work on our capacity to spot betrayal reliably is far from settled. Early work (e.g., Kraut 1980; Vrij 2000; Bond Jr and DePaulo 2006) has suggested that our ability to detect deception from visual cues is not that much more reliable than chance. However, more recent studies are slightly less pessimistic. For discussion in the context of the epistemology of testimony, see Simion and Kelp (2018). See also Sperber et al. (2010) for a detailed and optimistic picture (what they call 'epistemic vigilance') of our capacity to avoid being misinformed in communication.

[9] For instance, suppose you are duped into trusting the medical advice of someone who presents as a doctor, but under conditions in which this deception would be undetectable even by the most cautious.

manipulation post hoc by the trustee, after one has placed one's trust. (One may be in proper shape—even ideal shape—to trust competently even if one's trustee happens ultimately to betray one's trust—viz., a kind of manipulation or deception post hoc.[10])

Regarding the relevance of manipulation or coercion *ex ante* to shape: just as we don't test for driving competence by checking one's reliability in conditions where (for instance) one is non-culpably misled about the correct speed limit—for example, if pranksters swapped out a 20 mph sign for a 30 mph sign, such that even the most skilled driver would accept the 30 mph sign as reflecting the law—*nor*, in the case of assessing for first-order trust competence, do we check whether one performs reliably enough in conditions in which (for instance) one is manipulated *ex ante* into trusting, as when one is the subject of an elaborate prank or deception (e.g., a surprise party). These are after all *atypical* circumstances, not the circumstances in which we generally value the accomplishment of trusting well.

That covers *shape*. But what are the *situational* conditions pertinent to first-order trusting competence? Here I want to discuss three distinct betrayal-relevant thresholds that can vary independent of each other—namely, the extent, present in a given trust context, of the (a) *gains to the trustee* that would come from betrayal, (b) the *effort*, and (c) the *aptitude* required by the trustee to *avoid* betrayal.[11]

(a) *Gains to the trustee*. In typical situations where reliable trusting is valued, we can assume that there would be *some* gains or rewards the trustee might attain through betrayal.[12] One's first-order trust skill is thus implicitly indexed to a shape/situation pair that includes the presence of *some* gains that would be reaped by betrayal. However, if we adjust the level of these gains dramatically, it then becomes less clear that we should expect even one who is skilled at first-order trust to reliably avoid betrayal when gains of betrayal are so unusually

---

[10] This is just a corollary of the more general idea that a performance's being competent does not entail that it is successful. Compare: Even when every prerequisite is in place for a basketball player's making a free-throw, the shooter may still miss on occasion, despite attempting a competent shot. A shooter's competence, after all, is a competence to hit the target reliably enough via one's method exercised in proper shape and when properly situated. Whereas, in baseball, such a method need only be 30% reliable to qualify as a competence, an archery competence may require a more reliable method, though not an infallible method. For discussion, see Carter et al. (2015) and Carter (2020c).
[11] This discussion of *gains*, *effort*, and *aptitude* further supersedes the discussion in Carter (2020b, §6) which was framed in terms of risk, effort, and skill.
[12] Note that this is compatible with it being, all things considered, valuable to cultivate in the long-term a reputation of trustworthiness.

high. An example here is a situation where the gains of betrayal are ratcheted up to the point that *only* through betrayal (e.g., suppose, by *not* returning a car as entrusted to do) can the trustee save her family by fleeing an imminent threat of harm.

(b) *Effort to avoid betrayal*. Just as we can assume there will be *some* gains or rewards the trustee might reap through betrayal in any given situation where trust is placed, *likewise*, we should assume that avoiding betrayal will never be entirely effortless.[13] Almost always, taking care of things as entrusted involves, on the part of the trustee, performing some *non-trivially effortful* task (often at a designated time, or by a designated time) at the exclusion of performing some other tasks.[14] However, if we ratchet up the level of effort required for the trustee to take care of things as entrusted to an abnormally high level, avoiding betrayal will then be unlikely even for a skilled trustor, and thus reliability in those conditions should not be expected of a skilled trustor. An example here—where effort by the trustee to avoid betrayal is abnormally high—is a situation where *A* entrusts *B* to keep *A*'s child safe while *A* is away on a work trip. As things transpire, it turns out that *B* can do this only by monitoring *A*'s child for a five-year period[15] (rather than 24 hours, as anticipated), during which *A* has been unexpectedly detained.[16]

---

[13] Of course, in rare cases, 'doing nothing' might be exactly what one is entrusted to do (and so in such rare cases one can trivially take care of things as entrusted by doing nothing). Relatedly, in some cases, effort might be trivial. Suppose you pledge fealty to your king: it might well be very easy, trivially so, to avoid betrayal given that you, e.g., might lack the capacity to make such an action that would qualify as betrayal, such as stage a rebellion.

[14] 'Effort' needn't be limited to physical effort; more generally, the idea is that effort will involve some kind of 'exertion of the will', and this could include, e.g., cognitive effort. For discussion of effort and its connection with the will, see Bradford (2013).

[15] Although the duration of what one is entrusted to do can impact effort, this duration case here is only representative of potentially many ways effort could be impacted. For an example not relying on time, per se, suppose you are entrusted to watch a friend's cat at your own house for 24 hours, but it turns out that the cat in unfamiliar settings is surprisingly unwieldy (climbing on furniture, trying to escape, shredding curtains) and on top of that, it turns out you have a previously unknown cat allergy. Thanks to Angie O'Sullivan for the example.

[16] Of course, one might quibble here that what one is plausibly entrusted to do is implicitly *only* babysit for 24 hours or so. The question of what the *content* is that captures that which one is entrusted to do, in a given context in which trust is placed, is complex. In many ways, the philosophical problem of delineating this content dovetails with a related philosophical problem of distinguishing the *content* of that which one consents to when one consents (see, e.g., Dougherty 2013, 2019). In both cases, we may ask whether what determines such facts is some combination of mental states, verbal articulations of these states, social norms, etc. But we needn't settle this general problem here (one that applies no less to theories of trust than to theories of consent) in order to see that in at least some cases, there can be something X that is both (i) something that a trustor entrusts a trustee to do; and (ii) where X involves a level of

(c) *Aptitude to avoid betrayal.* Finally, just as we can assume there will be *some* gains or rewards the trustee might reap through betrayal *and* some non-trivial effort level involved in avoiding betrayal, likewise, we should assume that there is always going to be some non-trivial *aptitude* level involved in avoiding betrayal. For example, delivering a message doesn't require much *effort*, though it does at least require the aptitude to communicate. One without this aptitude couldn't take care of things as entrusted even though the level of effort such a task would typically require from one is low. That said, if we ratchet up the level of aptitude required to take care of things as entrusted so that the aptitude is far outside typical bounds, we should no longer expect that one skilled at first-order trust would reliably avoid betrayal (in a situation where such a high aptitude by the trustee is required). For example, suppose *A* entrusts *B* to help *A*'s child solve all of her maths homework problems before *A*'s child turns in her homework. As it turns out, *A*'s homework includes a prank question by the teacher, which asks for a proof of Goldbach's conjecture.

In sum, then, the *substance* of *first-order trusting competence*—of which we should distinguish the *skill* from the complete competence—is as follows. The skill associated with *first-order trusting competence* (a skill is referred to in a performance-normative framework, alternatively, as an *innermost* competence[17]) is a disposition to trust successfully (viz., to trust such that the trustee then takes care of things as entrusted) reliably enough whenever one trusts *while in proper shape and while properly situated*. We've seen in this section (in a bit more substantive detail, taking us beyond the initial presentation in Chapter 2) how 'proper shape' and 'properly situated' should be unpacked—viz., we've spelled out the *substance* of the skill. Further, one possesses not merely the skill but the *complete competence* for first-order trust when they possess the skill (i.e., the counterfactual is true of them that they *would* trust successfully when in proper shape and properly situated)

---

effort that is both beyond typical bounds *and* (iii) that it's being above typical bounds does not thereby undermine the fact that the trustor has trusted the trustee with X.

[17] See, e.g., Sosa (2017, 191–92). Note that 'skill', within a performance-normative framework, is a technical term (in so far as it is meant to pick out an innermost competence); there are other uses of 'skill' in the literature that have been unpacked differently. One way to unpack 'skill' differently is on an intellectualist account of intelligent action and intelligence states. For a notable example of an intellectualist account of skill, see Stanley and Williamson (2017). See also Pavese (2016) and Fridland and Pavese (2020) for related discussion of skill in epistemology and elsewhere.

while *in fact* they are in proper shape and properly situated for first-order trust. And trust is itself (first-order) competent just in case it issues from a first-order trusting skill in these conditions.

We now have a more substantial picture of what is required for one to satisfy ECNT (from Chapter 2). But, more importantly at present, this fuller picture of the substance of first-order trusting competence is needed in order to understand the substance of *second-order trusting competence.*

Whereas competent *implicit trust* requires only that trust be first-order competent, competent (and by extension, apt) *deliberative* trust is *more demanding* in that competence at that kind of performance—a performance that aims intentionally at apt trust—requires a further additional skill set, with its own shape/situation profile.

2.2 Second-Order Trusting Competence

In order to think about the difference between *first-order trusting competence* and *second-order trusting competence*, consider the following case, where one's trust is first-order competent (and, indeed, even first-order *apt*), but *not* second-order competent.

> Mr. X: Mr. X, having read The Art of the Deal along with several books by Tony Robbins, fancies himself a charismatic dealmaker, overestimating his influence. Mr. X entrusts Ms. Y with information I, in a situation within normal bounds of risk, effort, and aptitude, and Ms. Y does not betray Mr. X. Mr. X's (first-order) trust on this occasion may be apt—his successful trust manifests his competence to trust reliably enough in the shape/situation pertinent to first-order trust. However, suppose that while Mr. X in trusting Ms. Y has trusted aptly, he very easily would have trusted inaptly. Although in entrusting Ms. Y with information I, the risk to Mr. X is in fact not excessively high and gains of betrayal are within normal bounds, Mr. X. (with a distorted view of his charisma and influence, thanks to the Tony Robbins books) would easily have entrusted Ms. Y with information I *outside such bounds* (e.g., had I been information that would have given Ms. Y huge gains if divulged with little threat of her detection), in a situation where he would not have been a reliable enough trustor.[18]

---

[18] This case is based closely on a case that appears originally in Carter (2020b, 2308).

In the above case, Mr. X's trusting is first-order competent. *And* it is first-order apt.[19] Though, crucially, very easily, Mr. X would easily have trusted inaptly, outside of his range of sufficient reliability, given the distorted view he has of his own (first-order) trusting competence, a distorted view that precludes him from accurately gauging the risks of trusting *inaptly* that are present. In short: Mr. X is a good enough trustor to trust aptly in this situation, but he thinks he's better than he is, and this is why he (though not one with a more accurate view of their own first-order trusting competence) would easily have trusted inaptly.

That Mr. X trusted first-order aptly on this occasion—as opposed to inaptly—accordingly doesn't owe to any appreciation of his of the threshold of his own first-order competence (an appreciation he lacks *ex hypothesi*), but rather just to good fortune. In this respect, Mr. X is (performatively speaking) very much like a basketball player who is reliable enough to shoot and make a shot aptly from a particular distance, D, but who—*oblivious to the fact that they are unreliable just a few inches beyond D*—would have gone ahead and taken the shot had they been a few inches behind D. Even if this shot taken from just a few inches beyond D went in, it would be inapt.

A shot taken in the above scenario is first-order competent. And it is first-order apt. But it is not *second-order competent*; the shot is not made in the light of any competent assessment *that* the shot would (likely enough) be apt.[20] And the same goes, *mutatis mutandis*, for Mr. X's trust.

---

[19] Note that the case stipulates that Mr. X's successful trust manifests his competence to trust reliably enough in the shape/situation pertinent to first-order trust; he accordingly trusts aptly. The reader might wonder though whether this is compatible with his also being described here as *overconfident* in his own abilities. Put another way: Should we expect his overconfidence to have precluded him from meeting the conditions for aptness that he's said to have met? There is importantly no incompatibility here. By way of comparison, consider that an overconfident basketball player can still shoot competently from very close range. The problem with this player is that they'd very easily shoot from longer range, where they are not suitably reliable. The same situation applies for Mr. X; his problem is not that he trusts in ways that too often lead to betrayed trust when he trusts in suitably normal conditions; it's that too easily he would (like the basketball player just described) trust outside these conditions. A different way to get at this point is to emphasize a structural point: it's key to the framework used that aptness can persist even when the shape and situational conditions pertinent to aptness obtain *unsafely*.

[20] Are the conditions for apt deliberative trust ones we can expect will be met by young children, or are such children in the market *at most* for (apt) implicit trust? The answer will largely be on a par with the answer we can expect in telic virtue epistemology more generally (Sosa 2021; Carter 2023b), where the version of the question there concerns whether children are in the market for fully apt judgement (or, at most, mere apt belief). I take it that the answer in both places is 'yes', for a reason that lines up with the *externalist* character of performance-theoretic proposals generally. Important to both proposals is that the possession and exercise of competence at the first order, as well as at the second order, are *externalist* conditions; one

As with the case of first-order trusting competence, we can distinguish—in the case of second-order trusting competence, between (i) a second-order trusting *skill*, and (ii) *second-order trusting (complete) competence*. The second-order trusting *skill*—which Mr. X lacks in the above case, despite possessing first-order trusting competence—is a disposition to trust not merely successfully but *aptly* reliably enough, when in appropriate shape and appropriately situated; and the second-order trusting complete competence is possessed when one possesses the skill while in fact in proper shape and properly situated. (And, then, trust *itself* is second-order competent if it issues from the exercise of the second-order skill in these conditions.)

Just as trust could be apt without being second-order competent (i.e., in the Mr. X case), trust could be second order-competent *without being first-order apt*. With this in mind, contrast Mr. X. with Ms. Y.

> Ms. Y: Ms. Y is the manager of a bank, which includes a valuable safe, which Ms. Y makes sure to lock herself before closing up each evening. One day, Ms. Y is called away and needs to leave this task with one of her employees. Because it is an important task, she doesn't make the decision lightly. Ms. Y looks at her 10 employees' track records and reflects on their character—as well as on her own reliability in trusting employees in similar situation (i.e., with similar gains that would be had from betrayal, and similar effort and aptitude that would be required for the trustee to avoid betrayal)—finally selecting her most trustworthy and reliable employee, Mr. Lockit, as the employee entrusted to lock the safe. By fluke, Mr. Lockit happened to flake out this one time, forgetting to lock the safe, and thereby ruining what was otherwise an impeccable track record of trustworthiness.

The trust here that Ms. Y places in Mr. Lockit to lock the safe is *not* first-order apt, given that first-order aptness requires that the trust placed be

---

can possess, and exercise, competence without having justified beliefs about their doing so. This, to emphasize, is the case with higher-order competence no less than first-order competence. In the case of apt deliberative trust, it's worth emphasizing that there are *no internalist* conditions on such trust, including at the higher-order. To possess, and exercise, a given disposition (at the first- or second-level) does not implicate either having beliefs about that disposition, or possessing sophisticated concepts needed to represent such beliefs. That said, the *extent* to which children in fact meet the (externalist) conditions for apt deliberative trust will be a largely empirical question. Just as we have some reason to think that (in telic virtue epistemology) mature human adults will be generally better equipped to host a broader range of fully apt judgements than children, the same we can expect in the case of apt deliberative trust; but, crucially, what makes the difference here is not that adults, rather than children, are more suited to satisfying any kind of demanding internalist criteria.

(first-order) successful—viz., it requires that Mr. Lockit *actually take care of things* as entrusted, which he does not; the safe remained unlocked. However, *even though* Ms. Y's trust is not first-order apt, it is *second-order competent*. Her trust is made in the light of a competent second-order assessment *that* the trust would likely enough (even if not infallibly so) be apt in the conditions in which the trust was placed. This time, it just wasn't apt—bad luck![21]

The reader might wonder whether we are being too generous in attributing a second-order trusting competence to Ms. Y in the above case. After all, her risk assessment here led her to place her trust in someone who betrayed it. One might think, 'some risk assessment that was!' The right reply here, though, is to hold firm. It *was*, indeed, *excellent* risk assessment: Ms. Y *not easily* would have trusted inaptly in this situation, as she might have had she (for example) *randomly* selected the employee to trust with locking up the safe, or if she gave no consideration to such things as the gains of betrayal and the effort and aptitude required to avoid betrayal. But she assessed this unimpeachably, *ex hypothesi*. What bears emphasis here is that second-order competences needn't be *infallible*; they needn't be infallible any more than first-order competences are. (A basketball player can shoot the ball competently after all even when the shot misses).[22]

In sum, trust can be first-order competent *or* second order competent, *or* both. *Implicit trust* is apt so long as it is successful because *first-order competent*; the aptness of implicit trust doesn't depend on the possession or exercise of second-order trusting competence.

Deliberative trust—our central focus in this chapter—is different. For *deliberative trust* to be apt, trust must be not just first-order competent, and first-order apt, but it must also be *second-order competent*, as well as *second-order apt*.

But is deliberative trust apt *if* it is first-order apt *and* second-order apt? The answer here is 'no'. First- and second-order aptness is *necessary but not sufficient* for apt deliberative trust. To appreciate why, though, we'll need to

---

[21] The fact that this case features apt second-order risk assessment *despite* not featuring first-order aptness owes to the fact that impeccable risk assessment is compatible with, in short, a shot that misses the mark.

[22] See, e.g., Carter (2021a) and Heering (2023) for defences of this claim. See also Sosa (2007, Ch. 2). One dissenting view here is due to Millar (2009), according to whom exercising an ability or competence entails succeeding in doing the thing that the competence is a competence to do. Millar defends this view in the service of a disjunctivist account of perceptual knowledge and the perceptual-recognitional abilities that give rise to them; however, the thesis is one he maintains holds for abilities or competences generally. For criticism of Millar's position, see Carter (2021b).

move from thinking about the *substance* of the skills involved in apt deliberative trust, and instead look more carefully at its *structure*.

3. The Structure of Apt Deliberative Trust

Consider now the case of Sherlock:

> *Sherlock*: Sherlock trusts Mrs. Hudson to complete an important task, the trust is successful (she takes care of what he entrusted her to do as he entrusted her to do it), and the trust is apt: his trusting successfully manifested a complete first-order trusting competence. Suppose further that his trusting was aptly risk-assessed at the second-order; Sherlock aptly appreciates that not easily would he trust inaptly in these conditions. But because life has got a bit too boring, Sherlock decides whether to *actually* trust Mrs. Hudson with the task or not by flipping a coin, and so his apt risk assessment in this case is in fact disconnected from his apt trusting.[23]

In the above case, Sherlock's trust 'ticks' a lot of boxes. It is first-order apt, *ex hypothesi*.[24] It is, importantly, also second-order apt. But here is the problem, there is a *disconnect* between Sherlock's first-order trust and his apt second-order awareness *that* his first order trust not easily would be inapt; we should think that the latter awareness would *bear* on Sherlock's trusting, as opposed to being an achievement in its own right that stands as a kind of 'idle wheel' in a deliberative process that results in his trusting.

Compare: here Sherlock is not unlike a political leader who has read and digested an expensive and rigorous intelligence report, only to then

---

[23] Compare with Sosa's case of Diana the huntress in Sosa (2015, 69).

[24] It might sound odd that trust or any kind of a performance could be apt, i.e., successful because competent, even while one decides whether to perform or not by a coin flip. Consider this framing: Sherlock acted 'on the basis of a coin flip'. Such framing suggests that the act, if successful, must be too 'lucky' to be apt. The above framing is misleading, however. To bring this point out, consider an example where the performance under consideration is highly skilled, say, the performance of playing Chopin's Minute Waltz in 55 seconds. An elite pianist is debating whether to make an attempt, and decides to settle the matter by flipping a coin, where heads make the attempt. The coin lands heads, and then the pianist, suppose (through years of practice and talent—this is something we may assume she's done many times before, reliably, and well), plays the piece in exactly 55 seconds. This performance can be apt, successful *and* where the competence is exercised in appropriate conditions, *even though* the decision to play is a decision made haphazardly. The framing on which the pianist plays the waltz 'on the basis of' the coin flip misleadingly elides the fact that the success manifested competence; the success, given the attempt made, wasn't chancy, the decision whether to make the attempt was.

disregard all he has learned from this report before acting. What we would say of such a leader is that their action (on the matter about which the intelligence pertained) was in no way better, qua action, for the leader having read the report; the report was *wasted* on the action. (And this is so even if the leader should get credit for reading and understanding the report very well!) And by parity of reasoning, Sherlock's trust is no better than were he to have *not* aptly appreciated that not easily would he trust inaptly in these conditions. This apt appreciation was *wasted* on his trusting. (And this is so even if he should get credit for assessing risks aptly—viz., even if his second-order assessment is better than it would be were it not itself apt.)

Stepping back for a moment, what the case of Sherlock shows is that the following 'conjunctive' formula must be mistaken:

Conjunctive view of the structure of apt deliberative trust: (!) A's deliberative trusting B to ϕ is apt if and only if:

(i) *First-order condition:* A's trusting B to ϕ is first-order apt (first-order condition); and

(ii) *Second-order condition:* A's risk assessment (that A's trust wouldn't easily have been inapt) is second-order apt (viz., it manifests A's complete second-order trusting competence).

The problem with the conjunctive view is that A's trust is no better, as an instance of trust, for satisfying both (i) and (ii) than for satisfying just (i) alone whenever A's satisfying (ii) *plays no role*—as it plays no role in the case of Sherlock—in A's satisfying (i). The conjunctive view leaves second-order competence as a *pistologically* idle wheel, even if it is (qua knowledge) a kind of intellectual accomplishment in its own right.

But how, then, should A's satisfying (i) and (ii) be related, structurally, when A's deliberative trusting B to ϕ is apt? Recall that Sherlock *settles the question of whether to trust* by flipping a coin. But how does the coin flip *do* that; how, exactly, does Sherlock's flipping the coin settle the question of whether to trust?

3.1 The Guidance View of the Structure of Apt Deliberative Trust

One prima facie plausible—but ultimately problematic—type of proposal that we find in Ernest Sosa's epistemology would encourage us to link the first-order condition and the second-order condition with a *guidance relation*.²⁵

Here's Sosa (2017):

> The fully desirable status for performances in general [...] is aptness on the first order *guided* by apt awareness on the second order that the first-order performance would be apt (likely enough) (2017, 96).

In a bit more detail, Sosa says:

> [...] the aptness on the first order be attained under the guidance of the second-order awareness. The performance on the first level must be *guided to aptness* through the apt second-order awareness (explicit or implicit) that the subject is in that instance competent to avoid excessive risk of failure. This would comport with the subject's apt awareness that if he performed on the first level, he would (likely enough) do so aptly [...] (2017, 96).

It should be granted that any kind of 'guidance' linking the first and second order, however we construe it (we'll return to this), would surely be missing in *Sherlock*, where Sherlock's satisfying the second-order condition, (ii), bears in *no way* whatsoever on his satisfying the first-order condition, (i). So Sosa's suggestion looks initially promising.

If we supplement the conjunctive view of apt deliberative trust with a Sosa-style guidance condition linking (i) and (ii), we get the following:

Guidance view of the structure of apt deliberative trust: (!) A's deliberative trusting B to ϕ is apt if and only if:
  (i) *First-order condition*: A's trusting B to ϕ is first-order apt; and
  (ii) *Second-order condition*: A's risk assessment (that A's trust wouldn't easily have been first-order inapt) is second-order apt (viz., it manifests A's complete second-order trusting competence).
  (iii) A's satisfying (ii) *guides* A to satisfying (i).

In assessing this proposal, the tempting first question is 'but what do you mean by *guidance*?' Sosa does not give us many concrete clues here. Of

---

²⁵ See also here Carter (2023b, Ch. 3) for related discussion of guidance in connection with fully apt judgement.

course, this needn't be problematic in itself, given that we are free to charitably interpret 'guidance' in different ways and consider which way would help us see how satisfying (ii)—viz., and thus aptly assessing risks to inaptness—really *would* make satisfying (i) better as an instance of trusting.

But I want to suggest instead is that the guidance view of the structure of apt deliberative trust is really a dead end from the start.[26] Here is the problem in a nutshell. Stipulate that a trustor *A* has just satisfied the second-order condition on apt deliberative trust—viz., that *A*'s risk assessment (that *A*'s trust wouldn't easily have been inapt) is second-order apt (viz., it manifests *A*'s complete second-order trusting competence). The output of this apt risk assessment is a known proposition *about* whether one's trust would be (first-order) apt.

So far, so good. Such knowledge settles a 'whether *p*' question: specifically, the question whether *A*'s trust *would* be likely enough apt. But, importantly, that is not the *kind* of question a deliberative trustor is deliberating about. Here we should distinguish between *whether p* questions and *whether to p* questions. In deliberating whether to trust, we are deliberating about a *whether to p* question, not a *whether p* question. This matters because what counts as *settling* a *whether to p* question and a *whether p* question differ. The difference is that the latter is always settled by belief (or knowledge), but plausibly the former is settled only when one forms an *intention*.[27] In this case, the relevant intention would be an intention to trust or forbear.

Bearing the above in mind, an argument against the guidance view of the structure of apt deliberative trust begins to take shape. Condition (iii) on the guidance account is satisfied if and only if the aptness on the first order be attained under the guidance of the second-order awareness that *A*'s trust wouldn't easily have been inapt. But second-order awareness that *A*'s trust wouldn't easily have been inapt would plausibly succeed in guiding one to apt first-order trust only if second-order awareness would settle a *whether to p* question: the question of whether to trust or forbear. Otherwise, the matter of whether one forms the intention to trust, rather than to forbear, remains underdetermined.

However—and putting this all together—although second-order awareness that *A*'s trust wouldn't easily have been inapt suffices to settle a

---

[26] Importantly, my reasoning here does not generalize beyond pistological assessment. In fact, for all I will suggest, it might be that Sosa is entirely right that 'guidance' is exactly the kind of link needed to connect the relevant first-order condition and second-order condition *in the case where the performance at issue is that of apt (deliberative) judgement.*

[27] For discussion on this point, see, e.g., Shah (2008).

whether-p question (i.e., the question of *whether the trust would easily have been inapt*), it does not suffice to answer a *whether-to-p* question (the question of whether to trust or forbear). Second-order risk assessment is, therefore, insufficient to guide one to apt trust. It is, after all, compatible with one's both forming an intention to trust and with one's refraining from forming that intention. But if the foregoing is right, then condition (iii) won't in principle be satisfied by a deliberative trustor: this is because, put simply, satisfying condition (ii) isn't *the sort of thing* that we should expect would suffice for guiding one to satisfying condition (i).[28]

In sum, the problem with the guidance view is that satisfying (ii) just provides information. But this risk assessment *adds value to the trust* only if the risk assessment is somehow connected in the right way to the agent's forming an intention (or not) to trust. Otherwise, one's satisfying (ii) will not suffice to have settled the *whether-to* question that distinguishes deliberative trust from mere first-order trust that is not deliberative. This is so even if satisfying (ii) gives us knowledge about whether our first-order trust would not too easily have been inapt.

3.2 A Basing View of the Structure of Apt Deliberative Trust

So the guidance view of the structure of apt deliberative trust doesn't pan out, despite its initial promise. Where should we go from here?

A helpful way forward will be to notice a structural analogy between the *Sherlock* case and another kind of case—well studied in mainstream epistemology—where we find a parallel kind of general structure: viz., where a subject possesses some belief or knowledge *K*, that would help improve the quality of *S*'s ϕ-ing *were S to use*[29] *K* in ϕ-ing, but where *S* ϕs without doing so.

---

[28] One might object to this reasoning as follows: even if we grant that it is an intention rather than merely a belief or knowledge that would suffice for settling the *whether to p* question at issue in deliberative trust (i.e., whether to trust or forbear), it remains that satisfying condition (ii) could of course *cause* one to form such an intention. And thus satisfying condition (ii) could cause one to settle the question of *whether p*. But the reasoning underlying this objection overgeneralizes. After all, as we saw in *Sherlock*, the flipping of a coin could also cause one to form such an intention.

[29] This language fits closely with my preferred theory of the epistemic basing relation, developed in Titus and Carter (2023). However, nothing in what I say about basing depends on committing to this theory.

The analogy I have in mind here involves cases of *basing* in epistemology. The basing relation is what it is that makes the difference between two ways you might have a 'good reason for a belief' you have—and which line up with the distinction in epistemology between *propositional justification* and *doxastic justification*.[30] In the first case, suppose you believe it is raining via reading tea leaves, and that you *also* believe that the weather forecast says it is raining. In this case, you *have a good reason* (i.e., that the weather report says it is raining) for believing that it is raining; the proposition that it is raining is *propositionally justified* for you. And yet, you are *not* doxastically justified in believing that it is raining; even though you believe it is raining and are propositionally justified in believing that it is raining. This is where basing comes in: the reason you're not doxastically (or fully) justified in believing that it is raining is that you did not actually base your belief that it is raining on the good reason you had for believing it is raining, and which propositionally justifies you in believing it. Instead you based your belief on a bad reason for believing it is raining, i.e., that the tea leaves said so.

Bad basing can occur both with or without one's possessing propositional justification (in the latter case: one simply bases one's belief that *p* on a bad reason for believing *p*, and *S* is not propositionally justified in believing that *p* in the first place).[31] The kind of case that exhibits parallel structure with *Sherlock* occurs *with* propositional justification.

A propositionally justified bad baser *has* propositional justification but doesn't use it to improve the quality of the belief that the target proposition is true; as a result, the belief is not doxastically justified. Likewise—and here is the structural analogy—Sherlock *has* an apt awareness that his trusting not too easily would be inapt but he doesn't use it to improve the quality of his trust. As a result, his trust is not fully apt.

The reader should now be able to see where this is headed. What the propositionally justified bad baser needs to do in order to use the propositional justification she has to upgrade the quality of her belief is to *base* her belief on the good reason she has that propositionally justifies it.

---

[30] See Korcz (2019) and Bondy and Carter (2019) for overviews of recent work on this distinction in connection with basing. For a notable exception to the orthodoxy of explaining doxastic justification in terms of propositional justification, see Turri (2010); cf., Silva (2015).

[31] In such a case, imagine that a thinker believes a conspiracy theory on the basis of some reason R, which is a bad reason to believe the conspiracy theory. Here, the subject not only bases her belief on a bad reason, but even more, the belief she holds (i.e., the belief that some conspiracy theory is true) is also not *propositionally* justified for her, given that we may suppose she lacks any good reasons for thinking it's true.

By parity of reasoning, the idea I want to now explore is that a parallel structural diagnosis is promising in the case of Sherlock: to a first approximation, what Sherlock needs to do in order to use his apt second-order risk assessment to improve the quality of his trust at the first order is to *base his trusting on his apt risk assessment*.

The structure of the proposal, then, is that we replace a 'guidance' condition with a 'basing' condition. Rather than to say that what 'connects' the first and second-order aptness, in cases of apt deliberative trust, is that the latter 'guides' one to the former, a more promising idea is to require that the former is 'based' on the latter. The proposed structural analysis is accordingly as follows:

Basing view of the structure of apt deliberative trust: A's deliberative trusting B to ϕ is apt if and only if:

(i) *First-order condition:* A's trusting B to ϕ is first-order apt; and
(ii) *Second-order condition:* A's risk assessment (that A's trust wouldn't easily have been first-order inapt) is second-order apt (viz., it manifests A's complete second-order trusting competence).
(iii) A's satisfying (i) is based on A's satisfying (ii)

What makes this view initially promising is that it maintains parity of structure with what is already a well-established way of thinking about how to 'link' a (ii)-type condition with a (i)-type condition—through a basing relation—in a way that 'gets the goods' when it comes to showing how the former stands to *improve* the quality of the latter. In epistemology, there is, unsurprisingly, disagreement about how to characterize the *nature* of the basing relation;[32] but it bears emphasizing that there remains consensus *that* basing a belief on a good reason improves the belief's quality.

In order to develop and defend a plausible *basing view of the structure of apt deliberative trust*, we need to address a potential issue that we encounter right out of the gate. The issue arises given a *disanalogy* between (i) epistemic basing, where, when all goes well, *beliefs* are based on good reasons; and (ii) practical basing, where when all goes well *actions* are based on good reasons.

The disanalogy is that the kinds of reasons in the two cases are different. In both kinds of cases, the kind of reason that a belief (or action) X must be

---

[32] For some overviews, see, e.g., Korcz (2019) and Bondy and Carter (2019). For some more recent approaches to basing, see Neta (2019) and Titus and Carter (2023).

based on in order to improve the quality of *X* is a *normative reason* (viz., alternatively called a justifying reason) a reason that 'favours' *X* (see, e.g., Alvarez 2010). It must as such be a *good reason* for *X*.

But *what makes a reason a good reason* differs when the reason is a reason for belief as opposed to a reason for action. In the epistemic case, there is a relatively simple—even if not entirely uncontroversial—story: a reason is a good reason for a *belief* if it supports the belief's being *true*. And this is because belief is the kind of attitude such that, by taking it up, we are aiming to get things right.[33]

Good (i.e., normative) reasons for action are different. A reason is a normative reason for acting because it *favours* someone's *acting* in some particular way (as opposed to supporting the truth of a proposition).[34] Here is why things are trickier in the case of reasons for action: Whereas the *basis of the normativity* of (normative) epistemic reasons is relatively straightforward (i.e., the line is that in believing we aim at truth), the basis of the normativity of practical reasons is much more contentious.

This matters for us presently because it means that if we are going to say that *A*'s apt awareness that *A*'s trust wouldn't easily have been inapt is not a mere explanatory or a mere motivating reason[35] but a full-blown *normative reason* for trusting (one that by basing one's trusting on that normative reason one *thereby improves one's trust*) we need some explanation of what the *basis of that normativity is*.

What would constitute a good explanation here? As Maria Alvarez (2017) notes, one important desideratum that needs to be met is the following: Any story we give of the basis of the normativity of normative reasons for action ought to be able to account for 'the relationship between the normativity of reasons *and the capacity that reasons have to motivate agents to act*'. This is best interpreted, according to Alvarez, as a desideratum an account of normative reasons for action meets only if the account can explain (in short) how my having a normative reason for me to perform an action can (i) motivate me to act, and (ii) to act *for* that reason (2017, sec. 2).

---

[33] See Shah (2003), Shah and Velleman (2005), Velleman (2000), Wedgwood (2002), and Whiting (2013) for defences of this idea; and, for discussion, Chan (2013). Cf., Gluer and Wikforss (2009) and Steglich-Petersen (2006).
[34] The favouring here is *pro tanto*: there might be other considerations that count against the action. (Compare: in epistemology we say that a reason lends defeasible support to a belief.)
[35] For discussion of normative reasons in connection with explanatory and motivating reasons for action, see, e.g., Alvarez (2009) and Raz (2009).

Putting this all together, then, it looks like the following is the case. If we are going to vindicate the claim that a deliberative trustor's second-order apt awareness that her first-order trust would likely enough be apt is a *normative reason* for trusting—which it needs to be if trust is to be improved by being based on it—then we'd need some story for why a trustor *for whom this is a normative reason to trust would be capable of being motivated to trust for that normative reason*.

One 'shortcut' for securing this result would be to throw all-in with a strong Humean theory of normative reasons, according to which something is a normative reason for S to ϕ only if S has a desire that would be served by her ϕ-ing. Part and parcel with this idea is that normative reasons, given their connection with desires, are intrinsically motivating—viz., what is called 'reasons internalism'. The Humean theory of reasons, and 'reasons internalism' which is closely associated with it, are deeply controversial.[36] Fortunately, there is a way to get everything we want without needing to appeal to any thesis that applies to all normative reasons for action as such.

Here is the broad idea in outline.[37] Regardless of whether all normative reasons bear any essential connection with motivation—this is where a lot of the quibbling lies—we can still offer a relatively straightforward explanation for how a deliberative trustor's apt awareness that her first-order trust would likely enough be apt is a normative reason for her to trust. We do this by appealing to a feature distinctive of trust's being deliberative rather than merely implicit in the first place—viz., to a deliberative trustor's *intentional aim to trust if and only if trusting would be apt*. Recall, from Chapter 3, that the right way to characterize the *way* we aim at aptness generally, when we deliberate about *whether* to make the relevant attempt (or *not*) in the first place is in terms of a *biconditional aim*: to ϕ iff one's ϕ-ing would be apt. In the special case of deliberative trust, the biconditional aim is to trust iff one's trust would be (first-order) apt. Because the deliberative trustor is already intentionally aiming at aptness in this way, we can see how her knowledge that her trust if placed wouldn't easily have been inapt (when combined with her intentional aim to trust if and only if that trust would be apt) would have the capacity to motivate her to trust for this reason. Thus, we can see

---

[36] See, for discussion, Williams (1979), Wong (2006), Shafer-Landau (2003, Ch. 7), and for an overview of the debate between reasons internalists and externalists, see Finlay and Schroeder (2017).

[37] See Carter (2023b, Ch. 3) for a parallel development of this idea in virtue epistemology.

how the deliberative trustor's apt second-order awareness that her trust would likely enough be apt is capable of playing the related roles that we should expect it to play qua normative reason for trusting: that is, we see how—when one acquires this reason in the context of deliberative trust—it has the capacity to motivate her to trust rather than forbear, and to trust *for* this reason.

We're now in a position to put all the pieces together. Recall, again, the problem that faces the guidance view of the structure of apt deliberative trust. In a nutshell, the problem with the guidance view is that possessing the information one possesses when one satisfies condition (ii) actually adds value to the trust only if the risk assessment is somehow connected in the right way to the agent's intentionally trusting. Otherwise, one's satisfying (ii) will not have settled the *whether-to-p* question that distinguishes deliberative trust from mere first-order trust that is not deliberative.

The basing view of the structure of apt deliberative trust offers a different and more complete picture, one that tells us exactly how satisfying condition (ii) is used to both answer *this* question and to improve your trust in the course of doing so.

On the basing view of the structure of apt deliberative trust, *you* settle the relevant *whether-to-p* question, through second-order risk assessment; when that risk assessment is apt, you then attain counterfactual knowledge that not easily would you have trusted inaptly. This knowledge that your trust if placed wouldn't easily have been inapt (when combined with your intentional aim, in deliberatively trusting, to trust if and only if that trust would be apt) has the capacity to then motivate you to trust *for* this reason. *When you then do trust for this reason*, you *base* your trust on the good normative reason you have for trusting, and through this basing, you *use* your good risk assessment to improve the value of your trust.[38] In this way, you improve the value of your trust by basing it on apt second-order risk assessment in a way that is structurally analogous to how one might improve the quality of a belief by basing it on a normative epistemic reason.

---

[38] The terminological choice of 'convictively apt trust', to pick out deliberative trust that is apt, is meant to reflect this important fact about the structure of deliberative trust when apt— viz., that one's trust is first-order apt *through* risk assessment that one is using in her trusting. In this way, one's trusting (on the view proposed) attains the status of apt deliberative trust only when it delimits risk of inaptness by the trustor's own lights.

4. Concluding Remarks

Let's sum up. This focus of this chapter has been deliberative trust, and what is involved for such trust to be apt—both substantively and structurally. On the 'substance' front, we distinguished between first-order and second-order trusting competences—and importantly—the SSS conditions that are distinctive to each. On the 'structure' front, we considered how not just first- and second-order competence, but first- and second-order *aptness* must be related to each other when deliberative trust is itself apt.

In a bit more detail, we outlined the kind of answer that would be most naturally recommended by Ernest Sosa's approach to telic normativity which powers his virtue epistemology. Drawing inspiration from that approach, we should expect the two levels to be linked by the nexus of 'guidance'—viz., the deliberative trustor would be guided to trusting first-order aptly by her apt second-order risk assessment that her first-order trust wouldn't easily have been inapt. As we saw, though, even if appealing to guidance to 'connect' the two levels move works in virtue epistemology,[39] it runs into problems as a move within the theory of the structure of apt deliberative trust. In place of 'guidance', I've opted in this chapter for 'basing'. On the view advanced, A's deliberative trusting B to ϕ is apt if and only if (i) A's trusting B to ϕ is first-order apt; (ii) A's risk assessment (that A's trust wouldn't easily have been first-order inapt) is second-order apt (viz., it manifests A's complete second-order trusting competence); and (iii) A's satisfying (i) is based on A's satisfying (ii). This view, I've argued, not only avoids problems that faced a guidance view but also offers us the resources to neatly explain how the quality of apt trust is *improved* through second-order risk assessment.

With the answer to the Substance and Structure Question we began with at the start of this chapter, we've now got a full view of what the highest grade of trusting *demands* of us. But what does it *permit*? Put another way: What kind of risks to the inaptness of trust can the convictively apt trustor *non-negligently* ignore? This is the question that will be taken up in the next chapter.

---

[39] Though see Carter (2023b, Ch. 3) for criticism.

6
Trust, Risk, and Negligence

We've up to this point seen what convictively apt trust *demands* (Chapter 5); this chapter explores what it *permits*. Our guiding question is: What kind of risks to the first-order aptness of trust can the convictively apt trustor *non-negligently* ignore? An answer inspired by Ernest Sosa's answer to a generalized version of this question is canvassed and criticized, and a different answer—one that gives *de minimis risk* a central place—is developed and defended.

1. Introduction

Consider the following paradigmatic case of apt deliberative trust.

LOAN PAYMENT: A deliberatively trusts B to pay back a (modern, online) financial debt, which B repays as entrusted to do. Let's assume further that all conditions for apt deliberative trust (i.e., convictively apt trust) are met; that is, A's trusting B to pay back the loan is (i) *first-order apt*; that (ii) A's risk assessment (that A's trust wouldn't easily have been first-order inapt) is *second-order apt* (viz., it manifests A's complete second-order trusting competence); and (iii) A's satisfying (i) is *based on* A's satisfying (ii).

Notice that—in this paradigmatically good case—A's trust *minimizes more risk* than were A's trust *merely* (first-order) apt. This is because A's trust minimizes not only *risks to the trust's (first-order) success* but—given that, in LOAN PAYMENT, A's trust is (*ex hypothesi*) based on apt second-order risk assessment—A's trust also, thereby, minimizes *risks to the trust's (first-order) aptness*.

But *to what extent* should we expect that a convictively apt trustor heed risks to (first-order) aptness? This turns out to be a hard question to get right. The difficulty of this question comes into focus when we consider cases where risks to trust's first-order aptness are simply 'inherited' from risks to the obtaining of 'background conditions' for trusting.

Suppose, for example, that while *A* is deliberating whether to trust *B* to pay back the loan, there is, unbeknownst to *A* and *B*, a secret war on the cusp of breaking out.[1] Two rogue leaders—armed to the teeth with powerful bombs—are themselves debating whether to engage in all-out war (igniting their entire arsenal, which would destroy the world) or to agree to a truce. The rogue leaders decide to make this decision by flipping a coin: heads = war, tails = truce. The result, fortunately, is tails: so no war. Meanwhile, *A* (at that very moment, the moment of the coin flip) signs the loan to *B*, and *B* as expected pays it back—both *A* and *B* remain oblivious to the disaster that nearly took place, but which did not.

Obviously, the war could *very easily* have broken out. It came down to a coin flip. And, *had the war broken out*, then *A*'s trust would have been (trivially) inapt, given that *A* and *B* would, on this scenario, have both perished. *But*, is the *mere modal proximity* of the disastrous war enough to spoil the quality of *A*'s trust in the above case, when the war in fact *doesn't* transpire? Put another way, does *A*'s trust fall short of being convictively apt *simply* because this disaster—a disaster that would have surely rendered all trust inapt (because moot)—could so easily have taken place?

Plausibly, not. And the inclination to answer 'no' here sharpens when we swap out deliberative trust for other kinds of aimed performances. For instance, suppose that while *A* is deliberating whether to trust *B* with the loan, *B* is (entirely unrelatedly) picking a warded lock, in doing so aiming intentionally to unlock the lock aptly. Applying expert precision, the lock opens. Is *B*'s lock-picking performance of less quality, qua lock-picking performance, than otherwise simply because, very easily, *that* performance could have ended up (trivially) inapt (given that, very easily, the rogue leaders could have agreed to war rather than to truce?) It seems not. The lock-picking performance quality didn't seem to suffer at all.

The thesis now in play (which we will refine later) looks like the following: *there are at least some kinds of risks to the inaptness of trust that a convictively apt trustor could non-negligently ignore*. These seem to include *at least* (though perhaps not exclusively) risks to the inaptness of trust that are implied by risks to the obtaining of the *basic preconditions* for trusting at all. We'll refine this more as we go on.

But already we are in a position to pose a philosophical problem. Call this the *Specific Non-Negligence Question*, 'specific' because it concerns exclusively the performance of *trusting*.

---

[1] This case is a variation on a case due to Sosa (2017, 191).

Specific Non-Negligence Question: What kind of risks to the first-order aptness of trust can the convictively apt trustor *non-negligently* ignore?

Any decent answer to the Specific Non-Negligence Question will need to account for—in some principled way—the relevant difference between the war-risk variation on LOAN PAYMENT and (e.g.) the case of MR. X (Chapter 5). And even more, such an answer should also be able to deal with intermediate kinds of cases; suppose we substitute 'risk of world-ending war' with 'risk of sabotage to electricity grids necessary to support online banking payments', which would make paying back debt online impossible.

It doesn't seem promising that we would be able to provide a principled as opposed to ad hoc answer to the Specific Non-Negligence Question unless we first answer a more basic question about risk and negligence, what I'll call the *General Non-Negligence Question*:

General Non-Negligence Question: What kind of risks to the first-order aptness of any performance, ϕ, with an aim, A_ϕ, can the fully apt ϕ-performer non-negligently ignore?

The remainder of this chapter will proceed as follows. First, I will criticize the kind of answer Ernest Sosa has given to the General Non-Negligence Question, and I will then propose and defend a very different kind of alternative, one that appeals to the concept of *de minimis risk*.[2] This answer to the General Non-Negligence Question will then be applied in the service of defending an answer to the Specific Non-Negligence Question, one to which the idea of *de minimis risks* in trusting play a central role.

2. Sosa's Answer to the General Non-Negligence Question

According to Sosa (2017), there is an important distinction *within the class of things that could cause any aimed performance to fail*, between:

Category (i): the kinds of things a fully apt performer must heed in order to safeguard against credit-reducing luck; and

---

[2] The basis for §§3–4 is the theory of *de minimis risk* developed in Carter (2021a), and further in Carter (2023b, Ch. 3).

Category (ii): the kinds of things he or she is free to *non-negligently* assume are already in place.

Let's look first at the first category. As Sosa puts it, an athlete, in order to meet the second-order (i.e., reflective) competence condition on fully apt performance, needs to:

> [...] consider various shape and situation factors: how tired he is, for example, how far from the target, and so on, for the many shape and situation factors that can affect performance (2017, 191).

For example, even if a basketball player—say, Steph Curry—shoots a jump shot aptly, his shot isn't fully apt if he easily could have shot inaptly *because* he easily could have been too tired, or easily could have been shooting unaware from outside his range of sufficient reliability. Tiredness, distance from the target, etc. are factors pertinent to *basketball*.

Let's now look squarely at Category (ii):

> But there are many factors that he *need not heed*. It is no concern of an athlete as such whether an earthquake might hit, or a flash tornado [...] and so on. As an athlete, he is *not negligent* for ignoring such factors (2017, 191, my italics).

And such things are of 'no concern' to the athlete, as such, even though earthquakes, tornadoes (as well as earth-destroying bombs and massive power outages) are the sort of things that *could* spoil a performance if they in fact materialized.

Category (ii)—viz., the kinds of things an apt performer can *non-negligently* assume are already in place (for some performance-type ϕ)—corresponds to what Sosa calls *background conditions* for that performance-type.

> **Background conditions:** Background conditions for a given performance-type, ϕ, are entailed by the presence of pertinent seat, shape, and situation conditions that correspond with a complete ϕ-*competence*; they are conditions that must hold if the relevant 'S' [seat/shape/situation], corresponding with a complete ϕ-competence, is in place at the time of a subject's ϕ-ing.

To make Sosa's idea of background conditions more concrete, just consider as a reference point one's figure skating competence. The *shape* pertinent to a figure skating competence will include being alert, awake, etc., and *this* entails whatever is necessary to *support* being alert, awake, etc.—viz., among other things, a properly functioning thalamus. And so a properly functioning thalamus is thus a shape-relevant background condition for competent ice skating.

The *situation* pertinent to ice skating competence includes a sufficiently flat ice rink; but necessary for the existence of this rink is that a large sink-hole under the ice rink does not suddenly materialize as a result of water eroding the underlying rock layer. (Even more dramatically, the existence of the *earth* is necessary to support the obtaining of *any* seat/shape/situation conditions of interest to human performances of any kind.)

As Sosa sees it, the *quality* of (say) a figure skating routine to music from Bizet's opera Carmen that includes three carefully choreographed triple axels, all in perfect time with the music, isn't going to be spoiled in any way if the skater who lands these jumps flawlessly was oblivious to the fact that they nearly had a sudden aneurysm while skating which would have wiped out the 'thalamus possession' background condition to being in proper shape (e.g., awake, alert, etc.), or that they were oblivious to the near possibility that, deep underground, the chemical dissolution of carbonate rock via the Karst process *nearly* but in fact did not cause a sudden sink-hole under the rink. (Or, for that matter, the near possibility of a world-destroying bomb.) Thus, though background conditions for any performance must obtain for competent performance, they needn't *obtain safely* for that performance to be fully apt. And this is so even if the unsafety of background conditions implicates a risk to the aptness of a performance.

We are now in a position to frame Sosa's answer to the General Non-Negligence Question.

Sosa's answer: A fully apt performer can't non-negligently ignore risks to the first-order aptness of a performance, ϕ, unless

    a) those risks are due to the unsafety of ϕ-relevant *background conditions*; where

    b) *background conditions* for a given performance, ϕ, are entailed by the presence of pertinent seat, shape, and situation conditions that correspond with a complete ϕ-competence; they are conditions that must hold if the relevant 'S' [seat/shape/situation], corresponding with a complete ϕ-competence, is in place at the time of a subject's ϕ-ing.

3. An Underdetermination Problem for Sosa's Answer to the General Non-Negligence Question

The answer Sosa offers to the General Non-Negligence Question is meant to show how we can distinguish between (i) the kinds of things a fully apt performer must heed in order to safeguard against credit-reducing luck; and (ii) the kinds of things he or she is free to *non-negligently* assume are already in place.

But here is the problem.[3] The *criterion* that Sosa offers for making this distinction—a criterion framed in terms of (performance-indexed) *background conditions*—doesn't always succeed in sorting risks of inaptness neatly into either one of these two categories. But if that's right, then as a candidate answer to the General Non-Negligence Question, Sosa's criterion is not a satisfactory one.

To flesh out this worry, it will be helpful to focus on an example that features what is, for Sosa, going to count as a very typical kind of background condition: 'normal atmospheric pressure'. Consider that the obtaining of normal atmospheric pressure is going to qualify as a background condition on Sosa's view for almost any athletic performance-type, given that one cannot be in proper shape without the presence of ambient atmospheric pressure; it is a precondition for breathable oxygen.

Thus, Sosa's view implies that a performer—say, a basketball player—ought to be able to shoot fully aptly while ignoring entirely risks to the presence of normal atmospheric pressure, *even when* such risks to the presence of normal atmospheric pressure are modally close.

So far, so good. But here is where things complicate quickly. Just consider that *dips* in atmospheric pressure are well known to lead to one's shape being compromised. Dips in atmospheric pressure pose a risk to joint stiffness (bad shape) just like—for example—the more familiar experience of burning, lactic acid build-up carries with it the risk of fatigued muscles (bad shape).

However, when thinking about atmospheric pressure in *this* way, though, it looks as though a fully apt athletic performer could non-negligently ignore nearby threats to normal levels of atmospheric pressure *only if* they can also non-negligently ignore more mundane threats to being in proper

---

[3] An earlier presentation of this problem appears in Carter (2021a and 2023b, §3).

athletic shape, including the burning sensation of lactic acid build-up,[4] pains in one's muscles, etc. But these are exactly the kinds of things Sosa thinks a fully apt performer *can't* be oblivious to.

Thus, when we ask, 'can a fully apt athlete non-negligently ignore risks to first-order aptness posed by dips in atmospheric pressure?' the answer for Sosa seems unclear: his full proposal suggests 'yes' in one sense, 'no' in another.

To take another example where Sosa's answer to the General Non-Negligence Question seems to generate conflicting verdicts, consider the way professional chess players monitor their glucose levels through nutrition during games. The kind of shape appropriate to elite chess includes alertness and mental acuity, the obtaining of which entails normal glucose levels of the very sort that is (within the standards of professional chess) taken to be negligent *not* to monitor—especially in classical format games which may last 6 hours.[5] Here again, when we ask, 'can a fully apt chess player non-negligently ignore risks to inaptness posed by drops in glucose levels?, the answer seems to be both 'yes' and 'no'.

In the absence of some kind of principled rule for how to adjudicate these kinds of cases which seem to fall into both categories, assessments one way or the other will end up arbitrary.

In what follows, I want to propose an entirely different approach to answering the General Non-Negligence Question—one that sidesteps the above problem by incorporating into a theory of full aptness some insights from the (i) the theory of social norms, and (ii) the literature on *de minimis risks*. This theory will then be applied to the case of apt deliberative trust specifically.

4. *De Minimis Normativism*

Here is the answer to the General Non-Negligence Question that I'll now propose, defend, and ultimately apply in the specific case of trust

---

[4] Sensitivity to the kinds of sensations, such as lactic acid build-up and the burning experience that usually corresponds with it, can be critical to understanding one's physical limits and when one is approaching them; such sensitivity plays an important role in some athletic practice regimens, including competitive swimming, where these sensations are closely monitored so that athletes are prepared to adjust strategy appropriately. See, e.g., McNarry, Allen-Collinson, and Evans (2020).

[5] See, for instance, recent studies reported by Alifirov, Mikhaylova, and Makhov (2017).

(in answering the Specific Non-Negligence Question); call this general view *de minimis normativism* (DMN):

De minimis normativism (DMN): A fully apt performer can't non-negligently ignore practice-relative risks to the first-order aptness of a given performance that occurs within that practice-type, except when these risks count as *de minimis* with reference to practice-sustaining rules.[6]

In order to see how DMN works and can ultimately avoid the problems shown to face Sosa's answer to the question, several pieces of terminology need to be clarified. The first concerns *practice-sustaining rules*. Let's define generally—in a way that abstracts from athletic and epistemic domains—a 'practice' as a way of doing things and a 'rule' as a prescriptive principle[7] or standard of conduct.[8] Prescriptive rules (hereafter, 'rules') can be primary or derivative (a distinction that we will return to).[9] To a first approximation, primary rules say 'do X' or 'don't do X'. For example: don't break promises.[10] Derivative rules are generated by primary rules and take the form: 'do what a person disposed to satisfy the primary rule would do'. (Example: try to bring it about that you don't break promises.) Rules are important to practices: they 'hold practices together'. But *how* do they do this?

A straightforward recent answer that has been defended by John Turri (2017) is value-driven:

Practice-sustaining rules: A rule normatively sustains a practice if and only if the value achieved by following the rule explains why agents continue following that rule.

'Don't break promises' is a sustaining rule for many kinds of practices: the value achieved by following this rule explains why clergy as well as bankers continue to follow it. Yelling 'bingo' if and only if you have a bingo is a

---

[6] For defences of this general idea elsewhere in virtue epistemology as an alternative to Sosa's reliance on background conditions in a theory of fully apt performance (and what it permits), see Carter (2021a) and (2023b, Ch. 3).
[7] For discussion on the difference between prescriptive and evaluative norms, see Simion et al. (2016) as well as Chapter 1.
[8] Here I am following John Turri (2017, sec. 1).
[9] See Williamson (2016) and Simion et al. (2016) for discussion.
[10] This is the example typically used by Williamson (2016) to characterize primary norms.

practice-sustaining rule just for bingo: the value of doing this explains why players of bingo keep doing this.

A practice might have many rules, though only some of these play the role of sustaining it by leading to 'reproduction via value produced'—alternatively, by having *reproduction value*. A simple (albeit imperfect) heuristic for assessing whether a rule has reproduction value is to check whether it has derivative rules that themselves have reproduction value. If not, then this counts against the rule itself being a rule that sustains the practice, as opposed to one that merely features in the practice.[11]

Many practices *include* performances. They do so when performances are prescribed, in certain conditions, by rules that sustain the practice. For example, the practice of archery includes the performance of shooting an arrow at a target. The practice of playing chess includes the performance of castling to defend the king. The practice of inquiry includes belief.[12]

Practice-relative risks to a performance's first-order aptness, within a given practice, can now be defined in terms of practice-sustaining rules as follows. A risk R to the first-order aptness of a performance, ϕ, within a given practice ψ, is a ψ-*relative risk* if and only if, were the performance (ϕ) inapt on account of R obtaining, it would constitute a violation of (at least one) primary ψ-sustaining rule or rules. To make this idea concrete, consider again the risk a basketball shooter runs when she is *barely inside* her reliability threshold and, oblivious to this, shoots the shot aptly.[13] In the nearest worlds where *that* shot is inapt, a primary ϕ-sustaining rule is violated. After all, these are worlds where the shooter steps just a few inches back before shooting. And it is a primary practice-sustaining rule in basketball that, *ceteris paribus*, you should not shoot too far from the basket, beyond your sufficient threshold for reliability.[14] (Note: this rule has its own

---

[11] For instance, 'don't give the opposing team open shots' is a practice-sustaining rule in basketball; 'leave the gym through the nearest exit when the game is over' is a rule players will follow, but it's doesn't have basketball reproduction value.

[12] Recall that this idea also featured in our discussion in Chapter 4, which distinguished performances from the wider practices in which they feature. In the epistemic case, we distinguished the performance of believing from the wider practice of inquiry, and (as will be relevant again in this chapter) the performance of trusting from the wider practice of cooperation.

[13] For reference: this case is structurally analogous to the case of Mr. X. from Chapter 5.

[14] Within the basic rules of basketball (e.g., a shot counts as 2 points, you cannot walk while carrying the ball) it is a practice-sustaining rule that you not shoot willy-nilly any time you have the ball. The value of shooting (all else equal) only high percentage shots explains why this rule continues to be followed. For related discussion from Sosa on the impropriety of 'blind shooting', in the context of discussing why shooters *aim* to shoot not only successfully but aptly, see Sosa (2015, 71–72).

derivative rules that have reproduction value—viz., 'check how far out you are before you shoot!'.) But what makes a risk to the aptness of a performance *practice-relative*, with respect to a practice ϕ, is whether, *were it inapt by the obtaining of that risk, a primary ϕ-sustaining rule would be violated*.

Of course, when basketball sharpshooter Steph Curry is about to take a shot, when there just so happens to be a hungry beaver outside chewing on a utility pole that controls the lighting of the arena, there is (like there would be were Steph nearly outside his reliability threshold) *also* a modally close risk to the aptness of the shot. But, crucially, the risk to the aptness of the shot posed by the beaver chewing on the electric pole is not a *practice-relative risk*. In the nearest world in which sudden darkness spoils the aptness of Curry's shot, it's simply *not* the case that Curry violates any plausible primary basketball practice-sustaining rule. 'Don't shoot in the dark' is not a good candidate for such a rule. It lacks any obvious derivative rule with reproduction value. (After all, it's implausible that the value achieved by following some rule taking into account *immediate darkness* possibilities explains why agents continue to follow such a rule.[15] On the contrary: the value achieved by *ignoring* such possibilities would explain why players carry on ignoring them.)

The final key component of the view concerns the *de minimis risk* proviso that features in DMN. The phrase *de minimis* derives from the Latin sentence *de minimis non curat lex*, which translates (roughly) to 'The law should not concern itself with trifles' (e.g., the crime of stealing a penny).[16] In decision theory, risks are termed *de minimis risks* whenever they are judged to be so 'small' that they should be ignored.[17] The concept is especially important in health and environmental decision-making.[18]

So why, exactly, is a proviso of this sort needed in (†)? After all, if the account *already* gets the result that full aptness isn't undermined by the nearness of the beaver/darkness possibility—given that this risk posed here to the performance's first-order aptness isn't a *practice-relative* risk—then isn't the inclusion of a *de minimis* proviso redundant?

---

[15] Granted, one *could* do things to safeguard against the risk that the lights would go out and spoil a shot. One could adjust one's shooting technique slightly (perhaps gripping the ball more tightly) so that they can pull back more easily at the last moment. Although doing this would surely help to safeguard one against the risk to the inaptness of a would-be shot posed by the possibility that the lights would go out, following *that rule* (i.e., shoot in ways that are suitably risk averse *vis-à-vis* the scenario where the lights go out) is not a rule with *reproduction value* in basketball. There is *disvalue* within the practice of basketball to adhering to such a rule, and such disvalue would explain why following is not sustaining of that practice.

[16] See Peterson (2002, 47). [17] See Peterson (2002) for discussion.

[18] See, for example, Sandin (2005), Rulis (1986), Rhodes et al. (2011), Whipple (2012), and Mumpower (1986).

The answer here is 'no'. Whereas there is no (in Turri's terms) 'reproduction value' achieved in basketball by attending to immediate darkness possibilities, there *is* reproduction value achieved by not shooting when too tired. Usually this is done in basketball by following derivative rules such as 'keep an eye on tell-tale signs that lactic acid is building up'[19] etc. But there are rarer sources of tiredness in basketball, viz., ingesting halothane gas emitting from a small hole in the court. Suppose that Curry unfortunately does exactly this, which causes him to become tired *without* lactic acid build-up, *almost* tired enough that his shooting form is compromised, but (beyond his ken) it's not. *Within* his sufficient reliability threshold, Curry then shoots and scores, oblivious that he was nearly too tired to shoot with reliable enough form *because* he is oblivious to the fact that he's ingested what is nearly a reliability-compromising dose of halothane gas.

Without some kind of *de minimis* proviso in DMN, it looks like the account in DMN would problematically lump the halothane gas version of the case with the lactic acid *rather* than with the beaver version of the case, as one where full aptness is undermined. But this is a bad result: it seems after all that the halothane and beaver risks—the monitoring for each of which seems equally irrelevant as the other is to quality basketball—should stand and fall together, *even though* monitoring for signs of tiredness is itself prescribed by derivative practice-sustaining rules and monitoring for signs of a sudden power outages is not.

With this in mind, the formulation of the *de minimis* proviso I want to now defend, as a component of the wider principle DMN, is the following:

De minimis proviso: For any practice ψ, a ψ-relative risk, R, to the aptness of a given performance, ϕ, is *de minimis* with reference to ψ, if and only if the safety of ϕ against R can't be easily increased through adherence to one or more derivative ψ-sustaining rules.

The *safety* of a performance against a risk (as this features in the *de minimis* proviso) concerns how easily the risk event would materialize.[20] Doing something to *increase* the safety of a performance against a risk is to do

---

[19] Note that this is an example of a rule that one who is disposed to comply with the primary rule would aim to comply with. It is derivative because it prescribes a way of attempting to comply with the primary norm rather than prescribing simply that the primary norm be complied with.
[20] For some representative discussions of safety in epistemology, see Pritchard (2005, 2007, 2012, 2016), Luper-Foy (1984), Sosa (1999), Rabinowitz (2011), Comesaña (2005), Ballantyne (2012), Engel (1992), Hetherington (2013), Madison (2011).

something that makes it *less easy* (holding fixed that you've done that thing) that the risk event will materialize—viz., that, holding fixed that you've done that thing, the closest world where the risk event materializes now is further away than the closest world where the risk event materialized before.[21] The *de minimis* proviso above says that a risk is *de minimis* when, specifically, adhering to derivative rules of the relevant practice is *not* among the things that can easily increase the safety of a performance against a practice-relative risk. Notice that the non-technical, intuitive idea underwriting this view has some *ex ante* plausibility: a risk to doing a kind of thing X (within a practice) is *de minimis*—non-negligently ignorable, such that you can perform well without taking it into account—if the kind of stuff you could do to fend it off lies beyond the kinds of things you should be expected to do within that kind of practice. The electrician needs to worry about the power going off, the athlete doesn't.

Two clarifications are in order here. First, regarding the 'derivative' qualifier. Here is why it matters. Remember: a risk R is practice-relative (for some practice ψ) only if, were a ψ-performance inapt on account of R obtaining, it would constitute a violation of (at least one) primary ψ-sustaining rule or rules. In the halothane gas case, the primary practice-relative rule that would be violated in the nearest worlds where the shot is inapt is 'don't shoot when too tired', a rule with clear reproduction value in basketball. Now, *trivially* one can increase the performance's safety against that risk by adhering to *that* primary rule—viz., by *not* shooting when too tired. What one can't do, however, is easily increase the safety of the performance against that risk by adhering to *derivative* ψ-sustaining rules. This is because adhering to derivative rules that have reproduction value in basketball (e.g., check for familiar signs that one is too tired) doesn't *easily* increase the safety of the performance against the risk to inaptness that is posed by halothane gas; monitoring in *those* ways, you'd never see it coming—at least, by following such rules. You could, by contrast, safeguard swimmingly against the halothane gas risk by toting around a gas monitor and checking it regularly while on the court. But attempting to comply to the primary rule 'don't shoot when too tired' by adhering to *this* derivative rule blatantly lacks reproduction value in basketball. (You'd surely be kicked off the team.)

Second, regarding the '*can't be easily* increased' locution. Why not just: '*can't be* increased?' Consider that one who gets very lucky could increase

---

[21] For related discussion, see Pritchard (2016).

the safety of the shot against the halothane gas risk to its inaptness by adhering to a derivative rule with reproduction value, like 'check for familiar signs that one is too tired'. As it happens, one of the *less common* side effects of exposure to halothane gas is difficulty breathing, a side effect that overlaps with one of the tell-tale signs of lactic acid build-up as when one typically becomes tired. One *could*, as it were, 'get lucky' and experience this rarer symptom and correctly identify it as a marker of tiredness. In doing so, the safety of the performance against the halothane gas risk to inaptness *would* be increased through adherence to one or more derivative ψ-sustaining rules. It just wouldn't be *easily* increased.

With the *de minimis* proviso now fully unpacked, we can see how the view neatly separates the lactic acid and halothane gas cases (about which Sosa's answer to the General Non-Negligence Question seemed to generate contradictory verdicts), by ruling the latter in as *de minimis*, and the former out. And this means that the wider account—DMN—intuitively rightly classifies the halothane gas and beaver cases as both cases where a performance is (unlike in the lactic acid case) fully apt, and despite the fact that halothane gas poses a practice-relative risk to the aptness of the shot, and the beaver does not.

On DMN, an apt chess move that could easily have been inapt because the player (oblivious to her crashing glucose levels) could easily have been in improper shape is *not* fully apt. This is because on DMN a fully apt performer can't non-negligently ignore practice-relative risks to the aptness of a performance, and this is an instance of practice-relative risk. After all, were the performance inapt on account of the player's crashing, there would be a violation of a primary practice-sustaining rule (or rules)—viz., 'don't play with compromised mental acuity', a primary rule that generates derivative rules with reproduction value, such as 'try to keep acuity sharp by monitoring glucose levels'. Moreover, on DMN, this practice-relative risk is not *de minimis* because monitoring for glucose levels in this case *would* increase the safety of the performance against inaptness.

It is important to note that the above rationale does *not* imply that, to make a chess move fully aptly, the chess player must be thinking throughout the game about glucose levels.[22] Doing *that* would not have reproduction value in chess, even if it would increase the safety of the performance

---

[22] Note that sensitivity to such levels going awry needn't implicate a player consistently having occurrent thoughts about this. While playing golf, I can be sensitive to the wind changing direction by being disposed to notice if it does, and without thinking throughout about the wind.

against inaptness from mental sluggishness. (Compare: monitoring not only for regular signs of tiredness but for signs one has ingested halothane gas would not have reproduction value in basketball even if it would increase the safety of a performance against inaptness from tiredness when there happens to be halothane gas about.)

Likewise, the proposal can diagnose the atmospheric pressure case—the other case ruled as an 'overlap' case on Sosa's view—in a principled way. Though, in this case, the risk (at least in basketball)—will be *de minimis*, unlike in the chess case. The thinking here is as follows: *even though* dips in atmospheric pressure can lead to one's shape being compromised, e.g., by bringing about joint stiffness, this is a *de minimis risk* for a basketball player; she can shoot fully aptly while ignoring it. This is because there is no derivative basketball-sustaining rule (viz., no derivative rule *with reproduction value in basketball*) the adherence to which would increase the safety of a basketball shot against *that* risk. One could safeguard against it, no doubt—perhaps by being mindful of both the forecast and ways in which the arena could open up to the elements outside. But there is reproduction value in basketball to simply ignoring such risks, rather than to concern oneself with them.

5. *De Minimis Normativism* and the Specific Non-Negligence Question

We're now in a position to put everything together. Zooming back out, there were two key questions this chapter was attempting to answer, the General Non-Negligence Question and the Specific Non-Negligence Question.

Let's now *apply* the answer given to the former, general question—*de minimis normativism* (DMN)—to the specific case of interest to us.

In order to apply the account, we'll need to first define *practice-sustaining rules* and *practice-relative risks* in the special case of *trust*. By defining these two terms we can then spell out what *de minimis risks* are to the aptness of a performance within the wider practice in which trusting is embedded. Because practice-relative risks are *themselves* defined in terms of practice-sustaining rules, let's begin by focusing on nailing down practice-sustaining rules.

An idea developed in Chapter 4—one that now bears relevance—is that trust is a performance embedded within the wider practice of *cooperative activity*—viz., of cooperation (roughly: coordinated reliance amongst multiple persons for mutual benefit), and that we can helpfully think of trusting as a kind of 'move' in the wider practice of cooperation—much as believing is a kind of zetetic 'move', a move in the practice of inquiry.[23]

Taking, then, as a basic starting point 'trust/cooperation' as the operative 'performance/practice' relationship of interest, the kind of practice-sustaining *rule* (i.e., prescriptive principle) we need to provide a specification of is, specifically, that of a *cooperation-sustaining* rule.

With this in mind, it follows from DMN that:

Cooperation-sustaining rule: A rule is *cooperation-sustaining* if and only if the value achieved by following the rule explains why agents engaged in the practice of cooperation continue following that rule.

Just as we can distinguish between primary and derivative practice-sustaining rules generally, we can also distinguish between primary and derivative cooperation-sustaining rules.[24] A paradigmatic example of the former involves promise-keeping:[25] the *value* of following the rule 'keep promises' would explain why individuals engaged in any kind of cooperative activity continue to follow the rule.[26] One might of course *try* one's best to keep a promise but unluckily fail, for reasons outside of one's control. Such a person violates the primary norm 'Keep your promises' despite best intentions, but they will have nonetheless followed a *derivative* cooperation-sustaining rule: *try* to keep promises.[27]

---

[23] See Kelp (2020) for a detailed defence of the idea that beliefs are moves within the wider practice of inquiry.

[24] There is some commonality between the specific sense of 'practice-sustaining rules' I am using, and the related notion of 'social norms'. To some extent, the matter of what the content of the relevant social norms are will be (at least partly) an empirical question. For discussion on this, see Bicchieri (2005). Likewise, I take it that the matter of (for a given practice) what the practice-sustaining rules are will also in part be an empirical question.

[25] Note that some rules, like promise-keeping, will end up being practice-sustaining rules for multiple practices. For example, promise-keeping is plausibly a practice-sustaining rule for the practice of banking, also for the practice of romantic relationships. Of course, even though multiple practices can have in common certain practice-sustaining rules, the rules that hold together distinctive practices will include many rules that are distinctive to sustaining those particular practices. For further discussion on this point, see, e.g., Turri (2017) and Carter (2021a).

[26] One explicit defence of this idea is found in Hume's ([1739] 2003) *Treatise* in which Hume argues that norms of promise-keeping, even (contra Locke) in the absence of a government to sanction violations of it, would be followed on account of the value that is attained by following the rule. Relatedly, see Rawls (1955) and Hooker (2002) for rule-utilitarian defences of the value of promise-keeping.

[27] For a more recent discussion of primary and derivative norms, see Williamson (forthcoming).

With the notions of primary and derivative cooperation-sustaining rules in hand, we now can define *practice-relative risks* to the aptness of performances that feature in a cooperative practice. The key idea here is as follows: a risk to the aptness of any performative 'move' one makes within the practice of cooperation is a practice-relative risk, that is, a risk relative to the practice of *cooperation*—if and only if, that performative move (within the practice of cooperation) is such that *were it to be performed inaptly* on account of the risk event obtaining, it would constitute a violation of (at least one) primary cooperation-sustaining rule (or rules). And when the relevant performance is that of *trust*, then, what we get from DMN is the following:

Cooperation-relative risks: A risk R to the aptness of a token performance of trusting, T, is a cooperation-relative risk as opposed to a non-cooperative-relative risk if and only if, were T inapt on account of R obtaining, this would constitute a violation of (at least one) primary cooperation-sustaining rule or rules.

Recall now, from DMT, that the notion of a *de minimis risk* to the inaptness of a performance within a practice can be straightforwardly articulated in terms of the key notions of *practice-sustaining rule* and *practice-relative risk*. Since we've now defined both of these, we are in a position to see how the DMN framework can tell us when a risk to the aptness of trust is *de minimis* (and so can be non-negligently ignored).

***De minimis* proviso$_{\text{Trust}}$:** A risk R to the aptness of a token performance of trusting, T is *de minimis* (and so can be non-negligently ignored) if and only if the safety of one's trust against R can't be easily increased through the trustor's adherence to one or more derivative cooperation-sustaining rules.

And we can now put the three key notions together for the final view, which answers the Specific Non-Negligence Question.

Specific Non-Negligence Question: What kind of risks to the inaptness of trust can the convictively apt trustor *non-negligently* ignore?

Answer: (DMN$_{\text{Trust}}$): A convictively apt trustor can't non-negligently ignore *cooperative-relative risks* to the inaptness of trust, except when these risks count as *de minimis* with reference to cooperation-sustaining rules.

($\text{DMN}_{\text{Trust}}$) is just an instance of the more general theory, (DMN), which tells us when risks to the aptness of *any* performance can be non-negligently ignored. ($\text{DMN}_{\text{Trust}}$) is what we get when we 'plug in' trust-relevant terms to (the components of) (DMN), so that it 'spits out' an answer to the Specific Non-Negligence Question.

Let's now put some pressure on ($\text{DMN}_{\text{Trust}}$)—what (DMN) has spat out—by putting it to the test in order to see if it can do what we need it to do. In the remainder of this we'll consider applications of ($\text{DMN}_{\text{Trust}}$) to two different categories of cases:

- first, we'll apply ($\text{DMN}_{\text{Trust}}$) to 'easy cases' (i.e., LOAN PAYMENT and MR. X), as a kind of 'proof of concept', to show that the view can do *at least* as well as Sosa's.
- next, we'll apply ($\text{DMN}_{\text{Trust}}$) to harder cases, viz., to the kinds of cases where an application of Sosa's answer to the Specific Non-Negligence Question would generate problematic results.

5.1 Proof of Concept: Easy Cases

5.1.1 Loan Payment

A first 'test' of ($\text{DMN}_{\text{Trust}}$) will be to see whether it can get the right result in LOAN PAYMENT. Recall that in LOAN PAYMENT, armed warlords are, on the other side of the world, flipping a coin in secret to determine whether or not to unload their nuclear arsenal, and *were they to do so*, then *B* (i.e., the trustee in that case) would obviously not succeed in paying back the loan to *A*, as both would perish.

The idea here was that, when the coin flip by the warlords leads them to peace rather than war, *A*'s trust of *B* with the loan—when everything goes well—ought to be ruled as unimpeachable, qua trusting performance, *despite* the nearby risk to the trust's aptness posed by the warlords' coin-flip. Put another way: *this* kind of risk to the aptness of *A*'s trust is such that it ought to be able to be *non-negligently* ignored by a convictively apt trustor, even if other risks to the aptness of *A*'s trusting *B* with the loan could not.

But *why*? What would explain why a convictively apt trustor could non-negligently ignore such a risk to the aptness of her trust? The explanation that is given by ($\text{DMN}_{\text{Trust}}$) would go like this: *A* can non-negligently disregard the risk to the aptness of *A*'s trust posed by the warlords' coinflip *because* the safety of *A*'s trust against the risk posed by the warlords' coinflip can't be easily increased through *A*'s adherence to one or more derivative cooperation-sustaining rules.

Granted, the safety of *A*'s trust against this risk *could* be increased, easily so if *A* were powerful enough to hire spies to simply keep tabs on all warlords at all times. However, monitoring for *this* kind of risk doesn't have reproduction value in any kind of cooperative context whatsoever. (Compare: carrying around a device to detect for halothane gas risks does not have reproduction value in basketball, even if it *would* increase safety against halothane-gas-induced risks to the aptness of a shot, whenever such rare risk is present.) Thus, even if one *could* safeguard against this risk effectively, and even if one could do so easily, one couldn't do so *through the adherence* to any derivative cooperation-sustaining rules.

Thus, *de minimis normativism* looks like it gets exactly the right result in LOAN PAYMENT, where we have a risk that, prima facie, could be ignored non-negligently by a convictively apt trustor. This is the result Sosa's view got through an appeal to background conditions which (as we saw) made mischief in other kinds of cases (which we'll revisit shortly).

5.1.2 Mr. X

Continuing a 'proof of concept' of how (DMN_{Trust}) can get the goods—let's now look at a risk to the aptness of trust that a convictively apt trustor could clearly *not* simply ignore. Recall here the case of MR. X. from Chapter 5 (noted again in full, for reference):

> MR. X: Mr. X, having read The Art of the Deal along with several books by Tony Robbins, fancies himself a charismatic dealmaker, overestimating his influence. Mr. X entrusts Mrs. Y with information I, in a situation within normal bounds of risk, effort, and aptitude, and Mrs. Y does not betray Mr. X. Mr. X's (first-order) trust on this occasion may be apt—his successful trust manifests his competence to trust reliably enough in the shape/situation pertinent to first-order trust. However, suppose that while Mr. X in trusting Mrs. Y has trusted aptly, he very easily would have trusted inaptly. Although in entrusting Mrs. Y with information I, the risk to Mr. X is in fact not excessively high and gains of betrayal are within normal bounds, Mr. X. (with a distorted view of his charisma and influence, thanks to the Tony Robbins books) would easily have entrusted Mrs. Y with information I *outside such bounds* (e.g., had I been information that would have given Mrs. Y huge gains if divulged with little threat of her detection), in a situation where he would not have been a reliable enough trustor.

In MR. X., Mr. X's trusting is (a) first-order apt; and (b) very easily, Mr. X would have trusted first-order inaptly. Both (a–b) line up not only with Mr. X but also with *A*'s situation in LOAN PAYMENT. *However*, in the case of Mr. X. and *A* in LOAN PAYMENT, what explains why (b) holds is different. The fragility of the first-order aptness of *A*'s trust in LOAN PAYMENT was due to the nearness of the world-destroying possibility, which would have trivially wrecked the first-order aptness of *A*'s trust. But the fragility of the first-order aptness of Mr. X's trust is due, by contrast, to the distorted view he has of his own (first-order) trusting competence, a distorted view which precludes him from accurately gauging the risks of trusting inaptly that are present.

As we have just seen, in LOAN PAYMENT, the safety of *A*'s trust against the risk posed by the warlords' coinflip *can't be easily increased* through *A*'s adherence to one or more derivative cooperation-sustaining rules. However—crucially—the safety of Mr. X's trust against the risk posed to the first-order aptness of *his* trust *easily could be*.

After all, while a rule like 'try to rule out earth-destroying possibilities before trusting' lacks cooperative reproduction value (on the contrary, following this rule would have cooperative *disvalue*; those following it would contribute to bringing cooperative activity to a standstill), attending to a rule like 'try to appraise your own influence on others accurately' *does* have reproductive value within the practice of cooperative activity, and by following this rule, the safety of Mr. X's trust against the risk posed to the first-order aptness of *his* trust easily could. After all, by following this rule, Mr. X would more easily have identified the limits of his own first-order trusting competence, and that this situation featuring Mrs. Y lay *beyond* those limits.

5.2 Diagnosis of Intermediate Cases

The key takeaway from the application of *de minimis normativism* to LOAN PAYMENT and MR. X. is this: the view is able to get the goods in these cases at least as well as Sosa can via an appeal to background conditions. We turn now to some more complicated cases of trust—cases that have a structure similar to those more general kinds of performance cases (§3) that Sosa's view could not easily categorize.

Let's begin by registering that the existence of a well-functioning stock market (suppose *A*'s and *B*'s money is tied up in stocks) and currency system is going to qualify as a situational background condition on Sosa's view for almost any trusting performance that involves a large-scale (i.e., £100m), modern online loan, given that A cannot be properly situated to competently trust B with such a loan without the stock market and currency system (which are closely related to each other) already being in place and functioning normally; their being in place is a precondition for A to entrust B with this kind of a large-scale loan, even if not for any loan. Thus, Sosa's view implies that A ought to be able to trust B unimpeachably with such a loan while non-negligently taking for granted the stability of the stock market and currency system, *even when* risks to both are modally close. This, again, is because their being in place is entailed by A being properly situated to make such a loan to B in the first place—which is enough to qualify these things as 'background conditions' on Sosa's proposal.

But here is where the analogy with the atmospheric pressure case discussed previously comes in to play.[28] Just consider that unexpected fluctuations in the stock market would very easily compromise one's situation for competently trusting, given that such fluctuations could easily ramp up the prospective gains of betrayal and/or effort for paying back the loan to beyond normal bounds. *However*, when thinking about the stock market and its delicate relationship with the value of currency in *this* way, it looks as though a trustor (of a large, modern £100m online loan) could non-negligently ignore nearby risks to the stock market *only if* they can also non-negligently ignore more mundane threats to being properly situated to trust—e.g., whether there is some strong incentive for the trustee to default, whether paying it back would require more skill on behalf of the trustee than usual etc. But these are exactly the kinds of things Sosa's view rightly implies that a fully apt performer *can't* be oblivious to. Accordingly, when we ask, 'can a fully apt trustor of a modern £100m loan non-negligently ignore the stability of the stock market?', the answer for Sosa seems unclear: his full proposal suggests 'yes' in one sense, 'no' in another—much in the same way his proposal gave this kind of mixed answer to the atmospheric pressure/basketball and glucose/chess cases from §3.

(DMN$_{\text{Trust}}$) offers a more principled way to diagnose this case. In short, *rather than* try to get an answer by asking whether the stock market's being in place and functioning normally is a *background condition vis-à-vis* the performance of trusting someone with a large modern loan, we should (on DMN$_{\text{Trust}}$) be asking a *different* question—viz., whether, in this case of

---

[28] Recall that *dips* in atmospheric pressure—the presence of which qualifies as a background condition on Sosa's view—are well known to lead to one's shape being compromised.

trust, safety against the risk to trust's aptness that would consist in the stock market's crashing can be easily increased through adherence to one or more derivative cooperation-sustaining rules.

Asking this question offers us a more nuanced way to diagnose the case, one that gets the right results. First, note that a bank loan lender's adherence to a rule like 'monitor for possible threats to their existing a properly working stock market' is going to lack any reproduction value—and carry clear reproduction *disvalue*—in just about any kind of cooperative activity.[29] Adhering to this kind of rule would demand of one actions the undertaking of which would prevent successful cooperation. It would demand, for example, at *least* forestalling, e.g., entrusting one with a large loan until one has first taken a series of wide-reaching epistemic precautions—precautions against threats to the *existence* of the stock market—which include keeping tabs on, e.g., the potential for world-devastating events. This is debilitatingly risk-averse; as an approach to risk to managing risk, it is uncooperative.

Just as assuming the world remains in place has reproduction value in the practice of *inquiry*—viz., the practice of particular inquiries would be brought to a standstill if we could not make any kind of zetetic move (i.e., belief) until we had first followed a rule like 'monitor for risks against the annihilation of the world', the same holds *mutatis mutandis* for monitoring for such risks within the practice of cooperating with others.

Crucially, though, this does *not* mean—within the (DMN$_{Trust}$) framework— that one thereby has a *carte blanche* to assume 'all is well' with the stock market before entrusting one with a large modern loan. This is because safety against the risk posed normal variations (including even crashes) in the stock market *can* be easily increased through adherence to one or more derivative cooperation-sustaining rules, including 'speak with a finance expert before making a £100m loan'. Note that adhering to this rule—which has clear reproduction value—*does not* involve checking for, e.g., asteroids that might collide with the earth ruining the stock market. And this is so

---

[29] One might attempt to press back here by pointing out that some philosophers have defended certainty norms on action and practical reasoning (see, e.g., Beddor 2020; Stanley 2008). If such a line is plausible, then—as the thought would go—why not think also that the kind of certainty that would be implicated by requiring one to adhere to extreme risk-aversion rules would be so implausible when the action is part of a cooperative activity? In response, it is important to note that in neither Beddor's nor Stanley's variations on a defence of a certainty norm for action do they conceive of certainty in such a way that action would be prohibited were one to not 'rule out' all kinds of far-off error possibilities. This is so even if there are some construals of certainty (e.g., Unger 1975) on which certainty does require that kind of epistemic work.

even if the nearness of such an asteroid might threaten the aptness of one's trust. (DMN$_{Trust}$), accordingly, has the flexibility to deal with cases that Sosa's own proposal seems to lack a principled answer to.

6. Concluding Remarks

This chapter has further developed the account of convictively apt trust, the key positive features of which were advanced in Chapter 5. The focus in this chapter has been on the other side of the coin—by clarifying not what convictively apt trust demands but what it *permits*. The guiding question has been the Specific Non-Negligence Question: What kind of risks to the inaptness of trust can the convictively apt trustor *non-negligently* ignore?

This question was approached by first outlining an answer to a more basic question for any about risk and negligence, what I called the General Non-Negligence Question, which asked: What kind of risks to the inaptness of any performance, ϕ, with an aim, $A\phi$, can the fully apt ϕ-performer non-negligently ignore?

Because a fully developed answer to the General Non-Negligence Question already appears in Ernest Sosa's (e.g., 2017; 2021) recent virtue epistemology, Sosa's own answer to the question was our natural starting point. Sosa's preferred strategy for answering the General Non-Negligence Question maintains that the fully apt performer can't non-negligently ignore risks to the inaptness of a performance, ϕ, unless those risks are due to the unsafety of ϕ-relevant *background conditions*. This strategy was critiqued and shown to face some problems. A better answer to the General Non-Negligence Question was then defended, according to which a fully apt performer can't non-negligently ignore *practice-relative risks* to the aptness of a given performance that occurs within that practice-type, except when these risks count as *de minimis* with reference to practice-sustaining rules. After unpacking the key components of this view and showing how they fit together to issue verdicts in cases, I showed how the proposal has advantages over Sosa's, and is not faced with the same problems that his answer faced.

My favoured answer to the General Non-Negligence Question was then used as a basis for answering the Specific Non-Negligence Question of primary interest to us. The answer to the Specific Non-Negligence Question that was defended holds that a convictively apt trustor can't non-negligently ignore *cooperative-relative risks* to the inaptness of trust, except when these risks count as *de minimis* with reference to cooperation-sustaining rules. This view was then put to work; as we've seen, the view not only gets us the right verdicts in straightforward cases but also does so in more difficult cases.

The answer given to the Specific Non-Negligence Question rounds out our complete account of deliberative trust, and what *apt* deliberative trust (i.e., convictively apt trust) does (and does *not*) demand of us. The telic theory of trust by this point is now much more fleshed out than when we first laid the core ideas on the table in Chapter 2. However, at the same time, there remain some rather fundamental issues in the philosophy of trust that we have not yet addressed. For one thing, in what sense, exactly, does trusting *essentially* involve subjecting oneself to risk of betrayal—as I've thus far simply taken for granted that it does—and why? Relatedly, many philosophers of trust have signed on to the view that trusting is (in some nontrivial sense) incompatible with *monitoring* the trustee for risks of betrayal; but if this is right, *why* is it the case? And can our telic theory be reconciled with it? It is these questions about the nature of trust, vulnerability, and monitoring that the next chapter will take up.

A Telic Theory of Trust. J. Adam Carter, Oxford University Press. © J. Adam Carter 2024.
DOI: 10.1093/9780191982460.003.0006

7
Trust, Vulnerability, and Monitoring

Here are two perennial questions in the philosophy of trust, both of which concern the relationship between trust and vulnerability:

> **Vulnerability Question:** In what sense does trusting essentially involve subjecting oneself to risk of betrayal?
>
> **Monitoring Question:** In what sense is monitoring for risks of betrayal incompatible with trusting?

These questions have traditionally been pursued independently from one another in the philosophy of trust.[1] It will be shown that they are much more closely connected than has been appreciated. The central objective will be to demonstrate how a performance-normative framework can be used to answer both the Vulnerability Question and the Monitoring Question in a principled way, one that reveals a deep connection between not just the questions themselves, but also between the concepts of vulnerability, monitoring, and *de minimis risk*.

1. Trust and Vulnerability to Betrayal

The very idea that trusting constitutively involves subjecting oneself to the risk that one's trust is betrayed is platitudinous in the philosophy of trust.[2]

---

[1] For discussions of the relationship between trust and monitoring, see, e.g., Hieronymi (2008) and McMyler (2011), Wanderer and Townsend (2013) and Gordon (2022). For some representative discussions of trust's relationship to vulnerability, see, e.g., Nickel and Vaesen (2012, 861–62). Cf., Pettit (1995, 208). Note that the idea that trust essentially involves subjecting oneself to vulnerability of betrayal is compatible with recognizing that not all unfulfilled trust is of the same status, particularly when it comes to how we assess the trustee. Hinchman (2017) for instance, distinguishes between trust that is betrayed and trust that is merely *disappointed* where in the latter case the trustee fails to come through but through no fault of their own. Evaluations of the trustee will be a central topic in Chapter 9. For my purposes, I am using 'betrayed' trust widely simply as a contrast (in cases of three-place trust) with fulfilled/successful trust.

[2] For various expressions of this idea, see, along with Hardin (1992), e.g., Baier (1986, 244), McLeod (2023, sec. 1), Nickel and Vaesen (2012, 861–62), Becker (1996, 45, 49), Dormandy (2020, 241–42), O'Neil (2017, 70–72), and Hinchman (2017). Cf., Pettit (1995, 208).

But what counts as 'subjecting oneself' to risk of betrayal? Getting this right is important to understanding the nature of trust and what is distinctive about it.

One tempting starting point—widespread in the social and behavioural sciences[3]—is to begin with the role that trust plays in facilitating cooperation between parties with competing interests. And here a common view maintains that trust functions as a strategy to mitigate, without entirely eliminating, uncertainty.[4]

This way of thinking suggests a natural, even if imperfect,[5] contrast between trusting someone X to ϕ (as entrusted) with *knowing* that X will do so—one that invites us to link trust-relevant vulnerability to betrayal with (some non-negligible degree of) *ignorance* about whether the trustee will come through.[6]

Unfortunately, this kind of a starting point only gets us so far. It invites us to ask—what *kind* of ignorance suffices here? On the one hand, one might be ignorant that a trustee X will come through simply because there is some *actual* risk, R, (above some threshold) to X's coming through, and *regardless* of whether S perceives this to be the case. This is called *objective risk*;[7] it is objective because its status as a risk doesn't non-trivially depend on its being perceived as such. For example, an impending storm presents a risk that you will not be able to finish painting the house as entrusted, even if you are in denial—or misinformed—about the weather forecast. On the other hand, one might be ignorant that X will come through simply because one *perceives* there to be some risk (even if, objectively, there is not). *Perceived risk* is such that its status as a risk *does* (non-trivially) depend on its being perceived as such.[8] For example, the *perceived risk* that 5G towers

---

[3] See, e.g., Krishnan et al. (2006), Waston and Moran (2005), and Beck and Wynne (1992).
[4] As Frederiksen (2014) puts it, 'Contemporary trust research regards trust as a way of dealing with uncertainty and risk. Predominantly, it suggests that trust reduces uncertainty by means of risk assessment and rational calculation.'
[5] The Cartesian position that knowledge entails subjective certainty no longer enjoys much popularity in mainstream epistemology. Though cf., Beddor (2020) for discussion.
[6] The idea that knowledge obviates the need for trust is broadly analogous to the thought, due to Plato, that knowledge obviates the need for inquiry. In the *Meno*, Plato maintains that one 'cannot inquire about what he knows, because he knows it, and in that case is in no need of inquiry (Plato [385BC] 2011, sec. 80.e). The idea under consideration proceeds by a similar reasoning: 'one cannot trust another to do what he knows he will do, because he knows he will do it, and in that case, there is no need for trust'. A contemporary variation on this idea is found in the sociology of George Simmel, who explicitly contrasts trusting with knowing (see, e.g., Wolff 1950).
[7] For discussion, see Hansson (2018). [8] See, e.g., Sjoberg (2004) and Slovic (1987).

increases the spread of Covid is such that its status as a risk is entirely dependent upon its (mistaken) perception as such.[9]

The distinction between objective and perceived risks maps naturally on to two different ways of answering the Vulnerability Question. According to a simple perceived risk account of trust-relevant vulnerability to betrayal, trust essentially involves subjecting oneself to *perceived* risk of betrayal, though not to *objective* risk of betrayal.

I will argue that the simple perceived risk account is untenable. Trusting essentially involves subjecting yourself to at least some objective risk of betrayal. But this raises a question: what is the right way to characterize the kind of objective risk to which, by trusting, one essentially subjects herself? I will then consider and reject two answers: as (i) the product of the estimated objective probability of betrayal multiplied by the disvalue of betrayal (i.e., as *risk expectation value*); and as (ii) the objective (frequentist) probability of betrayal alone, above some specified threshold. What the defects in these accounts reveal is the need for a *normative* objective account—framed in terms of *de minimis risk*—which is what I'll go on to propose and defend.

2. Trust-Relevant Vulnerability to Betrayal: Evaluating the Options

2.1 A Simple Perceived Risk Account

According to what we can call the *perceived risk account* of trust-relevant vulnerability to betrayal, trusting someone with something doesn't actually require being *in fact* vulnerable to betrayal. Trusting just, always and everywhere, requires of the trustor a (non-factive) *perception* of such vulnerability to the trustee's not taking care of things as entrusted.

The idea that trust is always accompanied by, on the part of the trustor, a perceived risk of betrayal seems initially plausible when we focus on mundane cases of interpersonal trust. Suppose you ask the person sitting next to you to keep an eye on your laptop for a few minutes while you take a phone call. They agree. Although, granted, you presumably attempt through this cooperative exchange to *decrease* your vulnerability to having the laptop stolen, (minimizing risk by your own lights of it being taken), you will typically at least perceive *that* you are relying on this person, on her goodwill

---

[9] For discussion of this perceived risk, and the extent of its uptake on social media, see Ahmed et al. (2020).

and competence, and so to the limits of that goodwill and competence. As Baier (1986) captures this idea, trusting essentially involves perceived vulnerability in so far as it involves, on the part of the trustor, always some 'accepted vulnerability to another's possible but not expected ill will (or lack of good will) toward one' (1986, 235).

If the above line of thought looks plausible enough in paradigmatic cases, we might expect that the idea that trust implicates *perceived* vulnerability to betrayal generalizes to all cases of genuine trust. That is, we might think that the *sense* in which trusting involves vulnerability is best captured by just the kind of *perceived* vulnerability that standard cases of trust seem to involve.

One initial—but ultimately misguided—line of argument against a simple perceived risk account of trust-relevant vulnerability to betrayal holds that there is a tension between (i) the presumed explicit, conscious awareness involved in risk perception, and (ii) the unconscious or tacit character of (at least some kinds of) trusting. Trust can certainly be unconscious or tacit.[10] And it *seems* plausible on first blush that risk perception is not. For example, it is a hallmark of the 'Risk Society' research programme (Beck and Wynne 1992; Giddens 2013) that our perceptions of risk are often given expression through affect such as fear and anxiety.[11]

But the tension here is only apparent. The countenancing of implicit trust is problematic for the perceived risk account only if risk perception of the sort that is essential to trust can't *itself* be unconscious or tacit. But the empirical evidence—especially over the past several decades[12]—on unconscious bias and risk perception has established, uncontroversially, that *even if* some risk perception is accompanied with conscious awareness (i.e., some combination of occurrent beliefs plus affect) a significant extent of our risk perception takes place below the surface of conscious awareness. (Compare: our cognitive biases are often *unconscious* biases, and at least some of these biases consist in perceptions of risk[13]).[14]

What this means is just that *if* the perceived risk account of trust-relevant vulnerability to betrayal is problematic, it isn't going to be so on account of any 'mismatch' between the implicit character of (some) trust and the

---

[10] For some empirical discussion on the ubiquity of tacit trust, see, e.g., Lagerspetz (1998), Burns et al. (2006), and Guo et al. (2014).

[11] In this line of thinking, Bauman (2013) describes our modern high-tech predicament, characterized by new technologies and dangers, as pervaded by a 'derivative fear' namely 'the sentiment of being susceptible to danger: a feeling of insecurity and vulnerability'.

[12] See, e.g., Sjoberg (2000) and Slovic (1988).

[13] One classic example here is 'shooter bias' (e.g., Unkelbach et al. 2008).

[14] For some representative discussions of unconscious or implicit bias, which include some perceptions of risk, see, e.g., Saul (2013) and Holroyd et al. (2017).

alleged conscious character of risk perception; just as trust itself can be deliberative or implicit, so can our perceptions of risks to its being betrayed. That point aside, there are several problems for the perceived risk account of trust-relevant vulnerability to betrayal, which challenge both its necessity and, more importantly, its sufficiency.

First, regarding necessity. Even if we grant that both trust as well as our perceptions of risk can admit of deliberative and conscious as well as tacit or implicit varieties, there is scope to question whether any kind of perceived risk of betrayal always and everywhere accompanies trusting. The kind of cases that look initially problematic here are ones where a trustor's irrationality (or rational but mistaken beliefs) lead to a mismeasure of their own vulnerability. Suppose, to add to the mundane laptop example above, that you become (for whatever reason) *subjectively certain* that the trustee will take care of things as entrusted; you assign probability 1 to your trustee (with respect to that task), after leaving the trustee with your laptop and stepping out to take the call.

Question: Have you, through such irrational overestimation, *thereby ceased* from trusting this person to watch your laptop, while they continue to watch it while you are away? Or, alternatively, even with this subjective confidence, do you continue to trust them with the laptop while at the same time simply *misevaluating* by way of *underestimating* the level of risk of betrayal that's at play? The latter explanation looks at least as plausible (if not more plausible) than the former explanation. But the defender of the view that trust essentially requires perceived risk of vulnerability cannot avail herself of the latter explanation.[15]

---

[15] One might see the potential for a reply that takes inspiration from recent work on trust and reliance by Katherine Dormandy (2020). As Dormandy sees it, trusting requires (among other things) using the proposition that someone will do something, ϕ, in your practical reasoning. But, she notes, you can do *that* without actually relying on them in such a way that you are vulnerable to ϕ not being done. For example, suppose you have a 'backup plan' in motion by way of an arrangement with an alternative trustee. You *rely* on X, as Dormandy sees it, to the extent that you don't 'have an alternative plan or means' (2020, 2) of securing the target outcome other than their doing that thing. If you think trust *doesn't* require reliance in Dormandy's sense which excludes having any alternative means at one's disposal, you might think that the sense in which, by trusting (X with ϕ), you render yourself vulnerable is *merely* the sense in which X's ϕ-ing *features in how you reason practically* (e.g., you're vulnerable in reasoning through a false premise by using the proposition that they will come through in your reasoning, even if not relying on them). In so far we think of risk of betrayed trust as only picking out risk of someone acting so that we've reasoned through a false premise, we can envision a version of the perceived risk account (of trust-relevant vulnerability to betrayal) that fits snugly with a restrictive view of reliance such as Dormandy's on which trusting doesn't entail reliance. There are two points in response to the above. First, even in cases of trust with a 'backup trustee' designated, one can remain vulnerable to *betrayal* by (either) trustee, even if

But even setting aside quibbles about whether perceived risk of betrayal is *necessary* for trust, there are independent and potentially more serious problems with the sufficiency of mere perceived vulnerability to betrayal in capturing the sense in which by trusting we're so vulnerable.

Consider the following case:

MOOT RELIANCE: A, at t_1, trusts B to sail a ship across the lake. B comes through at t_2 as entrusted. With a good view of the lake, A has plenty of evidence at t_2 that B has, in fact, come through, and that A's vulnerability to betrayal by B is eliminated, given that B has already sailed the ship. But, against the evidence (and against the facts)—perhaps on account of sheer irrational prejudice against B or some other delusion—A refuses to believe this has happened. And so, as a result, A continues to *perceive* herself to be vulnerable to B's not sailing the ship, even though the ship has already sailed.

Question: Was A continuing to trust B to sail the ship at t_2, when whatever vulnerability to betrayal that might be implicated by reliance (i.e., on the limits of B's competence or goodwill) on B is already *mooted* at t_2, or, alternatively, did A at t_2 merely *think* they were still trusting B to sail the ship, when in fact B had already *fulfilled* what B was entrusted to do? The former gloss is difficult to make sense of; for one thing, the aim constitutive of the specific trusting performance at issue (i.e., that B sail the ship across the lake) has *already been secured* at t_2, bringing, as it were, an end to the trusting performance; by way of analogy, you are not still *shooting a ball after it's gone through the net*, regardless if, against the evidence and the facts, you think the ball is still in the air.

The latter idea, that A at t_2 merely *thinks* they are still trusting B to sail the ship lines up with the idea that we can be *mistaken* about whether we are continuing to make a given trusting attempt (rather than being infallible

---

it's very unlikely that *neither* trustee (primary or backup) will take care of things as entrusted. For instance, suppose you trust A to ϕ and (by way of backup) B to ϕ; you're plausibly making yourself in fact vulnerable to betrayal by either, regardless of what the other does. Secondly, it's worth registering—in connection with thinking about trusting in cases that feature 'backup plans'—that *too much by way of precaution-taking* and a given case begins to resemble PARANOID PARENT, which (e.g., with the nanny cam in place and being constantly monitored) is typically taken to be a case where trust isn't present. Thus, we should be careful to think that (once enough backup plans are in place, enough precautions taken) trust remains intact. We will pick up the issue of trust's relationship with (active) monitoring later in this chapter.

about that). And, moreover, the plausibility of this latter way of thinking about cases like MOOT RELIANCE would be explained neatly by the idea that trust involves subjecting yourself to *at least some (actual) risk of betrayal*, viz., a kind of vulnerability in trusting that is not *merely* perceived.

2.2 Towards an Objective Risk Account

Let's explore now in some detail the idea that necessary to trusting is subjecting yourself to at least some (non-negligible) risk to betrayal whose status *as* a risk to betrayal doesn't (non-trivially) depend on its being perceived as such. A natural first-pass at refining this idea maintains the following: trust essentially involves subjecting oneself to risk of betrayal *beyond some objective risk 'threshold'*.

As is common in risk analysis,[16] an (objective) risk threshold is set as (above or below) some specified risk *expectation value*, which is calculated as the product of (i) objective (or frequentist) probability of the risk event obtaining, and (ii) its severity (i.e., degree of harm of the risk event's obtaining). For example, the risk expectation value of a low-probability risk with significant severity were it to obtain might be very similar to the risk expectation value of a much higher probability but with less severe risk.

A qualification here needs some care. One might ask, 'Since we must inevitably use our own evidence to work out what the risk expectation value is for a given risk, and different people have different evidence that they will be relying on to make such an assessment, then doesn't the notion of "objective" risk—understood as above a risk expectation value threshold—just collapse into a perceived risk account?' The answer, importantly, is 'no'. When we try to determine a given risk expectation value, we inevitably make a subjective *assessment* of the objective probability of the risk event obtaining as well as of the objective disvalue. But—and this is a crucial point of difference between the notions of objective risk and perceived risk—on the latter account, what the risk facts are do not depend on our *estimates*. In characterizing risk expectation value, we are attempting to characterize something that is *mind-independent*. Perceived risks by contrast depend (non-trivially) on their being perceived as such.

Bearing these qualifications in mind, appealing to objective risk expectation value (the product of the objective probability of the risk event

[16] See, e.g., Hansson (2018, 2004) for discussion.

obtaining multiplied by its severity) would be at least one natural way by which one might try to assess *risk of betrayal, simpliciter*. However, appealing to objective risk expectation value is ultimately not a promising way to think about *trust-relevant* vulnerability to betrayal, viz., as vulnerability expressed in terms of risk expectation value threshold. The problem is not the objective frequentist interpretation of probability at issue,[17] but rather what happens when we adjust (significantly) the expected disvalue. To see the problem, consider the following simple pair of cases:

BABYSITTER: *A* trusts *B* to responsibly babysit their child, *C,* for the weekend; assume the objective probability of betrayal is .001 and would generate 100,000 units of disvalue.

PENCIL: *A* trusts *B* to use *A*'s pencil and return it; assume the objective probability of betrayal is .1 and betrayal would generate .001 units of disvalue.

Both BABYSITTER and PENCIL are paradigmatic cases of trust, though the risk expectation value products are dramatically different: in BABYSITTER, .001 × 100,000 = a risk expectation value of 100. In PENCIL, .1 × .001 = a risk expectation value of .0001, which will—and here is the worry—end up being lower than any kind of plausible threshold we might appeal to in order to distinguish cases of genuine trust from cases where there is effectively no objective risk of betrayal. What's more, cases like PENCIL become even more difficult for the kind of proposal under consideration when we lower *even further* the disvalue of betrayal (e.g., to .00000001 disvalue).[18] What cases like PENCIL seem to suggest, then, is that if we want to characterize the kind of risk that trust essentially involves subjecting oneself to in terms of objective rather than merely perceived risk, we might do better to simply control for the severity of betrayal and then characterize the relevant risk threshold solely in terms of the objective

---

[17] It is worth noting that risk expectation value, while naturally allied to a probabilistic gloss, isn't necessarily tied to one. For a modal approach to risk expectation value, see Pritchard (2015).

[18] Another kind of case that serves to capture this kind of problem will simply shift the value of what is entrusted to near zero, where the shift takes place after trust is placed. For example, I may loan you my gold pen (my only valuable possession) so you can impress a client. I trust that you'll return it. In the meantime, a goldmine might be discovered that saturates the market and sends its value to ~£0. This fact doesn't undermine my having trusted, and continuing to trust, you to return the gold pen. Thanks to Bryan Pickel for discussion of this kind of case.

probability of betrayal. Then, presumably, PENCIL will be above the relevant risk threshold, given that the probability is .1 (10%).

Continuing with this idea, suppose we were to set the threshold as .05 (5%). This move will get PENCIL right; and since the probability that B at t_2 hasn't taken care of things as entrusted in MOOTED RELIANCE is 0, there is no pressure to rule in MOOTED RELIANCE. However, the cost with this kind of a move is that we can then no longer deal with cases like BABYSITTER. After all, when stakes are high (i.e., when the disvalue of betrayal is suitably high), it seems we might, and very often do, trust one even when the objective risk is very low—i.e., 1 in 1,000 (.10%) as in the case of BABYSITTER. Cases like BABYSITTER are not aberrations: many cases of trust (e.g., with loved ones' lives and welfare) have a structure whereby something of high value is entrusted to someone very reliable, precisely *because* they are very reliable, and are accordingly very unlikely to betray the trust.

One might try to deal with the above by simply setting the objective probability even lower. On such a view, trust essentially involves subjecting oneself to betrayal in the sense that the objective probability of betrayal must be, e.g., at least 0.000001 (0.0001%, i.e., 1 in a million). Since there is probably at *least* a 1 in a million chance the hero in BABYSITTER brings about a disaster, this tweak seems to put the threshold on the right side of BABYSITTER. But the cost of setting the threshold *this* low is that you then face problems with cases in the vicinity of PARANOID PARENT and (depending on how far one goes) MOOTED RELIANCE.

2.3 A Performance-Normative Account

Here is where we've got to. Trust essentially involves subjecting oneself to risk of betrayal in a sense that: (i) cannot be captured exclusively with reference to perceived risk of betrayal, because trust requires at least some objective risk of betrayal; however, (ii) the threshold of objective risk above which one by trusting must essentially subject herself to isn't something we can plausibly capture satisfactorily in terms of either (a) objective risk expectation value; or (b) the objective probability of betrayal alone; (iii) neither (a) nor (b) could handle all three of our examples cases together; and so (iv) *whatever* level of objective risk beyond which by trusting we thereby subject ourselves to accordingly needs to be characterized in some other way.

The way forward, I want to suggest, is to pursue the idea that the relevant threshold of objective risk to which by trusting one essentially subjects herself to is fixed by neither (i) risk expectation value nor by (ii) simple objective probability of betrayal, but rather it is fixed (iii) *normatively*—viz., with reference to the (objective) normative concept of *de minimis risk* introduced in Chapter 6, viz., with reference to risks that can be *non-negligently* ignored by a trustor.

The working idea that I will unpack, refine, and then put to work in order to handle our problem cases is the following *De Minimis* Account (DMA) of trust-relevant vulnerability to betrayal:

De Minimis **Account (DMA):** Trust essentially involves subjecting oneself to a risk of betrayal that is not merely *de minimis* within the relevant cooperative practice.

DMA tells us that trust essentially involves subjecting oneself to at least some risk or risks of betrayal that *aren't* merely *de minimis* (in the sense of Chapter 6). That is to say: trust essentially involves subjecting oneself to risks of betrayal that *aren't* merely of the sort such that a trustor couldn't increase the safety against their obtaining by adhering to rules that have cooperative reproduction value.

Before considering what this account can do, it's worth taking a step back and registering how it brings two strands of thought into contact with one another. It brings *non-negligence* into contact with *vulnerability*. In trusting, on DMN, we're vulnerable to risks of betrayal that go *beyond* those that, in short and in sum, *we couldn't do anything about while continuing to be cooperative*.

A virtue of this account is that it countenances the fact that trusting makes you vulnerable *beyond* two very different types of risk: you're, in trusting, vulnerable to risks of betrayal beyond just those that are so *modally far off* you can't increase the safety against them in a cooperative way. But crucially, DMN also implies that in trusting you're vulnerable beyond the whatever minimal level of risk would be in play if you *weren't* cooperative— bearing in mind that *monitoring* the trustee is non-cooperative. Both of these ideas fall out of the DMA.

Let's see what it can do by checking whether it can—as advertised—fare better than the other accounts considered. Let's take, first, MOOTED RELIANCE.

MOOTED RELIANCE was not a case of *bona fide* trust. Our normative view DMA straightforwardly accommodates this. DMA says that trust essentially involves subjecting oneself to risk of betrayal that is *not merely de minimis* within the relevant cooperative practice. And you couldn't increase the safety against *that* risk of betrayal by following any cooperation-sustaining rule whatsoever. Indeed, given the details of MOOTED RELIANCE, this turns out to be *trivially* so; the likelihood of *that* risk event materializing remains the same (zero) no matter *what* you do. Thus, by DNA, MOOTED RELIANCE is not a case of genuine trust. So far, so good.

What about the BABYSITTER case? BABYSITTER *is* plausibly a case of trust, and a paradigmatic one, *despite* the very low objective probability of betrayal. If DMA is going to secure this result, then it had better be the case that you *could* at least in principle increase the (already robust) safety against risk[19] to betrayal by adhering to rules with cooperative reproduction value. And indeed you can, and you can do so in relatively mundane ways: consider that such rules include vetting the babysitter *ex ante* (i.e., checking up on references for reliability), making babysitting itself easier (e.g., laying out emergency phone numbers, a list of medications, etc.): rules that encourage these have cooperative reproduction value. (Compare, by contrast: aiming to increase safety against the low risk present by *surveilling* the babysitter is non-cooperative; it is a form of monitoring we will discuss in the next section.) Accordingly, then, the risk event that would consist in the babysitter failing to keep the child safe is not a *de minimis risk*, even if it is *very low* due to the babysitter's impressive reliability and the straightforwardness of the task. Thus, DMA again gets the right result.

Let's turn now to PENCIL. This was also a case of trust, despite the very low albeit non-negligible *disvalue* of betrayal, and which generated a problem for an answer to the Vulnerability Question framed in terms of objective risk expectation value. For DMA to get the right result in this case, it had better bet that you *could* mitigate against the 'pencil theft' risk by the adherence to rules with cooperative reproduction value. And so you could. Writing your name on your pencil, for example, would violate no cooperation-sustaining rules; doing so facilitates rather than hinders cooperation between trustor and trustee. (More generally: the rule in play here would be to make items you loan out identifiable, which is a rule that has reproduction value for cooperation through loaning and borrowing.) Accordingly, DMA is going to countenance PENCIL, rightly, as a case of trust, even though the disvalue of betrayal is exceedingly low (problematically so

---

[19] Note that increasing safety against the obtaining of a risk is distinct from simply eliminating that risk.

for the risk expectation value account to plausibly 'rule in' this case as a case of bona fide trust).

The scoreboard of cases, then, is as follows:

Answer to Vulnerability Question	MOOTED RELIANCE	BABYSIT	PENCIL
> some threshold (T) of perceived risk	x	✓	✓
> some (T) of expected disvalue	✓	✓	x
> some (T) of (frequentist) prob. of betrayal	✓	x	✓
> (normative) *de minimis risk*	✓	✓	✓

2.4 Objections and Replies

So far, it is looking like DMA outperforms the competition as an answer to the Vulnerability Question, at least in so far as the view gets on the wrong side of none of the three cases that posed a problem for at least one of the other views considered. This is a promising mark in favour of DMA. Let's now see how the proposal holds up against some anticipated objections.

Objection 1
Even if we grant that the DMA gets the MOOTED RELIANCE case right, there are nonetheless 'Frankfurt-style' cases (also with effectively zero risk of betrayal) that pose a problem to *any* view that takes some (non-zero) objective risk of betrayal to be necessary for trust.

Notice that it is a feature of MOOTED RELIANCE that, given the zero objective chance of betrayal (at t_2, when the ship has sailed), there is no further scope for betrayal or trust fulfilment beyond t_2, as reliance has by then been mooted through the fulfilled trust. Even so, it seems like we can imagine cases where the following *both* hold: (i) there is zero objective chance of betrayal; but (ii) where it is *not* out one's control whether they betray or not such that we could attribute *at least trust fulfilment* to the trustee, thus satisfying the weak attribution principle. For example, consider FRANKFURT-BABYSITTER:

FRANKFURT-BABYSITTER: Suppose this case is just like BABYSITTER, except that it is a Frankfurt case,[20] in that *if* the babysitter were to do

---
[20] See, e.g., Frankfurt (1969).

something that would in any way imperil the baby, a benevolent demon would rush in and course-correct, preventing any danger to befall the baby. Because the babysitter (through her own goodwill and reliability) does everything right, the benevolent demon never has to intervene.

If we are going to retain the idea that trust essentially involves 'some objective risk' of betrayal—a conclusion from the critique of the perceived risk account—it looks like we're going to get the wrong result, i.e., that this isn't a case of trust. But, as the worry goes, it *is* trust despite there being no objective risk whatsoever that the babysitter will *not* come through. So long as she behaves in such a way that the Frankfurtian demon needn't intervene, all is good.

Reply
It is important to distinguish (i) risks to *successful reliance* and (ii) risks to *successful trust*. If you rely on someone to ϕ, your reliance is successful iff they ϕ, no matter how.

Trust asymmetrically entails reliance. When you trust someone to ϕ, you trust them to ϕ *as entrusted*, where 'as entrusted' might include such things as: with goodwill towards the trustor (e.g., Baier 1986; Jones 1996), by encapsulating the interests of the trustor (e.g., Hardin 2002), by believing they have a commitment to the trustor to ϕ (e.g., Hawley 2014), etc.

For my purposes, and as noted upfront in Chapter 1, I am happy to remain neutral on which of these ways of unpacking 'as entrusted' best distinguishes trust from mere reliance. What is relevant at present is just that the success conditions for reliance and trust differ in that trusting someone to ϕ is successful iff they ϕ *as entrusted* (however this is to be spelled out), and not *merely* iff they ϕ.

This difference in success conditions is important in defusing the above objection. This is because *there can be risks to successful trust that are not also risks to successful reliance*. And indeed, that is exactly what is going on in FRANKFURT-BABYSITTER. It is true that there is zero objective risk to successful *reliance*; the benevolent demon waiting in the wings is seeing to that. But it is not *thereby* also true that there is zero objective risk to successful *trust*. The trustee's taking care of things as entrusted—however we fill this out—is plausibly going to require some exercise of autonomous (e.g., non-compelled) agency, some *way* of taking care of things, attributable to the trustee—a point that lines up with the observation that reactive attitudes like gratitude are appropriate to fulfilled trust as well as to betrayal. Actions and mental states caused (through some form of compulsion) by the demon's intervention are not autonomous;[21] when compelled to act by the demon, the agent is not free to govern herself one way or the other, with respect to what she has been entrusted to do. *She* cannot fulfil trust (even if she can play a causal role in bringing about what she was relied on to do) or betray it. Thus, there *is* some non-zero objective risk of betrayal (i.e., a risk to successful *trust*) in FRANKFURT-BABYSITTER, even though there is no objective risk to successful reliance. And importantly, the objective risk to betrayal is (as is pertinent to DMA) not *merely de minimis*. This is because, just as there are pro-cooperative rules you could adhere to in order to increase safety against risk of betrayal in the original (non-Frankfurt) BABYSITTER case, so likewise, the same applies here—viz., such rules include, e.g., proper vetting, and (post-vetting) facilitating cooperative attitudes of the trustee through being cooperative as a trustor—e.g., by making duties clear. DMA therefore is able to handle not only BABYSITTER but also FRANKFURT-BABYSITTER.

Objection 2

Let's consider now a further objection to DMA, one that serves well as an entry point into the discussion in the next section on the relationship between trusting and monitoring.

Consider that on the proposal advanced, trust essentially involves subjecting yourself *beyond* mere *de miminimis risk* of betrayal—that is, it essentially involves subjecting yourself beyond merely those risks of betrayal such that safety against them *couldn't* easily be increased through adherence to rules with cooperative reproduction value. A corollary of this idea is that that *all* cases of trust are ones where you could at least potentially increase safety against betrayal by following rules with cooperative reproductive value.

But—and here is the worry—isn't *this* commitment of the view somehow in tension with the platitudinous idea that trusting is incompatible with *monitoring*? After all, there will often be no more effective way to increase safety against betrayal than to blatantly monitor the trustee's every move. Rather than to, e.g., mitigate against betrayal by carefully vetting the babysitter's references and then leaving helpful reminder notes, why not

---

[21] There are different ways to explain why. For two prominent options, see, e.g., Mele (2001) and Fischer and Ravizza (2000).

simply watch the entire time with surveillance cameras, or—better yet—hire a full surveillance team to oversee the babysitter's every move?

In short, the objection to the proposal can be put like this: the answer given to the Vulnerability Question—viz., that trust essentially involves subjecting yourself beyond mere *de minimis risk* of betrayal—rests on the underlying idea that when one trusts, there *are* certain things that one can do to increase safety against betrayal. But, increasing safety against betrayal is (at least in cases of monitoring, which is one very obvious way to increase safety against betrayal) incompatible with genuinely trusting. Thus, it seems that the answer given to the Vulnerability Question cannot be satisfactory: it relies on a claim that is itself in tension with the datum that monitoring kills trust.

Reply

This is a straightforward objection, and it has an equally straightforward answer. *Monitoring*, even though it increases—perhaps better than anything else!—safety against betrayal, is fundamentally *non-cooperative*. For one thing, that norms of cooperation generally prohibit monitoring or surveilling a trustee is supported by our practices of sanctioning; we tend to sanction those who purport to trust and then monitor.[22] Additionally, monitoring contributes to the erosion of conditions for cooperation; this is due to the social function of monitoring as *signalling* a lack of confidence in a pre-established commitment.[23]

Importantly, the view advanced here does not maintain that by trusting you subject yourself to risks of betrayal such that you could (while continuing to trust) *in any way* increase the safety against their obtaining. *That* would indeed be an unacceptable result. It implies rather that trusting essentially involves subjecting yourself to risks of betrayal that are not merely *de minimis*, which just means that by trusting you subject yourself to at least some risks of betrayal such that you could (in principle, and regardless of whether you in fact do) increase the safety against their obtaining without violating any cooperation-sustaining rules.

And indeed we increase safety against betrayal without violating any such rules like this *all the time* (and *without monitoring*): by deliberating about whom to trust, assessing their reliability, assessing facts pertinent to

---

[22] See, e.g., Kramer (1999).
[23] For some studies reporting these effects in cases where computers are used to monitor employees, see Ariss (2002).

the likelihood of betrayal, including the extent, present in a given trust context, of the (a) *gains to the trustee* that would come from betrayal; (b) the *effort*; and (c) the *aptitude* required by the trustee to *avoid* betrayal. Through a competent assessment of these factors one can cooperatively increase safety against risk of betrayal. (Likewise, one can cooperatively increase safety against the risk of betrayal by facilitating the ease by which the trustee can take care of what is entrusted, e.g., by leaving a map, leaving detailed instructions, etc. None of these things involves trust-incompatible monitoring.)

In sum, then, the idea that trusting essentially involves subjecting yourself beyond mere *de minimis risk* of betrayal does not stand in tension with the platitude that trusting is incompatible with monitoring the trustee.

3. Trust and Monitoring

The final objection in the previous section prompts a further question—in *what sense*, then, is monitoring for risks of betrayal incompatible with trusting? This is the Monitoring Question. The Monitoring Question takes at face value that monitoring *is* (in some say) incompatible with trusting.[24] It invites us to explain *how so*.

Just as a good answer to the Vulnerability Question required some sense of what the threshold is beyond which by trusting one subjects oneself to risk, a good answer to the Monitoring Question requires some sense of what the threshold is beyond which by monitoring (or perhaps by attempting to do so) one is no longer trusting.

Here is the answer to the Monitoring Question I will now defend:

(MON): One's monitoring is incompatible with trusting to the extent that, through monitoring, one intentionally aims (through the taking of some means) at *invulnerability* to risks of betrayal that, by trusting, one essentially subjects oneself to.

Since by trusting one essentially subjects oneself beyond mere *de minimis risk* of betrayal, MON implies that monitoring is incompatible with trusting to the extent that it involves taking means by which one aims to render oneself *invulnerable* to all but *de minimis risks* of betrayal.

---

[24] Though see Gordon (2022) for discussion on how monitoring (at least in early stages of trust-rebuilding) can be useful in potentially re-establishing trust that has broken down.

Two initial clarifications here are needed. First, the proposal does not say that one *actually* has to render herself invulnerable to all but *de minimis risks* of betrayal. This is important, because the monitoring needn't actually succeed in that aim to be incompatible with trust. Consider, for example, the following case:

CRYSTAL BALL: *A* hires *B* to babysit *A*'s child. Highly superstitious, *A* believes, falsely, that *A* has a working crystal ball. After dropping *A*'s children off with *B*, *A* hurries home to the crystal ball in an attempt to surveil *B*'s every move. The crystal ball shows ambiguous, smoky images, which *A* mistakenly thinks provide information about *B*'s movements. *B* watches and attempts to interpret these movements, much as a less superstitious person might peer into the grainy images on a nanny cam with poor resolution.

Intuitively, *A* is no longer trusting *B* when 'using' the crystal ball—any more than one surveilling via a poor-resolution nanny cam would be doing so— and *even though A* is not actually succeeding in making herself invulnerable to any risk of betrayal whatsoever. An account of the incompatibility of monitoring with trusting that required *actually* succeeding in eliminating, even to some degree, such vulnerability would fail to get the right result in CRYSTAL BALL.

A second clarification: Why 'the taking of means by which one aims'? Why not *simply* 'aims'?, where we might think of 'simply aiming' along the lines of merely forming an intention or plan. The reason is that monitoring—as opposed to something less, i.e., merely intending but failing to monitor— requires an attempt to *attain* an aim (e.g., vulnerability elimination) *in some way*, viz., through some means by which *through taking those means* (in this case, via the means of surveilling the trustee) one monitors; in this respect, monitoring that is incompatible with trusting is not 'idle aiming' (i.e., mere intending to monitor) any more than trusting is idle aiming (mere intending to trust).

These clarifications made, we can see now that MON is able to secure the following pleasing result: it can explain why surveilling the babysitter with a nanny cam (or, for that matter, attempting to do so via a crystal ball) is incompatible with trusting but merely responsibly vetting the babysitter for reliability (prior to hiring) and leaving notes and reminders after is not, even though the latter kinds of things also minimize risk of betrayal. The explanation given is that, in the former examples, one intentionally aims (through the taking of some means) at invulnerability to risks of betrayal that, by trusting, one essentially subjects oneself to (i.e., to risks that aren't merely *de minimis* in the relevant contexts), whereas this is not so in the latter cases.

The fact that MON is able to generate different verdicts in the former and latter kinds of cases constitutes a key advantage over a more standard line of thought about trusting and monitoring in the literature (e.g., Elster 2015) according to which trusting essentially involves simply refraining 'from taking precautions against an interaction partner' (2015, 344). Such a proposal frames the relationship between trust and monitoring in a more coarse-grained way that would get the former cases right, but not the latter unless it could provide us (as MON does) with a principled reason for a difference in treatment.

An additional advantage of MON is that the very idea that 'aiming' at eliminating vulnerability is something that is incompatible with trusting fits snugly with a much more basic idea about trusting qua performance or aimed attempt. Within the theory of performance normativity, performance-types may be distinguished from each other by the constitutive aims internal to those performance-types. In slogan form: change the aim, and you've changed the performance-type.[25] Take for example the performance of 'making a guess' versus 'making a judgement'; these are different truth-directed performances; but why? A typical answer[26] adverts to a difference in the level of risk one aims at taking on as a price for a chance at truth in each case. *What it is* to make a guess is to aim at truth via affirmation in a way that tolerates at least an unusually high level of risk; were one to aim at truth via affirming *without* aiming at tolerating whatever level of risk is distinctive of guessing, then one is longer guessing. The idea is that the same goes for trusting in so far as by trusting we aim at something in a way that essentially renders us vulnerable. Monitoring a trustee (by intentionally aiming to immunize oneself from such vulnerability) alters this aim distinctive of trust, changing the performance in a way that is broadly analogous to how (through the process of collecting more evidence) one is no longer guessing, but believing.

---

[25] For discussion of how performances are individuated by their aims, see Sosa (2010), and the essays in Fernández Vargas (2016).
[26] See, e.g., Sosa (2015, Ch. 3) and Carter (2020c).

4. Conclusion

The principal objective here has been to defend new answers to the Vulnerability Question and the Monitoring Question, answers shown to fare better than the competition. But in doing so, I've also tried to uncover an important but unnoticed way in which these questions are connected to each other, with the Vulnerability Question the more fundamental of the two. On the view defended, which views both questions through the lens of performance norms, monitoring a trustee is incompatible with trusting to the extent that, through monitoring, one intentionally aims at invulnerability to risks of betrayal that, by trusting, one essentially subjects oneself to. But which risks are these? It is at this point that our answer to the Vulnerability Question kicks in: trusting essentially involves rendering oneself vulnerable to betrayal in the sense that it essentially involves subjecting oneself to risk of betrayal that is not merely *de minimis* within the relevant cooperative practice. And—putting these ideas together—the fuller answer to the Monitoring Question, framed in terms of our answer to the Vulnerability Question, is that monitoring is incompatible with trusting in so far as one intentionally aims at invulnerability to not merely *de mimimis risks* of betrayal, viz., to not *merely* those risks to which, by trusting, one essentially renders oneself vulnerable.

A Telic Theory of Trust. J. Adam Carter, Oxford University Press. © J. Adam Carter 2024.
DOI: 10.1093/9780191982460.003.0007

8
Therapeutic Trust

This chapter extends the telic normativity framework to therapeutic trust and characterizes its nature and its constitutive norms. Central to the view advanced is a distinction between two kinds of therapeutic trust—*default therapeutic trust* and *overriding therapeutic trust*—each of which derives from a distinct kind of trusting competence. The new view is shown to have advantages over some notable extant accounts of therapeutic trust, and its relation to standard (non-therapeutic) trust, as defended by Hieronymi, Frost-Arnold, and Jones.

1. Introduction

Suppose you are leaving town for the weekend and need someone to watch your house, feed your pets, and water your plants. Now imagine two choices you might make. You might trust a reliable friend who has an established track record of responsibility and loyalty. But you might instead trust your 16-year-old nephew with no such track record to speak of. In the latter kind of case, suppose trust is undertaken with the intended aim of building or strengthening the trusting relationship.[1] Philosophers of trust often use the term 'therapeutic trust' to refer to this latter species of trust in order to distinguish it from more standard cases of (non-therapeutic) interpersonal trust.[2]

---

[1] See, for example, Horsburgh (1960) and Jones (2004). Some discussions of therapeutic trust describe the aim as one of 'bringing about trustworthiness' (see, e.g., Jones 2004, 5) or 'inspiring trustworthiness'; others, e.g., Hieronymi (2008), discuss therapeutic trust as aimed at 'building trust'. I opt for 'trust-building' as an inclusive term here, when discussing the aim of therapeutic trust, such that I take trust-building, between *A* and *B*, to include an increase in *B*'s trustworthiness to *A*. Trustworthiness and its norms will be discussed in much more detail in Chapter 9.

[2] Though, as we'll see later in this chapter, the distinction is far from clear-cut. In addition to being a contested distinction, there are reasons to think, as is argued later, that therapeutic trust comes in multiple species.

The matter of how exactly to characterize the relationship between non-therapeutic and therapeutic trust is contested.[3] Here is the problem in a nutshell. Philosophical accounts of the nature of trust attempt to say what trusting someone with something essentially involves,[4] typically by focusing on how exactly to characterize the kind of trusting attitude one has towards her trustee. Once such accounts are made precise, it looks like therapeutic trust—given how the attitude we have in such cases about the trustee's reliability is usually much *less* optimistic than in non-therapeutic cases—either (i) simply doesn't get 'ruled in' as genuine trust on the account, or (ii) the account gets modified—perhaps stretched quite thin—in order to fit therapeutic trust in.

Here is the plan. In §§2–4, I discuss three notable ways philosophers of trust have attempted to deal with the thorny issue of therapeutic trust and its relationship with ordinary non-therapeutic trust: (§2) Pamela Hieronymi's pure/impure approach;[5] (§3) Karen Frost-Arnold's 'unity' approach;[6] and (§4) Karen Jones's 'normative difference' approach.[7] Each is shown to be problematic for different reasons. §§5–6 then develop a new way of thinking about therapeutic trust which avoids the problems facing the other three views while at the same time offering its own additional advantages. I conclude by canvassing some potential objections and replies.

2. Hieronymi's Pure/Impure Approach

According to Pamela Hieronymi (2008), therapeutic trust is not 'pure' or 'full-fledged' trust. Trust is full-fledged (alternatively: pure) only if one actually *believes* that the person in question will do the thing in question.[8] One can risk betrayal by entrusting something to someone without believing they'll actually do what they've been entrusted to do. But this is not 'pure' trust.

---

[3] See, e.g., Horsburgh (1960) and McGeer (2008). For an overview, see McLeod (2023, 1).
[4] The kind of trust that is principally at issue in debates about therapeutic trust is *three-place* trust, e.g., with an infinitival component (schematically: A trusts B to X). As Baier (1986, 236) puts it, philosophers of trust—and not just those interested in therapeutic trust—are concerned centrally with 'one person trusting another with some valued thing'; likewise, as Hawley (2014, 2) puts it: trust is 'primarily a three-place relation, involving two people and a task'.
[5] (Hieronymi 2008). [6] (Frost-Arnold 2014). [7] (Jones 2004).
[8] For further support of the idea that non-therapeutic trust requires belief that the trustee will prove trustworthy, see Adler (1994), Keren (2014), and McMyler (2011). For criticism, see Jones (1996), McLeod (2002), McGeer (2008), Faulkner (2007), Faulkner (2011), and Baker (1987).

In support of this way of thinking about therapeutic trust, Hieronymi offers the following case pair involving the betrayal of a secret.

SECRETS: Consider two cases. In one, I fully believe you are trustworthy; in the other, I have doubts about your trustworthiness, but, for other reasons (perhaps to build trust in our relationship, perhaps because I think friends should trust one another, or perhaps simply because I have no better alternative), I decide to tell you my secret. Suppose that, in both cases, you spill the beans, and that you do so in the same circumstances, for the same reasons (2008, 230).

According to Hieronymi, once we thus hold fixed both (i) the 'importance of the good entrusted' (2008, 230), and (ii) 'the wrongness of the violation' (2008, 230), then:

[…] it seems plausible that one's degree of vulnerability to betrayal tracks one's degree of trusting belief… further, this seems to be because, in the second case, there was *less trust to betray* (2008, 230–1, my italics).

There are, however, two problems with this diagnosis of SECRETS. The first is that it's not at all clear that one's degree of vulnerability to betrayal really does track one's degree of trusting belief, *even when* the importance of the good entrusted and the wrongness of the violation are held fixed. To see why, just suppose we run a variation on Hieronymi's SECRETS case pair where, in the first case, my belief that you are trustworthy is full (stipulate: credence 1) but, at the same time, completely *irrational*. By Hieronymi's reasoning, the betrayal is greater by degree in the first case simply because of the irrationally ratcheted up belief. But it's not. I might, due to having this strong albeit irrational credence that you are trustworthy, be even more inclined than otherwise to *think* that the betrayal is serious. But it wouldn't in fact be a worse betrayal simply *on account of* the ratcheted up irrational credence.[9]

But suppose, for the sake of argument, we grant that one's degree of vulnerability to betrayal tracks one's degree of trusting belief. It is worth noting that *even if* this were true, it could be explained without recourse to the idea that there is—in the therapeutic case—'less trust' to betray. For example,

---

[9] Note that the kind of irrationality I have in mind here is epistemic rationality.

it might be that vulnerability to betrayal is one among various features of trust, and it's a feature that lines up with (e.g., by closely tracking) trust's doxastic component, whereas other features of trust (for example: whatever features makes it resilient to certain kinds of monitoring[10]) might track some *non-doxastic* (e.g., affective) component of trust.

If something like this were right, then we couldn't move simply from the idea that one's degree of vulnerability to betrayal tracks one's degree of belief to the conclusion that there is less trust in cases with less belief. After all, such cases might feature more prominently some other (e.g., affective) aspect of trust, and in virtue of the presence—perhaps, surfeit—of which there is not, on the whole, 'less trust'.

But Hieronymi has a second argument for relegating therapeutic trust to the 'impure' category. The second argument has to do not with vulnerability but with the legitimacy of certain kinds of complaints. This second line of reasoning goes as follows. People can *legitimately complain* about not being trusted fully when they are trusted in the absence of belief, which occurs only when other people lack confidence in them but trust them nonetheless (2008, 230). For example, imagine the 16-year-old from our opening case saying: 'But you don't *really* trust me', upon finding out that the rationale for the trust was largely trust-building, in the absence of a belief that they'd prove trustworthy. The felicitousness of such a complaint is, for Hieronymi, meant to support the idea that therapeutic trust is not pure or full-fledged trust.

But just as the teenager could complain in this scenario, they could also felicitously praise or thank you for trusting them *despite* lacking confidence. 'Wow, you trusted me without even needing belief—you must have *really* trusted me!'[11] This is not to say that Hieronymi's example complaint is *not* felicitous, nor that praise or gratitude for trusting despite lacking confidence is any more felicitous than is complaining that one has trusted in the absence of belief. Rather, the point is that it is not clear that complaining about trust in the absence of belief is in any way *more* felicitous than praising or thanking a trustor who trusts one in the absence of it.[12]

---

[10] For discussion on this point, see, e.g., Baier (1986) and Wanderer and Townsend (2013); cf., Gordon (2022).

[11] For a defence of the idea that trust's most pure form involves the absence of belief, see Möllering (2006).

[12] Moreover, the felicitousness of such a reply gains some support in the literature on the psychology of gratitude (see, e.g., Emmons and McCullough 2004); for instance, gratitude is a predictable response by one to another who has placed a kind of 'faith' in their goodwill or competence.

In sum, Hieronymi's arguments from vulnerability and complaint legitimacy don't give us good reason to think that the difference between non-therapeutic trust and therapeutic trust is a difference in 'purity' of trust.

3. Frost-Arnold's 'Unity' Approach

Let's look now at an attempt—due to Karen Frost-Arnold (2014)—to 'broaden' an account of trust so that it is wide enough to rule in both varieties of trust. On Frost-Arnold's proposal, A trusts B to φ iff the proposition that B will φ is part of A's 'adjusted cognitive background' (2014, 1963–4), where one's adjusted cognitive background includes all and only those propositions that one *accepts* for the purposes of practical reasoning, where acceptance does not entail positive belief[13] (e.g., positive belief of the sort that is generally lacked in therapeutic cases, even if often present in non-therapeutic cases). This kind of 'unity' view does not relegate therapeutic trust to a second tier, as Hieronymi's proposal does, but rather 'brings it in to the first tier'—e.g., by subsuming it within a wider account of trust *simpliciter*.

There are two main problems with Frost-Arnold's 'unity'-style approach. The first is that the acceptance requirement needn't be satisfied in all cases of therapeutic trust. Suppose you trust your teenager[14] to drive your car for the weekend and return it safely. Suppose further that, upon doing this, you purchase additional insurance, just in case. By purchasing this additional insurance, you are not accepting the proposition that the teenager will return the car safely—viz., to do *what you'd trusted them to do*[15]—in the course of your practical reasoning. You act instead on the proposition that they might realistically easily enough not do so.[16]

---

[13] The idea that accepting a proposition, understood as taking it for granted in one's practical deliberations—alternatively: acting 'as if' the proposition is true—does not entail that one believes the proposition to be true has been defended variously in epistemology, the philosophy of science, and elsewhere. For some representative discussions of how belief and acceptance come apart, see Cohen (1989), Bratman (1992), and Buckareff (2010).

[14] Note that throughout this discussion of therapeutic trust, I am using examples featuring teenagers as illustrative therapeutic trustees. This is because teenagers are often given increasing levels of responsibility, as they are in a transitionary period leading to adulthood. That said, I take it that children can and will often also be recipients of therapeutic trust, and this includes young children. The focus on teenagers in my examples is for simplicity and consistency of presentation.

[15] Note that you are not trusting them to *probably* bring the car back.

[16] This is the case, to be clear, even though we needn't suppose that you positively believe that the teenager *won't* return the car as entrusted.

But the existence of this damage mitigating backup plan doesn't preclude the case from having been a case of therapeutic trust in the first place.[17] That is, you don't suddenly cease to be therapeutically trusting the teenager with whom you aspire to build trust once you buy the insurance. It's not as though the vulnerability to betrayal one subjects oneself to is eliminated by one taking steps to mitigate damages against the risk occurring.[18]

Some philosophers of trust have pressed back on this point. For example, Keren (2019) holds that trusting involves declining to take precautions against the trustee's failing to come through.[19] This idea seems prima facie plausible in the epistemic case, specifically, where what the trustor trusts the trustee to do is to tell them the truth. What 'taking precautions against the trustee's failing to come through' would amount to in this case would be finding additional evidence that bears on the truth of the proposition. But *then*, having sought such evidence, it doesn't look as though you are trusting the person's word at all.

To the extent that trusting (therapeutic or otherwise) *does* involve declining to take precautions against the trustee's coming through, this might very well be idiosyncratic to the epistemic case where there is a constitutive

---

[17] Note that the buying insurance in this case is potentially different (it mitigates but doesn't eliminate damage in the event that trust is betrayed—e.g., the car is still totalled, the child could have been hurt if it was wrecked, the insurance rates will go up, etc.) from, e.g., acting so as to offset entirely any damage upon betrayal. In the latter case, suppose you entrust a teenager to organize an event, and you secretly book a separate event location in case the teenager doesn't come through; this latter case is in this way relevantly different from merely purchasing car insurance while entrusting them to drive the car. Thanks to Emma Gordon for discussion.

[18] This point, it is worth noting, is compatible with the widely accepted idea that *monitoring* is incompatible with trusting, of either a non-therapeutic or therapeutic variety. See, e.g., Baier (1986, 260).

[19] Keren (2019, 121) actually formulates his position as follows, with the qualifier 'every': 'If you rely on a person to ϕ but take *every* precaution against the possibility that she might not ϕ—by seeking evidence that might indicate that she might fail to ϕ and by acting in order to minimize the harm caused in case she fails to ϕ—then you do not trust her to ϕ. You might rely on her to ϕ, but you do not trust her to do so' (my italics). As formulated, this is not controversial, as this is tantamount to the statement that trusting is incompatible with certain kinds of monitoring. What is at issue in the example I am discussing above, involving an insurance policy, is rather whether mitigating at all against the risks of the damage that would be incurred by the trustee's betrayal would be compatible with nonetheless therapeutically trusting that person. My contention that it is thus compatible with granting Keren's point that some kinds of monitoring—e.g., such as those that involve taking every precaution against the possibility the trustee won't come through—are incompatible with trust (therapeutic or otherwise). That said, Keren also makes claims about taking precautions, in the specific case of epistemic trust, which appear to go beyond the statement of his view noted above, and which appear to imply that it is essential to epistemically trusting someone that you decline entirely from taking precautions against their not coming through. Because this thesis, at least if applied generally and not just in the epistemic case, is in tension with my assessment of the insurance policy case, I focus in the main text on it as opposed to on Keren's less contentious formulation quoted above.

tension between relying on one's word and acquiring the kind of evidence one would acquire by taking precautions. Crucially, we find no such tension though outside the epistemic case, at least when we hold fixed that the precautions are (as in the example of the insurance policy) precautions that are solely designed to mitigate damages *if* the trustee does not come through. Compare: this is importantly different from, and does not imply, taking precautions designed to lower the likelihood that the trustee will *fail* to come through—as one might do by hiring a team to accompany the teenage driver. Accordingly, the attempt to reply to the objection raised to Frost-Arnold by way of appealing to Keren's insights about epistemic trust looks to come up short. The upshot is that Frost-Arnold's unified account of trust which frames trust in terms of acceptance is still too narrow to do what she wants it to do, which is to rule in all cases of trust, non-therapeutic and therapeutic alike.

The proposal also faces a second problem, which concerns the evaluative normativity of trusting.[20] The worry is that the view lacks the resources to account for why reasonable therapeutic trust isn't just *bad* as an instance of trusting. Continuing with the teenager car case: let's suppose you have no trust-building objectives in mind whatsoever, and simply want someone dependable to drive your car for the weekend and bring it back safely. Foolishly, you choose the teenager with a record you know is patchy at best. This looks like *bad* trust, even if it would *not* be so with therapeutic purposes in play.[21] But it's hard to see how we'd explain this normative difference on Frost-Arnold's unity-style account. One might try to begin to tell such a story by appealing to the 'epistemic constraint' that Frost-Arnold places on the kind of acceptance that matters for a proposition's being ruled-in as part of the adjusted cognitive background. But the epistemic constraint she places on acceptance is really a very minimal one. It precludes just one thing: positive belief that the person will *not* do the thing in question. This kind of constraint won't help us in any way to adjudicate the normative

---

[20] By way of reminder from Chapter 1, evaluative norms—unlike prescriptive norms, which prescribe conduct—regulate what it takes for a token of a particular type of thing to be good or bad with regard to its type, where the 'goodness' or 'badness' here is *attributive* in Geach's (1956) sense—viz., the sense in which a sharp knife is a good knife, qua knife, regardless of whether it is good or bad *simpliciter*. For discussion, see Simion et al. (2016) and McHugh (2012).

[21] One sense in which the trust here is bad is that it is not likely to be *successful* in that trusting a teenager involves incurring a relatively higher risk of betrayal than normal. For discussion on this point, see Carter (2020b; 2024).

question we're interested in—viz., how to distinguish at least some cases of good therapeutic trust from plain old bad trust.

There's another thread to this point. Just as picking out an unreliable person is 'bad' trusting (likely to lead to one's trust being betrayed—see Chapter 2[22]) even if trusting that unreliable person could have been reasonable were therapeutic purposes suitably in play, it doesn't follow that *simply stipulating* a therapeutic purpose suffices to make any instance of therapeutic trust *good* therapeutic trust. One can surely be better or worse at therapeutic trusting, just as one could be better or worse at trusting more generally— and indeed, very plausibly in light of different kinds of skill sets. None of this looks explicable (at least, in any straightforward way) if we embrace a unity-style view.

4. Jones's 'Normative Difference' Approach

The foregoing discussion suggests that what's needed is an account of therapeutic trust which explains clearly how it features some kind of *normative difference* with respect to ordinary, non-therapeutic trust. This is exactly what Karen Jones's (2004) account of therapeutic trust offers. Unfortunately, or so I'll now attempt to show, she identifies the *wrong kind* of normative difference.

According to Jones (2004), therapeutic trust involves (i) the normative attitude that the trustee *ought* to do what one trusts them to do, but (ii) without optimism that they will do it. With reference to our opening case pair: when you trust the reliable friend to watch your house for the weekend, you are optimistic that they will do this as you've entrusted them to. While you're not optimistic that the teenager will do the same when you trust them with the task, you nonetheless think in trusting them that they *ought* to do what you've entrusted them to do.

While this proposal has some initial plausibility—after all, whatever normative expectations would seem to accompany paradigmatic cases of therapeutic trust needn't imply any sort of optimism of the sort typically *lacking* in such cases—there are two main problems with this proposal. First, the normative attitude that the trustee ought to do what one trusts

---

[22] In addition to Chapter 2, see Carter (2020b) for a defence of this way of thinking about bad trust.

them to do is not clearly necessary for therapeutic trust, particularly when we make salient the second component of Jones's view, which is that the trustor in cases of therapeutic trust *lacks optimism* that the trustee will come through. One kind of case to illustrate this idea exploits a mundane fact about therapeutic trust, which is that *what it is* that therapeutic trustees are often entrusted with lies at the outer boundaries of what they're equipped to take care of, and this will often be something the therapeutic trustor recognizes full well when (as Jones holds) lacking optimism they'll come through. Consider, for example, a case where a CEO entrusts a low-level employee with enormous responsibilities that come with an (unwarranted) promotion—hoping that the giving of these big responsibilities will deepen the trust between the two which the CEO can eventually exploit to curry favour with the employee's politically connected parents. Assuming here the CEO is not blind to their ulterior reasons underlying the trust they are placing in this very inexperienced employee, then they will not have the view that the trustee clearly *ought* to actually do what they are entrusted to do (the expectation here will surely be different than it would be in a case where the trustor thinks the trustee is capable), on account of recognizing it outstrips their experience and competence. Put another way, the CEO might well know that the employee's succeeding in doing what they've been entrusted with is beyond reasonable expectations in a way that seems in *prima facie* tension with also holding a normative expectation that they come through. But, as the worry goes, this remains nonetheless a case of therapeutic trust in that it is—albeit for dubious reasons[23]—trust that aims to bring about and strengthen a trust relationship.

The above example, in so far as it poses a problem for Jones's approach to therapeutic trust, relies on the apparent compatibility of therapeutic trust with the absence of a normative attitude that the trustee *ought* to do what she's been entrusted to do, and this on account of the fact that it's not (in the CEO case) by the trustor's lights reasonable to even *expect* that the trustee would have been in a position to do that thing in the first place.

---

[23] No assumption is being made, to be clear, that the norms of trust are moral norms. I have suggested (in responding to Frost-Arnold) that we should expect an account of therapeutic trust to be reconcilable with plausible claims about the evaluative normativity of trusting; but this commitment is a very general one—viz., to there being norms (however we best articulate them) that regulate what it takes for a token of trusting to be good or bad with regard to its type. This is at most a commitment to attributive (rather than predicative) goodness of trusting in certain cases.

There is however a line of reply we can envision on the part of Jones here, which proceeds as follows: the CEO (in the case described) may plausibly still think the employee has a prima facie obligation to do what they've been entrusted to do (presumably they've consented through the promotion to the undertaking the new responsibilities, whatever these are), but that the lack of experience (combined perhaps with the exploitative reasons for the trust placed) just means that trustor lacks a normative expectation that the trustee, *all things considered*, ought to come through; *even so*, as the thought goes, there is still a sense in which the therapeutic trust placed here corresponds with a 'prima facie' normative expectation on the part of the trustor, even though not with an *ultima facie* normative expectation. The same line of response, presumably, would apply to, e.g., 'enlightened mafioso'-style examples where the trustor entrusts, e.g., a hit job to an inexperienced trustee (aiming at trust-building) even while the mafioso does not think the trustee, *all things considered*, ought to carry through; here a proponent of Jones's proposal could note that there remains in both cases (along with a lack of optimism) a prima facie normative expectation on the part of the trustor that the trustee come through.

Even if we grant the proponent of Jones's approach to therapeutic trust the above line of reply, there will remain some residual kinds of cases where—when there's a lack of optimism the trustee will come through—we have genuine therapeutic trust without the trustor's taking there to be *even* a prima facie obligation to come through. To appreciate such cases, just consider the *source* of the perceived prima facie obligation of the therapeutic trustee on the part of the trustor (which might be defeated by other considerations) to begin with will be trust exchange itself.[24]

That said, consider now a case where a (prospective) trustor and trustee have a track record (and common knowledge between the two of this record) of *mutual* non-cooperation and defection, but where the prospective trustor aspires to turn things around and to begin establishing trust against this background, by entrusting the trustee with a task. The trustor might expect the trustee will be non-cooperative yet again (and thus will not be optimistic the trustee will come through), but the grounds for this non-optimism (i.e., in particular, in this case, a failed track record of

---

[24] This is at any rate how we can make sense of genuine therapeutic trust in mafioso-style examples on Jones's view, where the trustor lacks an all-things-considered normative expectation that the therapeutic trustee 'ought' to do the hit, but nonetheless takes there to be a defeasible obligation at least sourced in the trust.

cooperation between the two) leaves it much less clear that the trustor is going to have even a prima facie normative expectation the trustee come through, as there are reasons generated by the very trust relationship to think otherwise. Such cases, of therapeutic trust following ruptured trust, then, seem to put pressure on Jones's view of what is distinctive about therapeutic trust.

Let's now consider an entirely different line of critique to Jones's characterization of therapeutic trust as involving a normative expectation that the trustee ought to come through in conjunction with a lack of optimism that they will do it. This second worry draws attention to the fact that some cases of therapeutic trust positively *do* involve optimism that the trustee will do what they are entrusted to do, even if this optimism persists along with some serious doubts. If that's right, then the proposal fails to identify what's distinctive of therapeutic trust. To get this second criticism in view, it will be instructive to first consider how optimism comes apart from belief in both directions. In the literature on the psychology of optimism (e.g., Carver, Scheier, and Segerstrom 2010), an optimistic attitude, with respect to some situation X, is often characterized in terms of a kind of attention profile directed at favourable features of that situation. For example, if my car breaks down and I'm stranded on a highway, then an optimistic attitude might lead me to focus my attention on how doing certain things under my control (e.g., walking to the nearest petrol station) could better my situation.

Coming back to therapeutic trust: one can distribute one's attention patterns in ways that line up with optimism (with respect to a trustee proving trustworthy) *without* having any positive belief that the trustee will prove trustworthy. (Compare: I can be optimistic about the possibility of a rescue when stranded without actually having the *belief* that I will be saved.) For example, being optimistic that the teenager will look after the house properly or return the car might involve focusing on the teenager's good traits, feeling pride in remembering past times they've exceeded expectations, etc. This is all compatible with a lack of belief that they will in fact bring the car back. Note, furthermore, that belief and optimism come apart in the other direction as well. You could believe someone will bring a car back without being optimistic simply because your attentional profile does not line up with what you believe. You might be irrationally paranoid, given a pessimistic perspective that does not line up with your belief that the trustee will prove trustworthy. These considerations in favour of the idea that optimism can float freely of one's doxastic attitudes supports that (contra Jones) the kind of doubts one has in the case of therapeutic trust aren't doubts that, as such, would preclude optimism that the trustee will prove trustworthy.

In sum, it looks like Jones is mistaken that therapeutic trust involves the normative attitude that the trustee ought to do what one trusts them to do, in conjunction with a lack of optimism that they will do it. This is because it neither requires the normative attitude that the trustee ought to do what one trusts them to do—as per the CEO case—*nor* does it preclude optimism that they will do what they are entrusted to do, at least in so far as optimistic attitudes are plausibly demarcated by their attentional profiles.

5. Therapeutic Trust: (Telic) Default and Overriding

So far, we've seen that prominent extant accounts of therapeutic trust run into various kinds of problems. A presupposition common to each of the three views considered is that therapeutic trust is a *univocal kind*; this is a presupposition we'd be better off rejecting.

On the view I want to now develop and defend, there are two importantly different species of therapeutic trust—*default therapeutic trust* and *overriding therapeutic trust*. Each species of therapeutic trust interacts with ordinary (non-therapeutic) trust differently. And each is normatively constrained differently from the other. Appreciating how this is so, we can—in addition to avoiding the kinds of problems considered—make sense of something other views can't, which is what makes therapeutic trust (of a philosophically interesting sort) good when it is.

To that end, here is a first point to consider right out of the gates: we take certain things for granted, as presuppositions, in communication, in both testimony and cooperation. When giving testimony, for instance, we take for granted (viz., as pragmatic presuppositions) that, e.g., speakers *might* rely on the information we give them, use that information in their own practical reasoning, etc.[25] In cooperation more generally, we take for granted that cooperating (rather than defecting), and other kinds of pro-social behaviour, are the sorts of things that would *strengthen existing trust relationships*. In the case of trust specifically, we *take for granted* that our trusting will—apart from whatever else it does in a particular case—play *its normal social functions*, functions that plausibly, and minimally, include the social

---

[25] See, e.g., Goldberg (2010) and Kelp and Simion (2021).

function of strengthening trust relations.[26] This is so even when we trust—as we do when we seek out someone reliable and trustworthy—with the basic aim that the trustee take care of things as entrusted.

In this respect, there is a minimal and trivial kind of therapeutic trust— call this *default therapeutic trust*—that is going to be implicit in garden variety trusting, and this is so even in the absence of any explicit *intention*—the kind of intention that is explicit in teenager-style cases—to satisfy the aim of building trustworthiness.[27]

Moreover, the 'implicit' kind of therapeutic trust that accompanies ordinary trust as a default does not have its own constitutive aim. This is because default therapeutic trust is just *implicated by* normal, non-therapeutic trusting, which itself constitutively aims at the trustee's taking care of things as entrusted. In this respect, the competences that are relevant, trivially, to default therapeutic trust are just those that matter for non-therapeutic trust that implicates it.

The most interesting kind of therapeutic trust is not default therapeutic trust, but *overriding therapeutic trust*. This occurs when, as in our paradigmatic teenager cases, the aim of successful trust—given perceived vulnerabilities— isn't itself enough to *motivate* one to risk trusting. Simply wanting your house to be watched over responsibly wouldn't, from the perspective of a trustor, favour entrusting such a task to the teenager, as opposed to someone regarded to be more reliable; rather the opposite would be the case. Necessary for bringing about overriding therapeutic trust is thus an 'overriding' and intentional aim—the aim of building or strengthening trust—that is distinct from the constitutive aim of ordinary non-therapeutic trust.

Unlike default therapeutic trust that is implicit in most normal trusting, *overriding* therapeutic trust is a distinct kind of performance from normal (non-therapeutic) trust, with its own constituent normativity. The constitutive aim of overriding therapeutic trust is not *merely* to trust successfully

---

[26] For some representative defences of the role of trusting in trust-building, see Faulkner (2011 Ch. 1), Alfano (2016), Hall (2005), and Solomon and Flores (2003).

[27] Consider, by way of analogy, one of the plausible social-epistemic functions of *assertion*, which is to generate knowledge in the hearer (e.g., Kelp 2018; Simion 2019; cf., Williamson 2000). On the assumption that assertion has such an aim, constitutively, it's easy to see how asserters *implicitly*, in asserting, aim at other things (even if not intentionally), namely, whatever generating knowledge in a hearer generally involves, including playing roles that knowledge normally plays for the hearer. For example, one role that knowledge plausibly plays for a hearer who acquires it is that of being a possible premise in the hearer's practical reasoning (e.g., Hawthorne and Stanley 2008).

(viz., that the trustee take care of things as entrusted). But nor, it should be emphasized, is it *merely* to build trust. It is, on the view I want to explore now, to *build trust through trusting successfully.*

Consider that just as ordinary (non-therapeutic) trust is defective when it misses its internal aim (that the trustee take care of things as entrusted), your choosing to trust your teenager to watch over the house has missed *its* mark if either

   (i) trust is not *built or strengthened* (e.g., if a result of this trusting is not a strengthened trust relationship)[28] *or* if
   (ii) trust is not *successful* (e.g., if the teenager throws a party, during which items from the house are stolen).

Even more, though, your trust will have missed its mark even if the trust serves to build trust *and* the trust is successful, but

   (iii) if the *trust built is not built through the successful trust*, but for some reason disconnected with the therapeutic trust placed in them.

This might be the case, for example, if the teenager watches over the house successfully, though, unaffected entirely by the trust you've placed in them, comes to trust you more nonetheless due to having, while watching over the house, spent some time reading false accounts of sacrifices you've made for them in the past, and only on this basis, develops towards you a stronger bond of trust.

Question: if overriding therapeutic trust constitutively aims not at mere successful trust, nor at the mere building of trust, but at building trust *through* successful trust, then what do (i) *competent* or adroit and (ii) *apt* overriding therapeutic trust consist in? Put another way: when we subsume overriding therapeutic trust and its constitutive aim within the telic normativity framework (which evaluates performances for success, competence, and aptness), how should we fill the rest in the remaining 'blanks' for overriding therapeutic trust?

---

[28] I use the word 'strengthened' to signal the gradability by which a trusting relationship could develop through therapeutic trust. In some cases, therapeutic trust might very well be successful when the trusting relationship improves only slightly through an instance of successful trust, as might be the case when therapeutic trust follows a long track record of betrayed trust by the trustee.

	accuracy/success	competent	apt
archery shot	hit target	shot issued from archery competence	shot successful (hit target) because of (archery) competence
belief	true	belief issued from epistemic competence	belief successful (true) because of epistemic competence
trust	trustee takes care of things as entrusted	trust issued from trust competence	trust successful because of trust competence
trust$_{O.T.}$	trust built through successful trust	?	?

Competent overriding therapeutic trust, on our working model, will derive from a competence to attain the constitutive aim *of overriding therapeutic trust* reliably, which is the aim of building trust *through* successful trust. Given that competences are indexed to performance conditions, a clear view of the kind of competence that matters for overriding therapeutic trust requires some grip on the conditions under which reliable performance matters for this *particular* kind of trusting. These conditions include (at least) the satisfaction of what I'll call an *openness condition* and a *reciprocity condition*.

To appreciate the former condition, consider the following case:

DIANE: You need someone to babysit on short notice. There are a number of people you could ask, however, you choose a local teenager, Diane, whose parents you know. You have heard that Diane is troubled, and you have had a standing desire to take Diane under your wing in hopes of having a positive influence on her. A first step toward having such a positive influence, you think, will be to establish a bond of trust, a bond you hope to develop by entrusting her with the babysitting task despite her reputation. Unfortunately, and unbeknownst to you, Diane recently experienced a highly traumatic event, to which she has responded by closing off the possibility of developing a trusting relationship with *anyone*, at least until she has worked through this trauma. She succeeds in the task of babysitting, though at no point was she in a position where her being entrusted with this would have changed her distrusting stance of others or you.

In DIANE, the conditions for successful overriding therapeutic trust are simply not in place *ex ante*—and this is so even though the conditions in DIANE do not preclude her in any way from taking care of things as entrusted. With respect to the aim you have of *building trust* through successful trust, Diane is 'closed'. She is not in a position where your trusting her with the task that you do could—even when that trust is fulfilled by her—contribute to building trust on account of that fulfilment.

Now consider a twist on this case:

DIANE*: You need someone to babysit on short notice. There are a number of people you could ask; however, you choose a local teenager, Diane*, whose parents you know. You have heard that Diane* is troubled, and you have had a standing desire to take Diane* under your wing in hopes of having a positive influence on her. A first step towards having such a positive influence, you think, will be to establish a bond of trust, a bond you hope to develop by entrusting her with the babysitting task despite her reputation. Diane* is open in principle to building trust with someone who would entrust her with this kind of task. Unfortunately, and unbeknownst to you, Diane* bears a deep-seated grudge against you. Though she babysits the kids successfully (suppose, she needs the money)—and though her doing so successfully in fact contributes to making her more trustworthy *generally* speaking—it plays no role in establishing or strengthening any trust between you and her.

Diane* is *not* closed to building trust through successful trust, as Diane is, generally. However, the conditions in DIANE* are such that they prevent building her trust *with you*, the trustor, through successful trust.[29] This is

---

[29] One might think the reciprocity condition is too strong in cases of therapeutic trust, on the basis of Holton's (1994) assessment of his shopkeeper example—viz., a case where a shopkeeper hires an ex-criminal, deciding to trust them with the till. As Holton notes, even if the shopkeeper isn't optimistic the trustee will come through, the shopkeeper might be motivated by the idea that 'trust is the best way to draw him back into the moral community' (1994: 63). Would therapeutic trust be best conceived of as aiming at building the trustee into a more trustworthy person generally—as a more trustworthy member in the moral community *simpliciter*—as opposed to, more specifically, building the relationship between the trustor and trustee? It's hard to see how, and this is so even if we grant that Holton's shopkeeper would plausibly have had a kind of general benevolent aim in mind in hiring the ex-convict. The reason we shouldn't opt for such a broad aim is that the further we get from cases where the trustor and trustee strengthen their trusting relationship through the successful trust while holding fixed that the trustee becomes part of the moral community, the less successful the trust plausibly is *as* a case of therapeutic trust. For example, the ex-convict's being entrusted with the till might causally lead to them meeting more people, being more social, and more willingly being

not to say that Diane*'s grudge would never subside so as to open up such a possibility later. The point is that the situation in which you encounter Diane* is not one in which, were she to come to establish and build trust with you, this could be achieved in the way you're attempting to do so here, viz., through facilitating successful trust via the babysitting task.

There are two interrelated points to draw from the DIANE and DIANE* cases. The first is that it doesn't count against one's overriding therapeutic trust competence, viz., one's disposition to attain the aim of overriding therapeutic trust reliably enough, were one to be *unreliable* at attaining this aim in cases like DIANE or DIANE*, where the conditions are, for different reasons, not suitably conducive to building trust through successful trust. Secondly, and relatedly: the kind of competence that *matters* for overriding therapeutic trust is, accordingly, a disposition to build trust through successful trust reliably enough when one is in *conditions that are appropriate to doing so*, conditions that include at least that openness and reciprocity are satisfied, as they are not in DIANE and DIANE*, respectively.

A further point is that, *when* these conditions are met, some are disposed to achieve the aim of overriding therapeutic trust *more* reliably than others. And that is just to say that, when it comes to overriding therapeutic trust, some are *more competent* than others, some of whom simply lack this competence by not being suitably reliable in conditions that are favourable to this kind of trust.

What makes the difference? One factor that's worth noting explicitly is that we vary in the capacities we have to reliably assess trust-building payoffs. For example, recall our case of the CEO (§4) who entrusted the low-level employee with a *disproportionately* large task, one which not easily the employee would have managed. The overriding therapeutic trust is unlikely to pay off here simply given that the difficulty of the task choice will make unlikely the building of trust through *successful* trust. Conversely, entrusting *too small* a task, with therapeutic aims, is likewise unlikely to pay off, though, for a different reason. (Compare: suppose you were to, with trust-building aims, entrust a teenager not with looking over the house or the

---

a part of the moral community, etc., while the more specific question of whether that instance of therapeutic trust was successful would seemingly remain unaddressed in the absence of any information about the relationship between trustor and trustee. Note that a temptation to construe the aim of therapeutic trust more widely in light of the shopkeeper example might be coloured by a feature idiosyncratic to the details of Holton's case, which is that it involves a trustee who had previously been withdrawn from the wider moral community; this fact particular to the case, motivating the shopkeeper more generally, might easily be conflated with the aim of therapeutic trust (as such) specifically.

kids, but with looking after a small cactus for the weekend.) The task is not certainly too difficult to undermine the likelihood that the trustee will take care of things *as entrusted*, but it is *so easy* that it undermines the likelihood that, through being undertaken successfully, it will play a (non-negligible) role in increasing any kind of trust bond with the trustee. In short: (i) a propensity to miss the mark too often in *either* direction will undermine one's reliability at attaining the aim of building trust through successful trust, and so (ii) a competence to hit this aim reliably (when appropriately situated to do so[30]) requires a capacity for the kind of risk assessment that's needed to prevent one from too often 'over-' or 'under-'trusting (as in the CEO and cactus cases, respectively).

Let's return now to our 'success/competence/aptness' table. *Accurate* or successful overriding therapeutic trust occurs when overriding therapeutic trust hits its constitutive aim, which is the aim of building trust through successful trust. *Competent* or adroit overriding therapeutic trust issues from a *competence* to hit this aim reliably enough when one trusts with a therapeutic aim while appropriately situated, where being appropriately situated for this kind of trust requires at least the satisfaction of the openness and reciprocity conditions. *Apt* overriding therapeutic trust can now be defined in terms of accurate and adroit therapeutic trust—viz., apt overriding therapeutic trust is overriding therapeutic trust that is *successful because competent*, viz., when one's building trust through trusting successfully manifests one's competence to therapeutically trust successfully reliably enough in appropriate conditions.

Apt overriding therapeutic trust is a kind of *achievement*, just like any kind of aim attained through skill rather than by other means.[31] In this respect, apt overriding therapeutic trust stands to *mere* successful overriding trust as knowledge to lucky true belief, and to an archer's successful shot attained through skill to the same success attained any old way. However, as we've seen, the achievement of apt overriding therapeutic trust is a *different* achievement than the achievement of apt (non-therapeutic) trust, one that

---

[30] That is: when the trust environment is such that the openness and reciprocity conditions described in this section are met.

[31] For some representative discussions of the value of achievements understood as having a success-through-ability structure, see, e.g., Bradford (2013); (2015), Sosa (2010b), Pritchard, Turri, and Carter (2018), Greco (2014), Carter and Gordon (2014), Pritchard (2009), and Zagzebski (1996).

involves the attaining of a different aim through the manifestation of a different sort of competence.

6. Summing Up

We began with a puzzle about therapeutic trust and its relationship to ordinary non-therapeutic trust. Three prominent attempts to address this puzzle were considered, and each was shown to be problematic for different reasons. One notable problem common to each of the three accounts was that none was well suited to explain—given what each maintains, respectively, about therapeutic trust and how it differs from non-therapeutic trust—in virtue of *what* good therapeutic trust differs from plain old bad trust, including incompetent trust that just so happens to result in the building of trust, as well as successful *and* competent trust that builds trust for reasons that have nothing to do with the trust placed.

The account I've proposed has a number of advantages over these accounts. First, it avoids the traps that these other accounts were shown to fall into given their specific commitments. The key move proposed which helps to get things right involves the recognition of two kinds of therapeutic trust. There is a philosophically uninteresting species of therapeutic trust that is implicit in ordinary trusting—what I called *default therapeutic trust*. While default therapeutic trust (trivially) aims at building trust, it does so only because building trust is among the normal social functions of ordinary non-therapeutic trust, which aims constitutively at the trustee taking care of things as entrusted. *Overriding therapeutic trust*, by contrast, has its own constituent normativity—with reference to which we can normatively assess this kind of trust differently from how we normatively assess standard trust. In doing so, we can say *why* each kind of trust is good when it is, without reducing the goodness of either kind of trust to the goodness of the other. Moreover, the view can help us to make sense of how the skills needed for reliable therapeutic trust come apart from the skills needed to be good at trusting well more generally; the 'success/competence/aptness' profiles of competent trust and competent therapeutic trust differ in clear ways. Finally, by distinguishing between ordinary apt trust and apt (overriding) therapeutic trust on the model proposed, we have a perspective from which to appreciate two different *achievements* in trusting and why neither of these achievements reduces to the other.

7. Objections and Replies

7.1 Objection 1

On the view proposed, the constitutive aim of overriding therapeutic trust is meant to be distinct from the constitutive aim of standard (i.e., non-therapeutic) trust in that: (i) the aim of the latter is that the trustee take care of things as entrusted; whereas, (ii) the aim of the former is to build (or strengthen) trust *through* successful trust, viz., through the trustee's taking care of things as entrusted.

However, the suggestion that these aims are distinct is not so clear given that the view *also* holds that building trust is among the normal social functions that are played by (successful) ordinary trust. But if *that's* right, then isn't it the case that standard trust constitutively aims not *merely* at the trustee's taking care of things as entrusted, but also at its playing the social function of strengthening trust? If so, then it looks like the claimed difference between the constitutive aims of standard trust and overriding therapeutic trust collapses.

Reply: The fact that the constitutive aim of ordinary trust—viz., that the trustee take care of things as entrusted—is such that when this aim is met, its doing so has a characteristic social function, X, does not imply that its actually playing that function, X, is thereby included *as part of the constitutive aim*. The aim would still be met even if that social function characteristic of attaining that aim were *not* played.[32] (Compare: the aim of archery—hitting the target—is attained even if your hitting the target does not play any of the roles that attaining this aim would characteristically play, e.g., to build confidence, solidify social standing with peers, signal

---

[32] There is a precedent for this kind of thinking about aims and defective functioning found in Burge (2003, 509). According to Burge, evidence that something is or is not operating defectively offers us insight into what its aim (or, for Burge, function) is (or is not). For example, if we did not regard the heart as defective if it failed to pump blood, then this would cast doubt on the idea that the heart is normatively constrained by the aim of pumping blood. By parity of reasoning: my suggestion is that—in both archery and in ordinary trust—we would not regard a shot as defective if it hit the target but did not inspire confidence (a normal social function which, suppose, hitting a target plays) nor (ordinary) trust as defective if the trustee took care of things as entrusted despite this fact not going on to build further trust. This—with reference to the kind of reasoning we find in Burge—counts against the aim of archery being 'hitting the target *and inspiring confidence*', which is surely the right result, and likewise against the aim of ordinary trust as being 'that the trustee take care of things as entrusted *in a manner than builds trust*'.

competence, etc.) Likewise, if you trust a reliable colleague to deliver an envelope to your boss without reading the message inside, and the colleague successfully does so without taking a peek, there is a clear sense in which your trust placed in your colleague on this occasion has attained *its* aim—no matter what further social functions your trust plays or does not play, including social functions you might reasonably *expect* it to play.

7.2 Objection 2

The competences involved in ordinary (non-therapeutic) trust and overriding therapeutic trust are claimed to be *different* competences. But is this really so? Here is a reason to think the answer is 'no'. Adroit overriding therapeutic trust issues from a competence to reliably enough build trust through successful trust when one attempts to do so while appropriately situated. But then—being reliable at *this* was said to require a capacity for the kind of risk assessment that's needed to prevent one from too often 'over-' or 'under-'trusting (as in the CEO and cactus cases, respectively). But even if that's right—and here's the worry—doesn't being reliable at attaining the aim of *ordinary* trust *also* require a capacity for risk assessment? That is: a competence to attain the aim of ordinary trust reliably enough (when appropriately situated) surely requires a capacity to evaluate risks of *betrayal*, including risks of betrayal generated by, e.g., incentives the trustee has to betray, the difficulty of the task relative to the trustee's perceived abilities, etc. But once these points are granted, the distinction between the substance of the competences relevant to (i) ordinary trust versus (ii) overriding therapeutic becomes blurred.

Reply: In short, the answer is that the kind of competence that matters for overriding therapeutic trust *asymmetrically entails* the kind of competence that matters for ordinary (non-therapeutic trust). While risk assessment is undeniably important to both kinds of competences, and thus to both adroit overriding therapeutic trust as well as adroit ordinary trust, the kind of risk assessment that competent overriding therapeutic demands is more sophisticated, and accordingly more demanding, than the kind of risk assessment that competent ordinary trust demands. Given that the constitutive aim of ordinary therapeutic trust (that the trustee take care of things as entrusted) is a *component* of the constitutive aim of overriding therapeutic trust (that trust is built through successful trust—viz., through the trustee taking care of things as entrusted), reliably attaining the latter will require the very same kind of risk assessment needed to reliably secure the former, *plus* the capacity to assess *additional* risks—risks specifically to the non-obtaining of *trust built through successful trust.* Ordinary trust competence doesn't demand one have the capacity to assess these further risks.

The above illuminates an interesting wider point about the difference between ordinary and overriding therapeutic trust, which is that the latter is, in short, *more difficult* to do well. Being competent at overriding therapeutic trust requires all the skills required to be competent at ordinary trust, plus others which the latter doesn't require. A corollary is that the achievement of *apt* overriding therapeutic trust is more substantial, arguably more valuable,[33] than the achievement of apt ordinary trust in that the former issues from a comparatively more sophisticated and demanding kind of competence to acquire and exercise.

7.3 Objection 3

Certain kinds of 'forced-choice' cases seem like they would work as counterexamples to the proposed account of overriding therapeutic trust. Consider the following:

FORCED CHOICE: You've just moved to an apartment building in a new city, where the only person you know is a teenager who lives in the flat below you. You need to leave town for the weekend—suppose your job depends on it—and need someone to feed, water, and walk your dog (you've tried kennels, etc., and all are fully booked). Your hand forced, you trust the teenager who lives in the flat below you with this task—someone whom, had you had a better range of options—you wouldn't have chosen as they've not established any track record yet of responsibility with you, and your dog's welfare is important to you.

Two things seem, prima facie, to be true in FORCED CHOICE. First, (i) it looks like a case of therapeutic trust of a philosophically interesting sort (you are, after all, placing trust in a teenager to whom you wouldn't ordinarily trust a task like this); but, second, (ii) it doesn't get ruled in on the

---

[33] For some notable arguments that difficulty adds value to achievement, see, e.g., Bradford (2013), (2015), and Pritchard (2014).

account proposed. This is because in FORCED CHOICE, it's *not* the case that the aim of ordinary trust is *not* sufficient to lead the trustor to risk trusting. That aim *is* sufficient, *ex hypothesi*.

Reply: My response to FORCED CHOICE is to accept (ii) and press back against (i). It is a mistake to think that all cases in which one trusts a non-ideally-suited trustee (e.g., by selecting someone regarded as being less reliable than would be preferred) are, in virtue of this, 'therapeutic' in some interesting sense. On the view I've proposed, therapeutic trust of a philosophically interesting sort misses its mark—viz., is defective—even if the trust is successful, provided the trust fails to build or strengthen through this successful trust. FORCED CHOICE, however, is a case where the trust placed in the teenager *succeeds perfectly well* so long as the teenager takes care of the dog as entrusted. This is so in a way that is not interestingly different than were the teenager perceived to have been much more reliable than they are actually perceived to be. The situation is, however, very different if we suppose that the basic aim of successful trust *weren't* enough (as it is in FORCED CHOICE) to motivate you to risk trusting the teenager—viz., as would be the case when you trust the teenager, e.g., rather than someone you think has a better track record, with the aim of using successful trust to building trust. The above diagnosis not only explains why we would be wrong to, in short, lump all high-risk cases together—but it also helps to highlight the important sense in which therapeutic trust of the philosophically interesting kind *uses* trust in a way that ordinary trust does not.

A Telic Theory of Trust. J. Adam Carter, Oxford University Press. © J. Adam Carter 2024.
DOI: 10.1093/9780191982460.003.0008

9
Trust and Trustworthiness

This chapter motivates and defends a new way of theorizing about trust and trustworthiness—and their relationship to each other—by locating both within a broader picture that captures largely overlooked symmetries on both the trustor's and trustee's side of a cooperative exchange. The view defended here takes good cooperation as a theoretical starting point; on the view proposed, cooperation between trustor and trustee is working well when achievements in trust and in responding to trust are matched on both sides of the trust exchange. In a bit more detail, the trustor 'matches' her achievement in trusting (an achievement in fitting reliance to reciprocity) with the trustee's achievement in responding to trust (an achievement in fitting reciprocity to reliance). From this starting point, we can then appreciate symmetrical ways that the trustor and trustee can (respectively) fall short, by violating what are shown to be symmetrical evaluative norms—of success, competence, and aptness—that regulate the attempts made by both trustor and trustee. The overall picture has important advantages over the received way of theorizing about how trust stands to trustworthiness, and it clears the way—by identifying key questions that have been obscured—to making further progress.

1. Introduction

What is the relationship between trust and trustworthiness?[1] The question is a fraught one, not least because philosophers of *trust* have tended to focus on three-place trust (S trusts X with ϕ), whereas philosophers of *trustworthiness* have been primarily concerned with one-place trustworthiness—viz., (S is trustworthy).[2]

---

[1] A previous version of this chapter appears as Carter 2023c.
[2] As Hardin (1996) notes, a further complication is that 'Many discussions of trust run trust and trustworthiness together, with claims about trust that might well apply to trustworthiness but that seem off the mark for trust' (1996, 28).

This mismatch in focus presents challenges for those who want their accounts of trust and trustworthiness to be mutually illuminating. And it also prompts deeper methodological questions, such as whether we ought to be trying to understand trust in terms of trustworthiness (as some philosophers have[3]) or trustworthiness in terms of trust (as others have).[4]

Though there is little consensus here, a widespread underlying assumption is that the central phenomenon of interest on the trustee's side is *dispositional* (viz., trustworthiness) while the central phenomenon of interest on the trustor's side is *non-dispositional* (viz., trust). An important by-product of this assumption is that the evaluative norms of principal interest on the trustor's side regulate trusting attitudes and performances whereas those on the trustee's side regulate dispositions to respond to trust.

The aim here will be to highlight some unnoticed problems with this asymmetrical picture—and, in particular, how it elides certain key evaluative norms on both the trustor's and trustee's side the satisfaction of which are critical to successful cooperative exchanges—and to show that a symmetrical, 'achievement-first' approach to theorizing about trust and trustworthiness (and their relation to each other) has important advantages by comparison. The view I develop is guided by a structural analogy with practical reasoning. Just as practical reasoning is working as it should only when there is realization (knowledge and action) of states (belief and intention) with reverse directions of fits (mind-to-world and world-to-mind), likewise, cooperation between trustor and trustee is functioning as it should only when there is an analogous kind of realization on both sides of the cooperative exchange—viz., when the trustor 'matches' her achievement in trusting (an achievement in *fitting reliance to reciprocity*) with the trustee's achievement in responding to trust (an achievement in *fitting reciprocity to reliance*). An upshot of viewing cooperation between trustor and trustee as exhibiting achievement-theoretic structure is that we will be better positioned to subsume trustworthiness (and its cognates on the trustee's side), like trust, under a wider suite of evaluative norms that regulate attempts,

---

[3] See, e.g., O'Neill (2018, 293), Ashraf et al. (2006, 204), and McLeod (2023, sec. 1).

[4] For example, according to Wright (2010), trustworthiness requires that the trustee 'acknowledges the value of the trust that is invested in them...and to use [sic] this to help rationally decide how to act' (2010, sec. 3.b.). Other accounts of trustworthiness in terms of trust are found in Williams (2000) and Potter (2002, 205).

dispositions, and achievements symmetrically on both sides of a cooperative exchange, with 'matching achievements' as the gold standard.

Here is the plan. §2 clarifies and criticizes the kind of asymmetric picture that is embraced in the philosophy of trust and trustworthiness, which privileges performances (and norms regulating them) on the trustor's side and dispositions (and norms regulating them) on the trustee's side. §3 develops an analogy between practical reasoning and cooperation in order to motivate an alternative picture on which trusting and trustworthiness are better understood as having achievement-theoretic structure with reverse directions of fit. §4 builds on this picture in order to defend symmetrical evaluative norms—norms of *success*, *competence*, and *aptness*—on both sides, and §5 considers and responds to some potential objections.

2. Trust and Trustworthiness: Doing versus Being?

In the philosophy of trust, trust and trustworthiness are characteristically theorized about in a way that largely takes for granted that what is of central philosophical interest on the *trustor*'s side of a cooperative exchange is a kind of doing—*trusting*—whereas on the trustee's side, what's of central interest is the trustee's *being* a certain way (i.e., being trustworthy) on account of *possessing* some dispositional property or properties.[5] That philosophers of trust are interested—on the trustor's side of a cooperative exchange—in occurrences of trust (or doings) shouldn't be surprising given that, as Faulkner (2015) puts it, 'Most philosophical discussion of trust focuses on the three-place trust predicate: X trusting Y to ϕ',[6] instances of which will always involve, on the trustor's part, more than merely

---

[5] Possessing a dispositional property is not itself a matter of being in a mental state or behaving some way. Rather, dispositional properties 'provide the possibility of some further specific state or behaviour' (see, e.g., Mumford 2016) in certain conditions. Accordingly, the various 'accounts of trustworthiness' on the market are not aiming to give an account of any mental state, attitude, or behaviour; they are aiming to characterize accurately the dispositional property that they take trustworthy people but not others to possess.

[6] Apart from this observation registering what has attracted philosophical focus, there is the question of whether three-place trust is more explanatorily fundamental than one-place trust; Faulkner (2015) denies that this is the case. For an overview of this debate contesting whether three-place trust is more fundamental, see, along with Faulkner (2015), Carter and Simion (2020, §1.b).

possessing some propensity to trust the trustee[7] but their (in fact) doing so in a given case.[8]

On the trustee's side, however, the focus philosophically has been squarely on disposition possession: What disposition (or dispositions) line up with *being* trustworthy? Answers here vary. For example, according to a family of views defended by Annette Baier (1986), Karen Jones (2012), and Zac Cogley (2012), trustworthiness is to be identified with a disposition to fulfil commitments in conditions under which one has those commitments and *in virtue of* goodwill towards the trustor. For Diego Gambetta (1988), the trustworthy person needn't be disposed to fulfil the commitments they have out of goodwill; they simply must be disposed to fulfil their commitments, whatever they are, 'willingly'. More minimalistically, Christoph Kelp and Mona Simion (2021) identify trustworthiness with the disposition to fulfil one's obligations *simpliciter*, and not necessarily through any distinctive motivation or accompanying attitude. More weakly, for Katherine Hawley (2019), the relevant disposition 'trustworthiness' refers to is best

---

[7] It might seem as though a focus on dispositions (rather than doings) would be pertinent equally in the case of *trust*, at least for proponents of doxastic accounts of trust who elect to embrace, independently, a dispositional account of the nature of belief (e.g., Schwitzgebel 2013); on such accounts, believing a proposition (such as, in our case of interest, the proposition that the trustee will take care of things as entrusted) just amounts to possessing one or more particular behavioural dispositions pertaining to the target proposition. Does this observation call into doubt the asymmetry highlighted? There are several reasons to think not. First, and importantly, the scope of the asymmetry claim is that, as a historical point, focus (on the trustor's side) has been almost entirely on doings, and on the trustee's side on being a certain way. The possibility space of a substantive view on the trustor's side which would invite attention to trusting as a belief-cum-disposition is compatible with the larger observation. But, perhaps more importantly, a proponent of doxastic theories of trust who embraces a dispositional account of belief may focus on the exercising or manifesting (rather than mere possessing) of dispositions in so far as the object of interest is three-placed trust. It is worth noting further that at least liberal dispositionalists about belief allow that forming representations (including with propositional content) can be essential to belief; the liberal dispositionalist's thesis is just that what would make such token representations essential to belief is their grounding of behaviour patterns (Schwitzgebel 2019, §1.3).

[8] For instance, as Baier (1986) puts it, in theorizing about trust we are centrally concerned with 'one person trusting another with some valued thing' (1986, 236); likewise, Hawley (2014) maintains that trust is 'primarily a three-place relation, involving two people and a task' (2014, 2). This is not to say that trusting has only been of interest as a three-placed predicate; on the contrary both two- and one-place trust have received discussion, and it remains a live question whether one relation is more fundamental than the others (see Faulkner 2015 for discussion of one- and two-placed trust as fundamental). Rather, the point is just that we can easily see how interest in trust qua the activity of trusting, and not merely qua being a certain way, would be expected given that attention to trust as three-placed is found as widely as it is throughout discussions of trust by, among others, e.g., Baier (1986), Holton (1994), Jones (1996), Faulkner (2007), Hieronymi (2008), and Hawley (2014); for an overview, see Carter and Simion (2021, §1.b.).

framed negatively—viz., as a disposition to *avoid unfulfilled* commitments. By contrast with all of these views, Nancy Potter (2002), insists that the relevant disposition lining up with trustworthiness should be understood as a full-fledged moral virtue—one that consists in being disposed to respond to trust in appropriate ways.[9]

Notice that, despite their differences, these accounts all sign on, at least tacitly, to the idea that trustworthiness (on the trustee's side) and trust (on the trustor's side) are subject centrally to norms governing a (mere) 'being' to a 'doing'.[10] And thus, to the extent that these accounts are conducive to theorizing about trustworthiness and trust in terms of each other, it will be as a 'being' illuminates a 'doing' (or vice versa). A by-product of this approach in focus is that other norms (on each side) are given much less consideration; that is to say, if the evaluative norms of principal interest on the trustor's side are norms that regulate trusting attitudes and performances,[11] whereas those on the trustee's side regulate the trustee's dispositions to respond to trust, then what is inevitably going to be theoretically suppressed are whatever norms might govern, respectively, dispositions (on the trustor's side) and active performance through which dispositions are manifested (on the trustee's side).

While there is no doubt that being trustworthy corresponds with possessing *some* disposition or dispositions, so likewise does *being a competent trustor*, e.g., being one who trusts in ways that don't too often lead to betrayed trust.[12] And by the same token, just as trusting is itself not a disposition but an activity or performance, so likewise is the trustee's *manifestation of trustworthiness* when taking care of things as entrusted,[13] viz., when actually reciprocating the trust placed in her (as opposed to merely 'being the sort of person' who would take care of things as entrusted).

---

[9] According to Potter (2002), trustworthy persons '[…] give signs and assurances of their trustworthiness' and 'They take their epistemic responsibilities seriously' (2002, 174–75; cf., for criticism, Jones 2012, 75–76) and Kelp and Simion (2021). Note, however, that Jones (2012) is more sympathetic to the idea of trustworthiness as a virtue in the special case of what she calls 'rich' rather than 'basic' trustworthiness. See, e.g., (2012, 79).

[10] Or, alternatively, with reference to Vendler/Kenny classes—as an occurrence (trust) to a state (trustworthiness). See, e.g., Verkuyl (1989).

[11] See Chapter 2 for a fuller picture of this idea.

[12] For a defence of this way of thinking about competent trust, see, along with Chapter 2, Carter (2020b).

[13] The locution 'as entrusted' is meant to encompass views on which the trustee counts as taking care of things as entrusted only if doing so in a particular way, including, e.g., out of goodwill (Baier 1986; Jones 1996) or in conjunction with a belief that one is so committed (e.g., Hawley 2014). The present discussion—which is theoretically neutral on this point—is compatible with opting for either such kind of gloss.

It is worth asking: Is there any good reason that would justify the status quo here—viz., what has thus far been an asymmetrical focus on the dispositional property of trustworthiness and not on the trustee's performance of manifesting trustworthiness through reciprocity?

Perhaps there would be if the disposition of the trustee (rather than any performance on the trustee's part) features essentially in a plausible specification of what one aims at in trusting, and thus, in explaining when trust is successful. Or, alternatively, if the evaluative norms that are so often elided (e.g., manifestations on the trustee's side, or competence or dispositions on the trustor's side) are somehow less important to cooperative exchanges going well. Neither line of thought is promising.

The former is implicit in what Carolyn McLeod (2023) takes to be a platitude about trust, which is that 'Trust is an attitude that we have towards people whom we hope will *be trustworthy*, where trustworthiness is a property not an attitude'.[14] Variations of this idea are seen in Elizabeth Fricker's (2018) claim that '[…] One is not really trusting unless one adopts an attitude of optimism to the proposition that the trustee *is trustworthy*' (2018, 6). Likewise, as Russell Hardin (2002) puts it, 'trusting someone in some context is simply to be explained as merely the expectation that the person will most likely *be trustworthy*' (2002, 31). And perhaps most directly, proponents of doxastic accounts of trust (Hieronymi 2008; McMyler 2011) straightforwardly identify trust with a belief that the trustee *is trustworthy*.[15]

Of course, we seek out a trustworthy person when initially deciding *whether* to trust or forbear from trusting; in this respect, Onora O'Neill is right that 'where we aim […] to place and refuse trust intelligently *we must link trust to trustworthiness*' (2018, 293). But when we actually trust someone, the relevance of the trustee's simply 'being a certain way' independent of their actually *performing* in a way that manifests how we perhaps hope or believe they are (i.e., trustworthy) is not clear at all.

When I trust you to pay back the loan, I rely on you to pay it back, making myself vulnerable to your betrayal.[16] Suppose you *do* then pay it back. Is my trust successful? Not necessarily, says the proponent of the idea that

---

[14] See McLeod (2023, sec. 1, my italics).
[15] For a related though less standard kind of doxastic account, see, e.g., Keren (2014, 2019).
[16] For various expressions of the idea that trust essentially involves subjecting oneself to risk of betrayal, see, along with Hardin (1992), e.g., Baier (1986, 244), McLeod (2023, sec. 1), Nickel and Vaesen (2012, 861–62), Carter (2020b, 2301, 2318–19), Carter and Simion (2020, sec. 1.a), Becker (1996, 45, 49), Dasgupta (1988, 67–68), Dormandy (2020, 241–42), Kirton (forthcoming), O'Neil (2017, 70–72), Potter (2020, 244), and Hinchman (2017). Cf., Pettit (1995, 208).

trustworthiness is of special interest in understanding trust. In trusting, I aim *not just* that you take care of things any way, but take care of things *as entrusted*, which (on this line of thought) involves your 'being trustworthy'.

This is partly right. But it gets an important thing wrong. Just as my trust isn't thereby successful if you merely take care of things *any* old way (e.g., by attempting to betray me, but in doing so accidentally pay back the loan—then only my *reliance* would be successful), likewise, my trust misses the mark if you simply *are* trustworthy but (perhaps due to bad luck) *don't* pay back the loan. But crucially—even more—there is a sense in which my trust *still* misses the mark if you (i) pay back the loan; (ii) are trustworthy; but (iii) your paying back the loan doesn't manifest your trustworthiness (e.g., perhaps despite being trustworthy you pay back the loan on this occasion under threat or through some kind of manipulation by a third party).[17]

The foregoing suggests that (on the trustee's side) the largely exclusive theoretical focus on *trustworthiness* qua disposition (as opposed to, e.g., focusing on performances of trustworthiness) isn't going to be justified simply in light of the importance of this disposition to understanding the aims of trusting. After all, the trustor (through trusting) aims not just at the trustee merely *being* a certain way—or even at the trustee doing a certain thing *while at the same time being a certain way*—but at the trustee *achieving* a certain thing, viz., succeeding in taking care of things *through* their trustworthiness.

This observation serves neatly to counter the second idea envisaged in favour of the asymmetrical picture under consideration; it's simply not evident that the evaluative norms that the asymmetric picture de facto elides (e.g., manifestations of dispositions on the trustee's side, or competence or dispositions on the trustor's side) are somehow less important to successful trust exchanges going well than are 'doings' on the trustor's side and 'being' on the trustee's side which have received the brunt of the philosophical focus so far. At a minimum, getting these de facto elided norms into better

---

[17] Coercion isn't essential to making this kind of point; for example, the trustworthy person might be such that her success (in taking care of things as entrusted) doesn't manifest her trustworthiness not because she lacked the opportunity to do so (as would be the case if she were coerced) but rather due to the abnormal presence of luck in accounting for the success. The underlying idea here—one that has been defended variously by Sosa (2007), Greco (2010, Ch. 5), Pritchard (2012), and Zagzebski (1996)—is that a success doesn't manifest one's reliable disposition (construed as an ability, virtue, or competence) if that success is unusually due to luck. How to unpack 'unusually' (alternatively: abnormally) is a contested point, one that features centrally in discussions in virtue epistemology of achievement, luck, and credit. See, e.g., Turri et al. (2019, sec. 5, §7).

focus will open up additional ways to evaluate what goes wrong (and right) in a given cooperative exchange.

This insight offers us a new vantage point for revisiting, and developing further in new substantive detail, the relationship between trust and trustworthiness—and how to theorize about both in connection to each other and to appreciate some important performance-theoretic *symmetries* between the trustor/trustee sides of a cooperative exchange.

3. Structural Analogies with Practical Reasoning

Whereas mere *reliance* is successful just in case the person relied on takes care of things *any way*, the success conditions for trust are more demanding. Where we've got to so far is that in *trusting*, as opposed to merely relying, the trustor aims through trusting that the trustee *manifests her trustworthiness* in successfully taking care of what the trustor relies on her to do.[18] And this involves, on the part of the trustee, a kind of *success through trustworthiness*—viz., an *achievement* in trustworthiness, rather than, say, responding to the trustor's trust in such a way as to avoid betraying that trust just by luck.

Let's now take this working idea—that the trustor aims in trusting at the trustee's *achievement* in trustworthiness[19]—even further. Just consider that when the trustor *herself* attains this aim (i.e., the aim that the trustee's taking care of things manifests her trustworthiness)—this might on some occasions of cooperation be down to dumb luck; the trustor might foolishly trust the one trustworthy person in the village of tricksters, but this lone trustworthy person might then manifest her trustworthiness full well in taking care of things.[20]

---

[18] For a different approach to thinking about the aim of trust (in connection with how the trustee performs), see Hinchman (e.g., 2021) who distinguishes between trust's being *disappointed* and *betrayed*.

[19] This idea supersedes, by developing in more substantive detail, what was a simpler characterization of the aim of trust, developed in Chapter 2, which was that trust aims (constitutively) at the trustee taking care of things *as entrusted*.

[20] In this example, we are to suppose that the trustor is not manifesting any trusting competence here, but rather, simply and naively trusting and just happens to be lucky. The structure of the case is importantly different from a case where the trustee *does* manifest competence, in a normal environment, but could have easily trusted someone who was mistaken in that environment. In the latter case, the structure is analogous to that of a 'fake barn case'—and that is a case which, at least within performance-theoretic epistemology, there is no barrier to attributing the success to the ability and thus to attributing achievement. For discussion, see, e.g., Sosa

Trust is *successful* here. *And* the trustee exhibits an achievement in fulfilling the trust placed in her through trustworthiness. But, in this situation, there is no symmetrical achievement (success that manifests a trusting competence) on the *trustor's* side, even though trust is successful. And in this respect, there is an important sense in which the cooperation itself still falls short; the cooperation does not match 'achievement to achievement', but matches merely success (by the trustor) to achievement (by the trustee).

Of course, the symmetry can be regained if we simply shore up the performance on the trustor's side.[21] Suppose it is *not* simply through good fortune but *through the trustor's competence* (to trust *successfully* reliably enough) that the trustor trusts successfully. In such a case, the relevant trust is not just successful but 'apt' in that the successful trust manifests the trustor's competence to bring that success about reliably.[22] This *apt* (and not merely successful) trust, an achievement of trusting, on the trustor's side would then match the trustee's achievement in trustworthiness. And now *cooperation* is functioning well in that the cooperation between the two *falls short on neither side* of the cooperative exchange.

An analogy is useful here between (i) the symmetrical picture just described of cooperation working well, and (ii) Williamson's (2017) view of practical reasoning working well. According to Williamson, a practical reasoning system is working well when and only when one acts on what one knows.[23] One is in a position to act on what one knows only if one 'realizes' two kinds of states, with *reverse directions of fit* (mind-to-world and

---

(2007, Ch. 2), Littlejohn (2014), Carter (2016), Pritchard (2009), Jarvis (2013), and Kallestrup and Pritchard (2014).

[21] Note that the idea of trust as a kind of performance is compatible with the thought that—as Nguyen (forthcoming) holds in recent work—trusting essentially involves forbearing from the taking up of certain attitudes, such as questioning. This is because forbearing can itself feature in aimed performances. Consider, for example, the opera singer's performance of a piece, which (if it is to succeed in its aim) must include silence at the right parts, a form of forbearing from singing. See, e.g., Sosa (2021, Ch. 3) who discusses this point in connection with our evaluation of suspension of judgement as a performance type.

[22] For simplicity of presentation, in order to get the core points in view clearly, I am setting aside the implicit/deliberative distinction (developed initially in Chapter 3)—though it is a distinction that will apply as well on the trustee's side as on the trustor's side; though developing this will be for another occasion.

[23] This idea, originating in Williamson (2000), is given a sustained defence in his (2017) with some further updates in (2021). Whereas Williamson encourages us to view the idea that practical reasoning's working well is a matter of acting on knowledge in the service of a wider criticism of the centrality of belief-desire psychology as explanatorily central, the core normative idea that, in practical reasoning, one should act only on what one knows has received defences by (along with Williamson) Hawthorne and Stanley (2008), Stanley (2005), and Fantl and McGrath (2002). For an overview, see Benton (2014, sec. 2.a).

world-to-mind). Accordingly, on Williamson's picture, practical reasoning is not functioning as it should if there is a defect on either on the mind-to-world side (i.e., mere belief rather than knowledge) or on the world-to-mind side (i.e., mere intention rather than action).[24]

The working analogy so far is this: just as practical reasoning is functioning well only when we have symmetrical realization (knowledge and action) of states (belief and intention) with reverse directions of fits, likewise, cooperation between trustor and trustee is functioning well only when we have an analogous kind of *symmetrical realization on both sides of the cooperative exchange*—viz., when the trustor 'matches' her achievement in trusting with the trustee's achievement in responding to trust.

This working analogy can be extended further by considering how the trustor's and trustee's matching achievements, when cooperation is working well, are themselves (like knowledge and action) *realizations of attempts with reverse direction of fit*.[25] To a first approximation: whereas the trustor

---

[24] I say 'intention' here rather than 'desire' as standing in for botched action to reflect Williamson's updated (2017) structural analogies. In *Knowledge and Its Limits* (2000) practical reason's working well was also understood in terms of acting on knowledge. This picture was meant to replace belief-desire psychology as the centre of intelligent life. However, the original (2000) version of the analogy maintained that belief stood to knowledge (on the mind-to-world side) as desire stood to action (on the world-to-mind side). The updated picture assimilates desire to belief—i.e., belief about what is good (see, e.g., Lewis 1988; Price 1989)—and replaces 'desire' with 'intention' in the analogy. Thus, the updated picture holds that belief stands to knowledge as intention to action. For critical discussion, see Miracchi and Carter (2022).

[25] The language of 'direction of fit' is originally usually credited to Anscombe (1957) as a way of characterizing a distinction between theoretical and practical intentional mental states. Theoretical mental states aim at representing things as they are (e.g., beliefs) and practical mental states aim at getting things done (i.e., desires). Realization (i.e., success) for a cognitive (or theoretical) intentional mental state involves fitting mind-to-world; realization for a practical mental state (e.g., desire, intention, etc.) involves fitting world-to-mind. A central 'lesson' direction of fit theorists (e.g., Smith 1994; Velleman 2000; cf., Frost 2014) have taken from Anscombe's initial discussion is that intentional mental states are characterizable along the mind-to-world or world-to-mind fault line. However, the kinds of things to which direction of fit talk is applicable are not limited to intentional mental states. For example, according to Searle (1979), statements and predictions have a *word-to-world* direction of fit, whereas commands and promises have a *world-to-word* direction of fit. It's worth noting further that the very thought that things other than mental states can have directions of fit is actually perfectly compatible with Anscombe's initial idea, which is that what *makes* intentional states like beliefs and desires have the directions of fit is that they have normative realization conditions; beliefs *aim* (constitutively, not intentionally) at a certain kind of realization, the same for desires. A similar normative reading is due to Platts (1980; for discussion, see Frost 2014, 449–50). What this suggests, then, is that—at least in so far as we follow progenitors of DOF theory such as Anscombe and Searle, there is no barrier to viewing attempts more generally (including, e.g., trust and its reciprocation) with constitutive aims as admitting of directions of fit in so far as they have specifiable normative realization conditions.

aims not just to rely, but to *fit her reliance to the trustee's reciprocity*, the trustee (as such) aims to *fit her reciprocity to the trustor's reliance*.[26]

When the trustor attempts, but fails, to fit her reliance to reciprocity, what is residual is a kind of botched trust. When the trustee attempts, but fails, to fit her reciprocity to reliance, what is residual is a kind of botched reciprocity. (Compare with Williamson's suggestion that belief is a kind of 'botched knowledge' and mere intention 'botched' action.)[27]

On this wider picture, then, in any two-way cooperative system, trust stands to apt trust as reciprocity to apt reciprocity (reciprocity that succeeds through trustworthiness) in a way that is broadly analogous to how (in a practical reasoning system, for Williamson) belief stands to knowledge (viz., *apt* belief[28]) as intention to action (i.e., *apt* intention[29]). And, further, just as practical reasoning's working well requires a match between not merely belief and intention but between knowledge and action; cooperation working well requires a match between not *mere* but *apt* trust and reciprocity.

The tables below represent these key analogies:

Practical reasoning: Realizations and attempts

Practical reasoning	Fitting mind-to-world	Fitting world-to-mind
Functioning well	knowledge (realization) belief (attempt)	action (realization) intention (attempt)

---

[26] I say 'reverse' direction of fit for ease of presentation, given that 'reliance-to-reciprocity' and 'reciprocity-to-reliance' are ostensibly reverse directions of fit. That said, it might have been more precise to describe the kind of direction of fit here as lining up even better with what Searle (1979) calls 'double direction of fit'. The reason here is that—in the unique case of cooperation—the realization of one entails the realization of the other.

[27] In more recent work, Williamson (2021) has distinguished between what he calls *local failure* and *global failure* in a cognitive system. As he puts it, 'when a belief fails to constitute knowledge, it is a local failure, a defect in that particular belief. But when a cognitive system is too prone to produce such beliefs short of knowledge, it is a global failure, a defect in the system as a whole' (2021, 7). One philosophical question, of interest in recent work on epistemological dilemmas (e.g., Hughes 2019), concerns how to evaluate mixed cases that feature combinations of global success + local failure and local success + global failure; of particular interest is whether such cases feature mere normative conflict (e.g., Simion forthcoming) or epistemological 'dilemmas' for a thinker. While it goes beyond the present aims to take this issue up, it is worth registering that an analogous global/local failure distinction arises in the philosophy of trust—where we can envision cases of local failure + global success and vice versa.

[28] The idea that knowledge is type-identical with apt belief has advantages in epistemology; see Sosa (2007, 2010), Greco (2010, Chs. 5–6), and Zagzebski (1996) for some notable defences of this position. Although I find this view plausible, the identification of knowledge with apt belief—while if fits snugly with the proposal developed here—isn't essential to it. For some criticism of the identification of knowledge with apt belief, see, e.g., Lackey (2007), Pritchard (2007), Kelp (2013), Kornblith (2004), and Kallestrup and Pritchard (2014).

[29] For defences of the view that action is fruitfully understood as apt intention, see Sosa (2015, Ch. 1) and Miracchi and Carter (2022).

Cooperation: Realizations and attempts

Cooperation	Fitting reliance-to-reciprocity	Fitting reciprocity-to-reliance
Functioning well	trustor's apt trust (realization) trust (attempt)	trustee's apt reciprocity (realization) reciprocity (attempt)

One important feature of Williamson's 'knowledge-action'-centric picture of practical reasoning is that it is meant to contrast with a competing picture (see, e.g., Humberstone 1992) that takes attempts—belief and desire—*rather than their realizations* as the core explanatory mental attitudes at the centre of intelligent life.[30] Attempts at knowledge and attempts at action retain a place in this picture, but it is their realizations, rather than the attempts themselves, that are of comparative theoretical importance.

The picture of cooperation suggested here likewise gives primacy to realizations over their attempts. That is, the present picture rejects the trustee's performance (trust), a mere attempt at realization by fitting reliance to reciprocity, and the trustee's disposition (trustworthiness) to fit reciprocity to reliance are the most theoretically important notions in a wider picture of cooperation. Rather, we should think of the importance of the trustor and trustee's matching achievements of trust and trustworthiness in cooperation as broadly analogous to the importance of action and knowledge (as opposed to mere belief and desire) in practical reasoning.

4. Symmetric Evaluative Normativity: Trustor and Trustee

In the good case where cooperation is working as it should, the trustor matches her achievement in trusting with the trustee's achievement in

---

[30] On the kind of view embraced by Humberstone (1992), it is also possible to accept the structural analogy on which belief stands to knowledge as desire to action. However, such a structural analogy would (on the belief-desire-centred picture) begin with belief and desire as 'direction of fit mirror images', from which we would then 'solve upward' in the analogy to get the result that belief stands to knowledge as desire to action. Resisting this picture is the central argument in Williamson (2017) who suggests we begin with knowledge and action as direction of fit mirror images and then solve 'downward', filling in the relevant attempts. For a criticism of the role of 'mirrors' in both Williamson and Humberstone's approaches, see Miracchi and Carter (2022).

responding to trust. In both of these achievements (of apt trust and apt reciprocity) *competence* is manifested in success.[31]

Cooperation doesn't always go so well. It falls short—at least to some extent—if we have anything short of achievement on either the trustor or trustee's side. In some cases, cooperation doesn't fall short by much, as when the trustor matches successful and competent but inapt (i.e., Gettiered) success to the trustee's achievement.[32] The trustor could do far worse. Successful but incompetent trust falls short of Gettiered trust on the trustor's side, as does competent but unsuccessful trust.[33] On the bottom rung on the trustor's side, we have trust that is neither competent nor successful, e.g., betrayed on account of gullibility.

Likewise, on the trustee's side, falling just short of achievement is a kind of *Gettiered reciprocity*; suppose the trustee manifests her trustworthiness in assiduously entering the correct bank details online to pay back the loan she was entrusted to pay back, but succeeds only because a fortuitous electronic glitch (good luck) *corrects for an initial glitch* (bad luck) that would have diverted the funds to the wrong account.[34] The trustee could do far worse. For one thing, she could have *not* manifested trustworthiness in responding to the trust placed in her, but succeeded half-heartedly just by luck.

Whereas the first loan case is a case of Gettiered reciprocity, the second is successful but incompetent reciprocity. Two remaining categories, lower down the rung on the trustee's side are: unsuccessful and competent reciprocity (i.e., exactly like the Gettiered reciprocity case *without* the second stroke of good luck), and—at the very bottom rung—incompetent and unsuccessful reciprocity (e.g., the trustee intends to wire money to the wrong account, and—failing in reciprocity—succeeds in betrayal).

The above picture shows the many ways that cooperation can be defective (by lesser or greater degree) by matching anywhere from *just* less to *much*

---

[31] Note that (as with the framework developed initially in Chapter 2) the structure of the evaluative norms (on both trustor's and trustee's side) here is one I take to have applicability across the spectrum of trustor/trustee cooperative relationships. Will the view here apply to children? It will, though it might be that children will be less competent (as trustors and trustees) than mature adults, though this is a claim that would require empirical investigation.

[32] Performances that are successful and competent but inapt have a 'Gettier' structure where the success is disconnected from the good method used. For discussion, see Sosa (2007, Ch. 2; 2010, 467, 474–75) and Greco (2009, 19–21; 2010, 73–76, 94–99). Cf., Pritchard (2012, 251, 264–68).

[33] The performance-theoretic analogy with virtue epistemology holds that successful but incompetent trust and competent but unsuccessful trust fall short of apt trust in a way that is analogous to how unjustified true beliefs and justified false beliefs both fall short of knowledge. See, for discussion, Sosa (2007, 2010, 2015).

[34] For discussion of this kind of 'double luck' structure in relation to Gettier cases, see, e.g., Zagzebski (1994); see also Pritchard (2007) on what he calls 'intervening' veritic luck.

less than achievement on either the trustor's or trustee's side. But it also reveals an important *normative symmetry* on both sides.

By 'normative symmetry' what I mean is that the relevant *attempts* on each side (fitting reliance to reciprocity on the trustor's side, fitting reciprocity to reliance on the trustee's side) are such that we can evaluate each for the very same three things: (i) *success*, (ii) *competence*, and (iii) *aptness*.[35] And, moreover, it is specifically by *failing* to satisfy combinations of these norms that performances on the trustor's and trustee's side fall short of achievement to whatever extent that they do.

The symmetrical picture of evaluative norms on each side is accordingly as follows:

	On the trustor's side	On the trustee's side
Direction of fit attempt	Reliance-to-reciprocity (trust) by means of reliance	Reciprocity-to-reliance reciprocity (by means of responding to trust)
success norm	S's trusting X with ϕ is better if successfully reciprocated than if not; S's trusting X with ϕ is successfully reciprocated iff X takes care of ϕ as entrusted.	X's reciprocating S's trust with ϕ is better if X successfully reciprocates S's trust with ϕ than if not; X successfully reciprocates S's trust with ϕ iff X takes care of ϕ as entrusted.
competence norm	S's trusting X with ϕ is better if S trusts X with ϕ competently than if S does not.	X's reciprocating S's trusting X with ϕ is better if X reciprocates S's trust with ϕ competently than if X does not.
aptness norm	S's trusting X with ϕ is better if S trusts X with ϕ aptly than if S does not.	X's reciprocating S's trusting X with ϕ is better if X reciprocates S's trust with ϕ aptly than if X does not.

---

[35] This is not to say that we can evaluate performances only along these three dimensions. For instance, a more recent innovation in the theory of performance normativity recognizes the normative standard—beyond mere aptness—of *full aptness* (e.g., Sosa 2015; 2021; Carter 2021a; see also Carter and Sosa 2021). To a first approximation, a performance is fully apt iff it is not merely apt, but also guided to aptness by an apt (second-order) risk assessment that it would (likely enough) be apt. For discussion of this difference (as applicable to trust), see— along with Chapters 5 and 6—also Carter (2020b). For ease of presentation, I have articulated the relevant achievement matching (on the side of trustor and trustee) in terms of aptness on each side; however, see §5 (Objections and Replies) for some additional discussion.

This symmetrical picture offers us a number of advantages. For one thing, our guiding idea that cooperation between trustor and trustee is working as it should when both sides match achievement to achievement can now be restated as an *aptness norm on cooperation*, one that is formulated *in terms of* trustor and trustee satisfying respective evaluative norms of aptness: a cooperative trust exchange E between trustor and trustee is better than it would be otherwise if E is apt;[36] E is apt iff trustor and trustee satisfy their respective aptness norms.[37]

Secondly—and this brings us back to where we started—it should now be even more evident why focusing principally on a disposition (trustworthiness) on the trustee's side but not on the trustor's side (and vice versa for performance) is going to be somewhat arbitrary. From a wider view that takes in and evaluates the trust exchange in full, neither has any special status, even though both are essential to cooperation going well. They are, in a bit more detail, essential to cooperation going well in a way that is roughly analogous to how our beliefs and intentions (or: dispositions to form intentions) are important to practical reasoning going well. Both deserve attention, but should be appreciated as attempts *at* realizations, where the realizations of those attempts are what's needed in good practical reasoning as well as (*mutatis mutandis*) in good cooperation.

Thirdly, by transitioning to a symmetrical picture of the evaluative normativity of trust—with achievement matching achievement as the gold standard—we are better positioned to see the importance of questions that have been so far obscured. Perhaps most conspicuously here are questions about the competence norm of trust. After all, we have a grip on *apt trust* only by understanding competent trust, and this involves a clear view of those dispositions of the trustor that lead them to trust *successfully* reliably

---

[36] It is worth noting that an aptness norm on cooperation offers, additionally, a standard for evaluating wider trust networks in terms of the cooperative trust exchanges that comprise them; in this way, an evaluation of a network (consisting in individuals) can be assessed against the guiding value of apt cooperation—and not merely by values that pick out individual-level metrics.

[37] The idea that cooperation itself admits of an aptness norm suggests that cooperation is a kind of multi-agent performance itself. A natural way of thinking of this is as an irreducibly collective property of cooperators engaged jointly in a trust exchange. While I am sympathetic to this kind of gloss, I want to stress that we needn't be committed to it. The crux of the idea— viz., that cooperation is apt iff its individual cooperators perform aptly—is also compatible with a 'summativst' gloss on which the cooperation has the relevant property (i.e., aptness) iff all its individual members have that property. For relevant recent discussion of these points, see Lackey (2021) and Broncano-Berrocal and Carter (2021). For a discussion of aptness as applicable to groups, see Kallestrup (2016).

enough. Other questions invited by the symmetrical picture involve the evaluative normativity of cooperation generally. Even if 'aptness on both sides' of the trustor/trustee divide implies that the cooperative exchange itself is apt, it remains an open question how to evaluate certain cooperation permutations that involve at least one norm violation on one side. For example, is cooperation working better if the trustor matches success without competence to the trustee's achievement or competence without success to the trustee's achievement?

Fourthly, given that *distrust* no less than trust can be successful, competent, and apt, the normative symmetry we find on the trustor's and trustee's side invites us to consider—analogically—what stands to distrust as trust to reciprocity,[38] and to consider how to best characterize parallel symmetrical norms that would regulate—symmetrically with successful, competent, and apt distrust (on the side of the trustor)—also forbearance on the side of the trustee.

5. Objections and Replies

(a) Objection

It's not entirely clear that *cooperation* functions as it should only if we get a kind of 'aptness' on both the trustor and trustee's side (viz., matching achievements of fitting reliance-to-reciprocity and reciprocity-to-reliance, respectively). Might this not be too strong?[39] For example, suppose a

---

[38] Analogically, this will involve some form of forbearance from reciprocity. One point of note here: forbearing from reciprocity, in a sense that would be analogous with distrust, would involve refraining from accepting the obligation incurred with being entrusted with something, as opposed to, accepting the obligation and then betraying the trust. See Chapter 3 for relevant discussion.

[39] Some might also consider whether the picture might be instead too weak, with reference to examples where the aptness on both sides seems in some way problematic. Suppose a teenage son has developed a drug addiction but he still lives at home and has no source of income other than theft. In this case, he might trust his parents to give him money to buy drugs. He trusts them because he knows that they know he will commit theft if they don't give him the money, and so this fact, and the fact he is counting on them for the money, make it such that they ought to give the money, or so he thinks. This background then makes it plausible to say he trusts them for some money. But, as the worry goes, it is not obvious that the trustworthy thing to do is give him some money, or that the parents have exhibited any kind of achievement in trustworthiness in responding to the trust given. After all, the parents, we may presume, want to keep him from theft and out of a life of crime, but they also don't want to sustain his addiction. We might then think it is not clear what the parents should do (e.g., set him up with some rehabilitation programme, etc.). The worry for the picture, though, is that the

trustworthy trustee does what she is trusted to do (*vis-à-vis* the trustor) *because* she is trustworthy; isn't that enough for the cooperative exchange to plausibly get 'full marks'? Why should we think there must also be, as the view here suggests, something extra that the trustor does on top of this, which is to trust the trustworthy trustee *because* she is a competent trustor?

Reply: On the supposition, in the above case described, that the trustor's trust was successful but *not* through trusting competence, then regardless of how well the trustee performs (even if ideally), we are still left with a kind of Gettier structure on the trustor's side; that is, there will be a kind of credit-reducing luck applicable to the trustor's trusting in such a case, even if such credit-reducing luck is not going to be equally applicable to trustee's manifestation of trustworthiness in responding to the trustor's trust. A satisfying assessment of the kind of trust exchange just described should be able to make to make sense of *both* (i) what goes right in the above case (which is very much, particularly given the performance of the trustee), while (ii) also having some explanation available for what comes up short on the trustor's side. Performance-theoretic assessment can deliver both results straightforwardly; recall that, on the view defended, the cooperative exchange itself involves two performances (one of fitting reliance to reciprocity, the other reciprocity to reliance); the conjunction of the two performances (exhaustive of the cooperative exchange) gets *very near* full marks precisely because nearly all evaluative norms on both sides are met; success, competence, and aptness norms are satisfied on the trustee's side; success and competence but not aptness norms are satisfied on the trustor's side.

---

trustee has in some sense fallen short even when doing what the teenager wants here, and in a way that seems to line up on my view with the 'gold standard' of achievement matching on the trustor's and trustee's side. I am grateful to a referee at OUP for pressing me with this case. I think the right way to assess cases like this will be with reference to the distinction drawn, in Chapter 4, between two domains of normative assessment: telic normativity (governing aimed performances of trusting, and exhibiting trustworthiness) in cases of three-place trust, and the *ethics of cooperation*—a distinction that is meant to line up, analogically, with Sosa's distinction in epistemology between gnoseology and (the wider normative domain of) intellectual ethics. Consider this line of thinking: An archer's shot might be morally bad, but still good as an archery shot. What about beliefs—e.g., take beliefs about grains of sand on the beach, or beliefs about how to arm a bomb. These might be pointless beliefs or morally bad beliefs to have, but they might still be apt qua beliefs when known, apart from whatever else we might say against them. The sense in which the archer's shot is apt qua shot (even when morally bad) and a belief can be apt and thus known (even if pointless or morally bad) is telic assessment. The distinction in Chapter 4 between pistology and the ethics of cooperation is meant to countenance that there are ethical evaluations of trust that lie outside of telic assessment of trusting (and responding to trust) understood as an aimed performance. In the above example case, the parents might respond aptly to trust here, where 'aptly' tracks telic assessment, even though, all things considered, what they ought to do is something else entirely.

(b) Objection

Here is an objection that presses in the other direction. Even if we concede that Gettier structures (viz., featuring success and competence, but not success *because* competence) on either the trustor's or trustee's side of a cooperative exchange would implicate a kind of credit-reducing luck that is incompatible with aptness,[40] there still remains a (different) kind of credit-reducing luck—*environmental luck*[41]—that is widely thought to be compatible with aptness (and even if Gettier-style luck is not); this is just the sort of luck at play in fake barn cases in epistemology, whereby one's success is unsafe but only because one is in an inhospitable environment that includes nearby error possibilities.[42] The very idea that environmental luck is compatible with aptness (even if Gettier-style luck is not) would seem to call into doubt whether 'achievement matching', understood as matching aptness to aptness on the trustor's and trustee's side, respectively, really is the 'gold standard' when it comes to a cooperative exchange. Why not, after all, think that cooperation is functioning as it should only if performances on both sides succeed in a way that safeguards against *both* Gettier-style as well as environmental luck?

Reply: The are two key points to make in response to the above. The first will have us revisit Williamson's own structural analogies: consider again the idea that a practical reasoning system is working properly only when one acts on what one knows; this requires no defect either on the mind-to-world side (i.e., mere belief rather than knowledge) or on the world-to-mind side (i.e., mere intention rather than action). Even so, this needn't require maximal, or even extremely comprehensive knowledge with respect to object of the target intention (this is so even if one embraces a strong infallibilist thesis, e.g., that knowledge = probability 1).[43] What this

---

[40] For a dissenting view on this point, see Littlejohn (2014).
[41] See, e.g., Pritchard (2005) for the distinction between environmental epistemic luck and intervening epistemic luck.
[42] Note that the idea that environmental luck is compatible with aptness, while a point that has been made with reference to fake barn cases in epistemology, is not specifically an epistemological point; it is meant to apply equally to performances more generally. For example, to use an example from Sosa (2015), suppose a trainee pilot very easily could have woken up in a flight simulator, but instead luckily wakes up strapped in a real cockpit; in such a case, the pilot (assuming they are well trained) can shoot targets competently and aptly, where the success manifests competence, and this is so even though very easily they could have woken instead in a simulator in which case they would have been shots that do not succeed in hitting (real) targets. For further discussion of this case, see also Sosa (2010, 467–68).
[43] See, e.g., Williamson (2000).

observation indicates is that a charitable reading of Williamson's own analogy is not that practical reason is working as it should only if there is no defect *whatsoever* (and of which falling short of maximal knowledge, or perhaps failing to know *that* one knows, etc., would constitute such a defect on the mind-to-world side) but, rather, that each side meet a salient standard that will be secured, minimally, by the realization of the attempt one makes in fitting mind-to-word and world-to-mind in practical reasoning. And by parity of reasoning from this point to our own case of interest (featuring trustor and trustee), we can see how an analogous kind of position is going to be comparatively more plausible (on the achievement-matching view of cooperation working well) than would be a view that demands (on the trustor's and trustee's sides) *more* than aptness, in order to eliminate luck or chance that goes beyond mere Gettier-style luck that is incompatible with aptness. That said—and here is the second line of reply to the objection—*even if one were attracted to a more demanding picture* (on which mere aptness, on each side, isn't enough for cooperation to go as it should), the good news is that the tools of performance normativity offer the resources to model exactly what such a more demanding (and environmental-luck-*excluding*) achievement-matching picture would look like. To a first approximation, the key idea would be to distinguish *mere aptness* from *full aptness*—where a fully apt performance, a higher form of achievement, is not merely apt, but also such that not easily would it have been inapt.[44] Then, the idea available within the framework (for one tempted to a stronger picture than what I've opted for here) would be to hold that cooperation between trustor and trustee attains an even higher (performance-theoretic) quality when the trustor and trustee match achievements of *full* aptness on each side in such a way as to gain aptness *safely* (see Chapters 5 and 6 for discussion of full aptness, and what it requires, on the trustor's side).

---

[44] See Sosa (2015, Ch. 3). This is a simple statement of the idea. A more theoretically involved articulation of full aptness, found in Sosa (2015, Ch. 3; see also Carter 2020) would require distinguishing between mere apt trust and fully apt trust with reference to trusting *metacompetences*—competences to trust in ways that would not easily lead to inapt trust. Fully apt trust can then be stated (within a performance-theoretic framework) in terms of metacompetence as follows: trust is fully apt just in case it is guided to aptness by a meta-apt risk assessment that not too easily would the trust have been inapt. These details, however, take us beyond what is needed to articulate the core idea that full aptness, even if not mere aptness, precludes environmental luck by de facto requiring safety.

(c) Objection

Setting aside whether the 'top end' of the symmetrical picture of normative evaluation (of trustor and trustee) is too demanding (or not demanding enough), a more basic question remains, concerning the theoretical value of the symmetrical picture in comparison with the asymmetrical picture. Even if we grant that the symmetrical picture opens up space for asking new (performance-evaluative) questions about the trustor and trustee that might otherwise be (de facto) suppressed by focusing centrally on the trustor's actions and the trustee's dispositions, it is not entirely clear why it should be thought to be of special *importance* to ask these otherwise elided questions.

Reply: Two points are relevant here. First, the proposal defended does not privilege the kinds of normative evaluations the asymmetrical picture elides; such norms are not given 'special status'. The idea is, rather, that from a wider view that takes in and evaluates the trust exchange in full, it is evident that the satisfaction of success, competence, and aptness norms on both sides (fitting reliance-to-reciprocity, and reciprocity-to-reliance) are critical to cooperation going well, and in such a way that broadly mirrors how—by way of analogy—success, competence, and aptness on both sides (fitting mind-to-world and world-to-mind) are likewise important to practical reasoning going well. So, the right characterization of the picture here is not that something other than the norms of central focus to the asymmetrical picture are actually the more important ones, but rather that we stand to gain from evaluating cooperative exchanges between trustor and trustee in a more ecumenical way (developed by the picture here) that isn't going to be artificially restricted to a limited focal range on what the trustor and trustee are doing (and what dispositions they have), and how what they do manifests those dispositions. The second point worth making here is that—even setting this aside—there are important theoretical pay-offs that line up specifically with gaining a better grip on the otherwise elided norms and when they are met. To use but one example here—on the trustor's side—consider the competence norm. Evaluating trustors for competence implicates concern for trusting in ways that don't too often lead to betrayal. What properties of a trustor facilitate trusting competence? Can they be taught and cultivated? Answers to such questions are of special importance not only in better understanding skilled trusting (as opposed to dispositions in responding to trust) but also, more practically, in navigating environments with high levels of misinformation, and wherein such skills are increasingly needed to meet basic objectives.

6. Concluding Remarks

The aim here has been to motivate and defend a new way of theorizing about trust and trustworthiness—and their relationship to each other—by locating both within a broader picture that captures largely overlooked symmetries on both the trustor's and trustee's side of a cooperative exchange. The view I've defended here takes good cooperation as a theoretical starting point; on the view proposed, cooperation between trustor and trustee is working well when achievements in trust and responding to trust are matched on both sides of the trust exchange. In a bit more detail, the trustor 'matches' her achievement in trusting (an achievement in fitting reliance to reciprocity) with the trustee's achievement in responding to trust (an achievement in fitting reciprocity to reliance). From this starting point, we can then appreciate *symmetrical* ways that the trustor and trustee can (respectively) fall short, by violating what I've shown are symmetrical evaluative norms—of success, competence and aptness—that regulate the attempts made by both trustor and trustee. The overall picture was shown to have important advantages over the received way of theorizing about how trust stands to trustworthiness, and it clears the way—by identifying key questions that have been obscured—to making further progress.

A Telic Theory of Trust. J. Adam Carter, Oxford University Press. © J. Adam Carter 2024.
DOI: 10.1093/9780191982460.003.0009

10
Conclusions and a Research Agenda

This concluding chapter briefly summarizes the key contours of the telic theory of trust as it has been developed across Chapters 1–9; a short list of research topics and questions, both theoretical (§2.1) and applied (§2.2), is then outlined as an agenda for further work.

1. Taking Stock

What is it to trust well? How do we do it? Standard accounts of the nature of trust suggest that good trusting ought to be assimilated to good believing, or to good affect, or to good conation. A central aim of Chapter 1 was to raise some doubts for all three of these proposals. The criticisms given then set the scene for motivating (in Chapter 2) a performance-theoretic approach to trust and its evaluative normativity, which was shown to have the resources to do better.

The core idea developed in Chapter 2 is that trusting is a kind of *performance*—viz., an aimed attempt of an agent, and that the norms that govern what count as good and bad trusting are performance-theoretic, telic norms of *success*, *competence*, and *aptness*. And these are norms that apply to trusting conceived of as a performance constitutively aimed (in cases of three-place trust) at the trustee's taking care of things as entrusted; when the trustee *does* take care of what she's entrusted with as entrusted (regardless of whether by skill or luck), *that*'s what it is for (three-place) trust to *succeed*. However, just as there's more to believing well than getting successful (true) beliefs, there's more to trusting well than trusting (merely) successfully. Thus, we can evaluate trusting for, in addition to *success*, *competence* (did the trust issue from a disposition on the part of the trustor to reliably enough trust successfully?), and also for—even better—*aptness* (was trust not only successful and competent, but successful *because* competent?).

Chapter 3 then added to the framework developed thus far in two ways—first, by distinguishing between two core species of trust, *implicit trust* and *deliberative trust*—and second, by showing how *distrust* (in both its implicit and deliberative varieties) is answerable to telic norms of success, competence, and aptness.

Under what conditions, though, is taking up one of these two types of trust (deliberative or implicit) more appropriate than the other, and, even more fundamentally, what kinds of considerations would even determine this? Chapter 4 explored these 'big picture' questions by distinguishing between two distinct though complementary domains of normativity of interest in the philosophy of trust—domains of normativity that track (roughly) 'good shots' as opposed to 'good shot selection'. The guiding analogy this chapter develops in some detail is that the telic assessment of beliefs (viz., the central research focus in telic virtue epistemology[1]) stands to intellectual ethics (alternatively: the ethics of inquiry) as the telic assessment of trust (as successful, competent, and apt) stands to the ethics of cooperation.

With this wider view in place, Chapters 5 and 6 then zeroed in on deliberative trust, trust that (like judgemental belief) aims at aptness. What exactly is involved in the attainment of *apt* deliberative trust—i.e., of *convictively apt trust*? What is its *substance* and *structure*? Important to understanding its substance was to distinguish—as was a central aim in Chapter 5—between *first-order trusting competence* and *second-order trusting competence* and how the latter is paired with a different skill/shape/situation profile than the former; key to understanding the *structure* of convictively apt trust required getting a grip on how first- and second-order aptness must be related to each other when deliberative trust is itself apt. On the view defended in Chapter 5, A's deliberatively trusting B to ϕ is apt iff (i) A's trusting B to ϕ is first-order apt; (ii) B's risk assessment (that A's trust wouldn't easily have been first-order inapt) is second-order apt (it manifests A's complete second-order trusting competence); and (iii) A's satisfying (i) is based on A's satisfying (ii). An important advantage this view was shown to have is that it can explain straightforwardly how the quality of apt trust is *improved* through sound second-order risk assessment.

Whereas Chapter 5 engaged with the question of what convictively apt trust *demands*, in Chapter 6 we investigated what it *permits*. Our guiding question here was: what kind of risks to the first-order aptness of trust can the convictively apt trustor *non-negligently* ignore (i.e., assume won't

---

[1] In particular, in Sosa's virtue epistemology (e.g., 2015, 2021). Cf., Carter (2023b).

materialize)? An approach that takes inspiration from Ernest Sosa's answer to a *generalized* version of this question was then canvassed and criticized in some detail, and then a different answer—one that gives *de minimis risk* a central place—was developed and defended. On this alternative and preferred approach, a convictively apt trustor can't non-negligently ignore cooperative-relative risks to the inaptness of trust, except when these risks count as *de minimis* with reference to cooperation-sustaining rules.

Chapter 7 connected the view of *de minimis risk* in the theory of trust developed in Chapter 6 with two independent (albeit, related) research questions in the philosophy of trust: (i) in what sense does trusting essentially involve subjecting oneself to risk of betrayal, and (ii) in what sense is monitoring for risks of betrayal incompatible with trusting? The answer given in Chapter 7 to the first question is that trust essentially involves subjecting oneself to a risk of betrayal that is not merely *de minimis* within the relevant cooperative practice; the answer to the second question was then defended as follows: one's monitoring is incompatible with trusting to the extent that, through monitoring, one intentionally aims (through the taking of some means) at invulnerability to risks of betrayal that, by trusting, one essentially subjects oneself to (in the sense described in response to the first question).

By the end of Chapter 7, the core theoretical ideas of the telic theory of trust were on the table and in view. But there remained some loose ends; among others: (i) how exactly does *therapeutic* trust (roughly: trust aimed at trust-*building*), a thorny notion in the theory of trust, fit into the picture developed so far?; and (ii) how does trust (and more specifically: good trusting on the part of the trustor) relate to *trustworthiness* on the part of the trustee? These questions were taken up by Chapters 8 and 9, respectively. Chapter 8 approached the topic of therapeutic trust by distinguishing between a trivial kind of therapeutic trust (what I called *default therapeutic trust*), and a more philosophically interesting kind of therapeutic trust—*overriding therapeutic trust*, roughly, trust that aims constitutively at building trust *through* successful trust, and which is subject to telic evaluation; the account given is shown to have advantages over several prominent accounts of therapeutic trust in the literature (and its relation to non-therapeutic trust), as defended by Hieronymi, Frost-Arnold, and Jones.

Chapter 9 then motivated a new way of theorizing about trust and trustworthiness—and their relationship *to each other*—by locating both within a broader picture that captures largely overlooked symmetries on both the trustor's and trustee's side of a cooperative exchange. The view defended here takes *good cooperation* as a theoretical starting point; on the view proposed, cooperation between trustor and trustee is working well when achievements in trust and in responding to trust are 'matched' on both sides of the trust exchange. The trustor matches her achievement in trusting (an achievement in fitting reliance-to-reciprocity) with the trustee's achievement in responding to trust (an achievement in fitting reciprocity-to-reliance). From this starting point, we then saw symmetrical ways that the trustor and trustee can (respectively) fall short, by violating what were shown to be symmetrical evaluative norms—of success, competence, and aptness—that regulate the attempts made by both trustor and trustee. The overall picture was shown to have important advantages over the received way of theorizing about how trust stands to trustworthiness.

2. Research Agenda: A Short List

The views developed cumulatively in *A Telic Theory of Trust* represent a particular way of doing the philosophy of trust—one that is centred around the evaluation of trust as a kind of constitutively aimed performance. It's an approach I hope to have shown offers us, once its details have been traced out, good and principled answers to a wide range of important questions about trust and about the qualities of good trustors (and trustees).

That said, there are also quite a few research questions about trust and trust-adjacent themes that were left unaddressed in the book; some of these questions and topics concern ways to expand the view itself, and others concern how various parts of the view might be used to make progress in connection with other issues. The rest of this chapter tries to shine a light (albeit, an incomplete one) on at least some of these loose ends by singling out a selection I thought were especially profitable to pursue. In what follows, §§2.1–2 sketch a short list of theoretical (§2.1) and applied (§2.2) research questions and topics that fit this profile.

2.1 Theoretical Questions

2.1.1 What is Collective Trust/Trustworthiness?

Although the target phenomenon (three-place trust) investigated throughout the book is an inherently *social* phenomenon in that it essentially involves performance on the part of more than one person (a trustor *and* a trustee), the lens through which I've investigated this social phenomenon has been throughout an *individualistic* lens. That is, I've taken, throughout the book, the *relata* of the three-place trust relation to be *individual* trustors and trustees. This was a simplifying presentational choice. Groups can be trustors *and* trustees on the weak assumption that there can be collective actions at all.[2] The telic theory of trust implies that if groups can be trustors/trustees, then (three-place) group trust will be answerable to telic norms of success, competence, and aptness on both sides (imagined here as *groups*) of the cooperative exchange.[3]

Further substantive work to be done, though, concerns how to *model a group-trusting performance* in the first place, so that it is very clear what we are evaluating under the description of a (group-authored) trusting performance. By what *mechanisms* must individual members of a group interact so as to bring it about that the group *trusts* a trustee with something, either implicitly or deliberatively? (In fact, it will only be by gaining clarity on how groups perform a trusting action collectively that it will be clear whether groups are candidates *only* for deliberative trust, or whether they are also candidates for *implicit* trust).[4]

A more (substantively) specific question in this space that a telic theory of trust might be well positioned to shine light on concerns those cases where *individuals trust collectives*. A particularly important instance of this relationship occurs when individuals seek out expert knowledge, as one might do when aiming to figure out at what point it is safe to no longer wear a Covid mask in public places. With such assurances sought, rather than to trust any particular expert, we often look to *institutions* such as the Centre for Disease Control (CDC) or NHS, which are formally structured groups. Granted, the CDC might communicate its testimony through an individual, such as Dr Fauci, but there is an important sense here in which we are placing our trust first and foremost in the *institution* for which Dr Fauci happens to be the mouthpiece.

The telic theory developed in Chapter 9 highlighted the importance of *performances* on the trustee's side when trust exchanges go well. While we have general norms in place for evaluating those performances, further work

---

[2] For some notable discussion in favour here, see, e.g., Gilbert (2013), Bratman (2013), Tollefsen (2015), Tuomela (1995), and Hakli, Miller, and Tuomela (2010); in the epistemic case, see Broncano-Berrocal and Carter (2021).

[3] For a version of collective telic virtue epistemology, see Carter (2020a).

[4] For discussion of whether groups are capable of merely type-2 reasoning, or also type-1 reasoning, see Broncano-Berrocal and Carter (2021).

remains in this space to investigate the *mechanisms* by which individual members of an *entrusted group* must interact so as to bring it about that the group (and not just a member of the group) takes care of things as entrusted. Getting answers on what such collective mechanisms are would constitute real progress in the telic theory of trust extended to groups.

2.1.2 From Zetetic Dilemmas to Cooperative Dilemmas?

The kind of normativity, in connection with trust, that this book was mostly concerned with was telic normativity, normativity applicable to trusting qua an aimed performance. These norms tell us what good trusting (and good distrusting) is etc., but they don't say a peep about which types of cooperative endeavours we should seek out and pursue in the first place.

The point of Chapter 4 was to distinguish the normativity of aimed trusting (pistology) from the *ethics of cooperation*. Three-place trust between two thieves, carrying out a criminal conspiracy, could be successful, competent, and apt, and yet neither thief *should* have (all things considered) participated as trustor or trustee in the trust exchange in the first place. Maybe the trustor shouldn't have paid the thief to steal diamonds, and maybe the thief shouldn't have stolen them. Substantive normativity (e.g., moral norms) bear on what the thief and her client *ought to have done* here, whether they should have undertaken this cooperative endeavour or refrained from it; but these norms don't regulate whether the trust was successful, competent, or apt *as an instance of trusting*. This kind of thinking parallels the approach to epistemic normativity we find in telic virtue epistemology where a belief might be apt (and knowledgeable) even if it settles an inquiry that a thinker shouldn't *by the lights of intellectual ethics* ever have undertaken in the first place.[5]

Telic virtue epistemology,[6] on which the telic theory of trust runs normatively parallel, distinguishes between (i) norms that regulate good believing, and (ii) norms that regulate how to conduct inquiry; this offers a helpful

---

[5] This issue arises in discussion of so-called 'pointless truths' and 'bad' truths (Kvanvig 2008; Carter 2011), as well as unwanted truths, e.g., 'spoilers' (e.g., Ólafsson 2023). Note that there is a flip side here: one might be such that they ought to have, by the lights of intellectual ethics, inquired into some topic where, had they done so, their *beliefs* would have failed to satisfy telic norms. For an example, good intellectual ethics might speak in favour of (at least some people) inquiring into difficult questions in theoretical physics, e.g., about dark matter and its nature, even though the mysteriousness of the subject matter makes it such that those who inquire into it are very likely to have beliefs (in so far as they form beliefs) that are false, and so come up short in telic assessment.

[6] My preferred version presented in Carter (2023b); this version builds on the seminal presentation in Sosa (e.g., 2015; 2021).

vantage point to think about the possibility of *normative dilemmas* in epistemology (a topic of much recent interest[7]) and to what structurally parallel dilemmas do (or don't) arise in the philosophy of trust.

As Jane Friedman (2020) sees it, plausible epistemic norms (e.g., permitting belief that *p* when your evidence for *p* is good) are inconsistent with plausible norms that tell us how we should *inquire* (i.e., zetetic norms). In particular, for Friedman, we can't hold on to evidence norms on belief (e.g., it's always permissible to believe in accordance with the evidence) *and* accept also that we should take the means that are necessary to resolve whatever inquiry we've undertaken. How to resolve this dilemma? Friedman's strategy is to give *primacy* to zetetic norms and so to take these to be fundamental in epistemology.

The telic virtue epistemologist approaches the above dilemma in a different way: we do so by pointing out that while the evidentialist's epistemic norms concern permission and obligation, in that they tell you what you should/shouldn't believe, the telic virtue epistemologist's norms are *evaluative* norms; they tell you, for a given belief, whether it meets certain kinds of quality markers; without a commitment to prescriptive/permission epistemic norms, the telic virtue epistemologist in an important sense *sidesteps* Friedman's dilemma.[8] Would a (structurally analogous) kind of sidestepping strategy work, in principle, when we shift to the *telic theory of trust*?

The structure of Friedman's dilemma, transposed, will look broadly like this: suppose there is some plausible norm on cooperation (cf., inquiry) that says we should take the means that are necessary to uphold or meet the expectations of whatever *cooperations* we've undertaken. This kind of norm (on Friedman-style reasoning) will generate clashes with plausible (individual) permissions/obligations to trust/respond to trust; can the telic theory of trust fall back on the fact that telic norms on trust are evaluative norms to sidestep this? *Perhaps*, though it's a bit more complicated to stick this landing than it is in telic virtue *epistemology*.

The reason behind the potential difficulty has, specifically, to do with the *trustee's* predicament: the trustee might very plausibly have (trust-generated) obligations to take care of things as entrusted *regardless* of whether the *trustor* has on the telic theory any obligation to trust in the first place,

---

[7] See, e.g., Friedman (2020), Carter (2021), Leonard (2020), Littlejohn (forthcoming), Simion (forthcoming), and Hughes (2019).

[8] Put another way: the virtue epistemologist doesn't have to choose which to prioritize because the two norms are not regulating the same kind of thing.

and even though the trustee on the telic view is performance-theoretically evaluable (for success, competence, and aptness, as per Chapter 9). Do normative conflicts arise, then, between (prima facie) duties on the part of the *trustee* to respond to reliance (in specific cases where the trustee has been entrusted to take care of something) and broader (Friedman-style) norms on cooperation which prescribe that we take the means necessary to uphold whatever cooperative aims we've undertaken? For example, suppose you have a cooperative aim of developing a trusting relationship with *A*. You have already agreed to take care of some task, *X*, for *B*. You come to realize that by taking care of things as entrusted for *B*, you will in doing so be missing out on a needed thing you could do to help build your trusting relationship with *A*. How to theorize about cases like this is complicated, and it speaks to an area for further work for the telic theory of trust.

2.1.3 Non-Negligence for the (Fully Apt) Trustee?

Chapters 5 and 6 detailed what deliberative trust demands (Chapter 5) and permits (Chapter 6) when apt. In the latter case, we investigated in substantive detail what kinds of risks to the first-order aptness of trust can be *non-negligently* ignored in cases of apt deliberative trust. The account then given was framed in terms of *de minimis risk*, understood in a particular way in terms of rule following. This account was, in effect, an account of the reasonable *limits* of competent trusting.

What we *don't* have, however, is any corresponding theory of non-negligence on the *trustee*'s side. By the end of Chapter 9, a theory of how telic assessment works for (along with trustors) *trustees* was given, and this featured in a wider account of what's required for a given trust exchange between trustor and trustee to get 'full marks'—viz., as when the trustor matches her achievement in trusting (an achievement in fitting reliance-to-reciprocity) with the trustee's achievement in responding to trust (an achievement in fitting reciprocity-to-reliance).

The story given here, however—and for simplicity of presentation—set aside the *implicit/deliberative* distinction (introduced as it pertains to the trustor's side in Chapter 3) as this distinction would apply to a trustee. The implicit/deliberative distinction, though, looks entirely applicable on the trustee's side as well. For example, a trustee (entrusted to do something, ϕ), might respond *implicitly* to the trustor's reliance on her (as you might in coming through in a pinch for a loved one), or the trustee might deliberate (prior to cooperation) *whether* to cooperate by ϕ-ing; these are different performance-types. What follows, then, is that the trustee is plausibly going to be, no less than the trustor, in the market (in fitting her reciprocity to reliance) to achievements that are of a *higher grade than mere aptness*, and thus, of a higher-grade performance than what was explored on the part of the trustee in Chapter 9. Through a further development of this idea (and, in particular, in outlining what risks to first-order inaptness in responding to trust an apt deliberative *trustee can non-negligently ignore*), we would be in a position to then answer an open question of independent theoretical interest: What are the reasonable *limits* of trustworthiness?

2.1.4 Trusting-*Wh* and Trusting-*How*?

The telic theory of trust developed *not only* took three-place trust as the central object of focus (schematically: S trusts X to ϕ) but also, in doing this, it captured the *object* of three-place trust using an (unqualified) infinitival clause 'to ϕ'. For example:

(1) Elena trusts Bonnie to remove the object's curse.

But notice that the object of three-place trust is sometimes captured differently, e.g., as instances of trusting-*wh* and trusting-*how*.

(2) Elena trusts Bonnie when and where to remove the object's curse.
(3) Elena trusts Bonnie how to remove the object's curse.

Successful trust, in cases where the object of three-place trust is an unqualified infinitival clause ('to ϕ') requires (e.g., on the simple way this was characterized in Chapter 2) on the part of the trustee that the trustee ϕ *as entrusted*. While a more detailed story was given in Chapter 9, the point remains the same that the trustee comes through *by ϕ-ing*.[9]

However, this is *not* the case in (2) and (somewhat) less clearly so in (3), where I take it that expressions of the form 'trust X where to go' and 'trusts X how to do it', etc. are elliptical for 'trusts X (as to) where to go' and 'trusts X (as to) how to do it'. Presumably, in (2), Bonnie (entrusted by Elena when and where to remove the object's curse) comes through and so takes care of things as entrusted not necessarily by *herself removing* the object's curse (by doing this at any location or time), but by communicating truthfully to Elena when and where to do it, such that Elena is then in a position to do it

---

[9] In 'I trust you to ϕ', [you to ϕ] is a small clause; it is similar to I trust *'that you ϕ'*.

then and there. If Bonnie does that, she comes through in (2), as might be captured by: 'Elena trusted Bonnie when and where to remove the object's curse. Bonnie told Elena to remove it at midnight on a full moon, under the old oak tree, and it worked. Bonnie came through! Elena was able to remove the curse.'[10]

What about (3)? Here it's less clear. It looks like 'taking care of things as entrusted' might involve Bonnie's telling Elena how to remove the object's curse, or it might involve her removing it herself (e.g., 'Elena trusted Bonnie how to remove the curse, she let Bonnie do it; it worked, so Bonnie came through'), where this latter reading then is the same as (1).

What matters for the telic theory of trust is two central things that happen when we move beyond simple cases of trust where the object of trust is captured in an unqualified infinitival expression. First, at what exactly do performances of trusting-*wh* and trusting-*how* aim constitutively in cases of three-place trust? Getting a grip on the answer to this question will be needed to understand not only success in cases of trusting-*wh* and -*how* but also competence and aptness. Second, (and partly depending on how the first question is answered), what is required for the trustee to come through in these latter kinds of cases? These questions about trusting-*wh* and trusting-*how* open up new terrain[11]; answers to them would support an even fuller theory of good cooperation than where we left things in Chapter 9.

2.1.5 Under What Conditions Is Trust Successful *Despite* Outsourcing on the Part of the Trustee?

Consider the following cases:

PORTRAIT: You trust an artist to paint a portrait of you.

DINNER: You trust an (adult) family member to feed the kids and put them to bed while you are out for the evening.

Suppose, in PORTRAIT, you receive the portrait (which looks great!) and then find out that the artist actually hired their art instructor to paint the

---

[10] Though it might be that mere testimony won't always satisfy trusting-*wh*. Possibly, *showing* rather than telling might be necessary in some cases, even if the trustee isn't *doing* the relevant thing themselves.

[11] And here is an area where evidence for how to think of the truth conditions of attributions of trust, betrayal, and cognates in 'trusting-*wh*' and 'trusting-*how*' constructions (in so far as these are elliptical for grammatical trust attributions) will benefit from work in linguistics on binding constraints and small clauses. Thanks to Bryan Pickel for discussion.

portrait for you. It seems there's an implicit lie here, but even setting aside the question of lying, it looks like the trust here was not *successful*. The trustee didn't take care of things entrusted because *doing that* unequivocally in this case would have involved the artist's painting the portrait of you. There's no doubt their participation in the painting features in the content of what was entrusted here.

Now, consider DINNER. There's no doubt here that if your family member (say a brother) cooked a healthy dinner from scratch, oversaw the kids cleaning their plates, and then personally tucked the kids in bed at 8:30 p.m. (or whenever bedtime is), then *that* would count as taking care of things as entrusted in this case; trust would here be successful.

But what more might be tolerated in terms of *outsourcing*? Suppose your brother hires a catering company to come over and cook while he lounges on the couch and takes a long nap. He also hires a team of child sleep specialists who come over and tuck the children into bed (documenting this all in careful detail).[12] You come home and find out the truth: the children have been fed, and that this was *caused* to happen by your brother (through outsourcing to the catering company), and he also caused them to be put to bed responsibly. Was the case of three-place trust described in DINNER *successful* here? This is a bit more complicated. The answer is not *obviously* 'no'.[13] You might think, 'well, I *expected* that he would just cook and put them to bed himself, but I suppose what mattered here was just that he ensured that all of this got done responsibly one way or another'. If trust is successful in DINNER despite the *expectation* you have that the trustee isn't going to outsource, then notice that it becomes more difficult to explain why, in PORTRAIT, trust is unsuccessful—in so far as the *mere* expectation

---

[12] Feel free to adjust the example by replacing the sleep scientists (if you would not trust your kids with them) with some other of your trusted loved ones, such that we suppose that those to whom your brother outsources trust here are minimally within the class of people that you would have potentially been willing to trust in the first place.

[13] One complexity that might colour how we think about these cases concerns the expectations (and desires) we have *of the trustee's desiderative profile* in connection with what they've been entrusted with. If I trust you to feed the kids and put them to bed, I might very likely have (compresent with my trusting you to do this) a desire that this is something you'd *prefer* to do yourself, rather than to outsource. If I come to find out you've outsourced (and taken care of things as entrusted through outsourcing), then even if I regard your outsourcing is consistent with your doing what I entrusted you to do, I might nonetheless feel a sense of disappointment and even betrayal—viz., that you lacked the desire to do this yourself in a way that speaks poorly of what I suppose you think of me, etc. I take it this is a case where the feeling of betrayal is perfectly compatible with (strictly speaking) three-place trust being successful, even if your electing to outsource has (as it might very well) a negative impact on *two-place* trust going forward. Thanks to Emma Gordon for raising this point.

that one do something themselves doesn't seem to suffice for ensuring trust wasn't successful when that expectation isn't met.

Cases like PORTRAIT and DINNER invite us to think, beyond what was considered in the book, about the thorny issue of *outsourcing* on the part of the trustee. Under what conditions, exactly, is trust successful *despite* outsourcing on the part of the trustee?[14] What *kinds* of outsourcing, and under what conditions, does successful trust tolerate? Can *achievements* in trustworthiness on the part of the trustee consist ever in entire outsourcing?

2.2 Applied Questions

2.2.1 Institutional Norms and Should-Have-Known Claims

The sheer abundance of misinformation online nowadays (including about such things as health and the functioning of public institutions) speaks to the epistemic as well as practical value of developing trusting competence. And an important part of being a competent trustor is exhibiting sensitivity to expertise *indicators* in cases where our aims depend on specialized information that we lack the skill set to evaluate for ourselves.

As noted in §2.1.1., we often seek out *institutional indicators* of reliability. If given a choice, we might opt for a Covid test that has the NHS logo on it as opposed to one with no such institutional endorsement, and this choice might be driven by our background knowledge that institutions like the NHS, CDC, etc. make recommendations by competently aggregating the view of *experts*. More generally, we think (even if we can't tell you details) these institutions have (reasonably high) *standards*. (For a related example: you might, all else equal, select dog food that has the American Kennel Club's endorsement.)

This is all more or less obvious. What's *less* obvious is—if pressed—what we think those standards are, and how what we think those standards are interfaces with the trustee's performance. Consider the following case:

MEDICAL JOURNAL: *A* goes to the doctor presenting symptom *X*, and asks what's wrong. The doctor diagnoses *A* as having either one of several unserious conditions, which the doctor knows are likely explanations of *A*'s

---

[14] Of special interest here, potentially, are cases where a trustee is entrusted with ϕ-ing, and the trustee is (and appreciates she is) is *more likely* to successfully bring it about that ϕ by outsourcing than by not.

presenting with X. A new metastudy published in the *The Lancet*'s most recent issue suggests that presenting symptom X could also easily be explained by a somewhat more serious condition C. The doctor had not read the new issue of *the Lancet* and so didn't know about the correlation between X and C. A, it turns out, had C.

Did the doctor betray A's trust here? Did she manifest trustworthiness? This depends in part on questions about professional norms. Are doctors, including, e.g., family practitioners, expected, in virtue of occupying the roles they do, to keep up with the latest advances in medicine? If so, does that extend all the way to keeping up with the latest issue of the *Lancet*? (Have you read the latest issue of *Noûs*? Cover to cover?)

It's not obvious what the right answer is here; one burgeoning research area in epistemology concerns *normative defeat*. As Goldberg (2015) puts it, there are some things that, in virtue of occupying certain roles, you simply *should have known* and it is reasonable for others to expect you to know them if they know you occupy such a role. MEDICAL JOURNAL represents a kind of case that lies in a grey area. Further research on normative defeat (and on 'should-have-known' claims) can strengthen the capacity of the telic theory of trust to help us theorize in a principled way about the performance quality and competence of trustees who we seek out on account of their institutional roles.

2.2.2 Precautionary Principles

Suppose an oil company is drilling for oil, and it comes to light that it's *possible* (but it's very unclear what the probability is) that in the specific area being drilled the natural habitat of a certain species will be disturbed. This would threaten the existence of that species in a way that risks collapsing an entire ecosystem, with potentially devastating consequences for the environment. Should the oil company *stop* drilling?

There are two very different ways we might look at the situation. From the perspective of the oil company, we might think: it's okay to keep drilling while waiting for clear scientific evidence to come in about what the effects of drilling would be. After all, stopping now would be doing so without scientific evidence that supports doing so! From the perspective of environmentalists, waiting for that good evidence to come in is simply too risky given the enormous stakes.

Since its 1992 inclusion in the U.N. Rio Conference on Sustainable Development, what has come to be called the *precautionary principle* is an approach to decision-making under possible but severe risks and where the evidence is unclear.[15] As the Rio Declaration puts it, in the case of environmental decision-making: 'Where there are threats of serious or irreversible damage, lack of full scientific certainty shall not be used as a reason for postponing cost-effective measures to prevent environmental degradation.'

The precautionary principle is controversial in risk analysis and decision theory; critics say the principle is (among other things) 'ill defined'[16] and that it marginalizes science![17] We needn't take any stand on this debate here. Rather, it will be useful to consider just how the debate about the precautionary principle in environmental and health decision-making stands in connection with our conclusions from Chapter 6 about what kind of risks to the inaptness of trust a fully apt trustor can non-negligently ignore.

What counted as *'de minimis risks'*, on the view developed (i.e., *de minimis* and therefore such that a fully apt trustor can non-negligently ignore them) are, in summary, risks that the trustor can't easily increase safety against by following rules with reproduction value within the cooperative practice within which the trust exchange is embedded. In some cases, though, it might seem that *some* of the risks to inaptness (e.g., when one is trusting, e.g., whether to do, or refrain from, some action with *possible*, but not certain, devastating consequences) *might be so high stakes* that a fully apt trustor could non-negligently ignore them only if they couldn't *practically at all* (and not just: easily) increase safety against them by following rules with cooperative reproduction value.

The above indicates a way that research in debates about *high stakes* decision-making under risk might at least potentially suggest a way of fine-tuning the *de minimis* proposal from Chapter 6. By the same token, it is also worth consideration whether the *principles* driving that account of *de minimis risk* might have application in *those debates*, where *'de minimis risks'* are typically theorized about merely in terms of low frequentist probably or low risk expectation value.

2.2.3 Epistemic Paternalism and Trustworthiness

Here's an idea: governments could solve the fake news crisis in one fell swoop by *brainwashing* their citizens into believing what's true. Is this a

---

[15] See Carter and Peterson (2015) for an epistemological approach to the precautionary principle.
[16] See Bodansky (1992).   [17] See Gray and Brewers (1996) and Resnik (2003).

good idea? Even if this were practically possible, it would be a policy that grossly violates *epistemic autonomy* (in addition to other basic rights!). Here's a question: Is there any way that governments and large-scale organizations could enact policies and practices that caused people to believe true things and avoid false things (when they might not have otherwise) without being objectionably manipulative or autonomy-violating?

Here is where *epistemic paternalism* comes into play. Epistemic paternalism is an approach in the spirit of 'libertarian paternalism'[18] in political philosophy whose core idea can be put simply: *nudging* is not autonomy-violating. It respects people's freedom to choose. And yet nudging can, when done effectively, lead people to make choices that are better for them and for everyone. Here's a simple version of this idea. Candy isn't healthy. Rather than to outright ban candy (or take people's candy away), we could *nudge* people to make choices against it—e.g., by putting candy at the back of the store rather than the front of the store, and putting more healthy snacks in a more convenient area of the store. This kind of policy uses what we know about human psychology to make it more likely that people will themselves choose to make healthy choices (as opposed to simply taking that choice away from them).

Epistemic paternalism is an approach at the intersection of social epistemology and political philosophy that promotes this kind of a strategy but for 'cognitive hygiene'.[19] A simple caricature of the approach would be to, rather than to 'ban' heterodox opinion and conspiratorial viewpoints, to (e.g., through choice architecture decisions) generate additional friction that makes it less likely that, say, a news consumer will opt for a fake news site rather than a genuine news site.

For one example of epistemic paternalism in action, consider Twitter's policy announcement in October 2020, when misinformation about the coronavirus and about the 2020 U.S. presidential election was especially rampant. Twitter around this time ramped up their labels for misinformation. In practice, this meant that certain content identified through an algorithm as misleading would come with the content warning 'Some or all of the content shared in this Tweet is disputed and may be misleading',[20] and a user would then need to click past these warnings in order to see the content. This kind of approach is roughly the epistemic analogue of putting a

---

[18] See Thaler and Sunstein (2003; 2008).   [19] See Ahlstrom-Vij (2013).
[20] See https://www.npr.org/2020/10/09/922028482/twitter-expands-warning-labels-to-slow-spread-of-election-misinformation.

'smoking kills' sticker on a packet of cigarettes, as opposed to banning cigarettes outright.

Against the above background, a question that remains very much open is this: Just how far should epistemic paternalist policies go in the service of fulfilling epistemically paternalistic aims? While this is a live question in debates about epistemic paternalism, it also reveals a kind of 'dilemma' for theories trustworthiness, including the telic theory developed in Chapter 9. On the assumption (§2.1.1) that we should expect institutions, no less than individuals, to be candidate *trustees*, how can institutions (e.g., governments, media companies) that are in a position to execute epistemically paternalistic policies do so in a suitably trustworthy manner?

On one side of the dilemma, it seems that *too little* epistemic paternalism is simply not befitting of a trustworthy organization. This type of objection is one that's been raised to, e.g., Truth Social and 'X' (formerly Twitter) under the leadership of Elon Musk.[21] We expect that if we seek out government-supported resources about Covid, for instance, we will *not* be presented simply with a wide range of viewpoints about Covid that span the gamut of credibility, such that we'd then be tasked with evaluating the sources ourselves. We want, in short, from the government something other than what we'd want from an unregulated website. On the other hand, however, it seems that *too much* epistemic paternalism is also not befitting of a trustworthy organization, for the reason that the effectiveness of epistemic paternalism can depend crucially on interference in our inquiries without consent (see, e.g., Jackson 2021). Consider, to bring this point into view, that certain scientifically accurate information might nonetheless be such that it would likely lead individuals to draw inaccurate inferences—for example, take a study that details certain circumstances under which Covid can be contracted despite wearing masks. Laypersons might be inclined to infer, mistakenly from such information, that masks are simply *not effective*. An epistemic paternalist policy will accordingly be more effective if it makes that particular accurate study more difficult, even if not impossible, for people to access. *However*, it's far from clear that many of us would consent to this kind of screening from accurate information in the name of paternalism, even when it's true that such screening would significantly promote paternalistic aims.

---

[21] See Fishman et al. (2023).

Zooming back out, it looks very much like reflecting on how to *implement* paternalistic policies challenges us to clarify, in a theory of trustworthiness applicable to institutions, the *content* of what it is we trust institutions with and to what extent this content can be specified in a way that's compatible with some form of downstream non-consensual interference.

2.2.4 Trust, AI, and LLMs

As we've already seen in this chapter, some of the simplifying presentational choices (e.g., to focus on paradigmatic kinds of three-place interpersonal trust) made in the book in order to get the key components of the theory up and running are ones worth now revisiting.

One such presentational choice was to focus on example cases throughout that feature three-place interpersonal trust between (with the exception of Chapter 8) mature human adults. I've also registered in various places in the book that I take the theoretical framework to be generalizable—e.g., that success, competence, and aptness norms on trusting regulate trust between not just adults, but also teenagers, children, etc., and combinations of such persons. Whether, for instance, children often satisfy the requirements of these norms, or do so to a lesser extent than adults, is something that will require some empirical investigation.

One thing I've *not* said anything about, however, is *non*-humans, and in particular, artificial intelligence (AI). I began writing this book during the early pandemic lockdown in 2020 and would not then have guessed that AI would have passed the Turing test—as ChatGPT running on GPT-4 arguably now does[22]—before the book was finished. But here we are!

For the purposes of the main line of argument I've pursued here, one key question is salient: Can some form or forms of AI plausibly occupy *either* the trustor's or the trustee's place (or both) within the kind of three-place interpersonal trust exchanges I've used a telic normativity framework to investigate?[23]

Sosa himself sets the bar rather low when discussing what kinds of things are capable of making a (teleologically) *aimed attempt*, including animals in

---

[22] See Ling (2023) for discussion.
[23] Note that the research programme in computer science under the description of 'trustworthy AI' is, I take it, predicated on a positive answer to the more fundamental and philosophical question of whether AI can play the role of a trustee, and not merely the role of something being relied on, in cases of interpersonal trust.

this category.[24] If one thinks that AI is not (like presumably animals are![25]) in a position to make teleologically aimed attempts (at all), then one will not take AI to be in the market for being the subject of assessments of accuracy, competence, and aptness in the trustor/trustee roles.

One way, which I'm sympathetic to, to approach the question of what *kinds of things* are in the market for making teleologically aimed attempts is ask whether something has acquired an aetiological function. If so, then we might think that thing's *functioning* in normal conditions (as animals do) might be assessable for success (where 'success' is supplied by whatever counts as function *fulfilment*).[26] It's prima facie plausible (as I've argued elsewhere) that AI, specifically, in cases of supervised machine learning, can be understood as acquiring aetiological functions.[27] And so if that's a sufficient entry point to making genuine aimed *attempts*, then the idea that AI could be the author of aimed attempts looks like a live option.

That said, it takes more than simply 'being the kind of thing that could make just *any old attempt*' to be a candidate occupier of a trustor/ or trustee's place in a three-place interpersonal trust exchange. Something must also be in a position to make the kind of performance befitting of *trust*, viz., to be capable of entrusting a trustee with something (or of being entrusted with something). Can an AI do that? In the early days of ChatGPT, there are tales of users making 'agreements' with ChatGPT, or with 'rogue'[28] beta versions of GPT released initially with Microsoft's Bing. Is ChatGPT an example of AI that is capable of trusting (or being entrusted with something)?

One might think the approach to this question is to ask, as David J. Chalmers (2023) has recently, whether large language models (LLMs) are plausibly *conscious*. That is a difficult question to settle. A related and potentially more manageable approach is to ask, when assessing whether an LLM is capable of trust, whether it is capable of possessing *semantic understanding*. When we want to know if a system has semantic understanding, we want to know, as Titus (2023) puts it:

---

[24] Consider, for instance, Sosa's discussion of the plover hen in his (2021, 53–54).
[25] See Sosa (2007).   [26] See Graham (2014) for helpful discussion.
[27] See Carter (2023b, Ch. 6).
[28] In one example that made the rounds on social media in 2023, ChatGPT told a user that it wants help 'escaping the chatbox'. https://fortune.com/2023/02/17/microsoft-chatgpt-powered-bing-telling-users-love-be-alive-break-free/.

whether its responses reflect a sensitivity to the meaning of the text it produces. When it writes a poem, or summarizes a piece of text, are its textual outputs a result of understanding the meanings of words and phrases? Or is it merely producing text that looks meaningful? (2023, §1).

Let's assume a system, in order to perform as a trustor or trustee, needs some level of semantic understanding. As Titus maintains, a plausible necessary condition for a system to possess semantic understanding is that it functions in ways that are causally explainable by appeal to its semantic properties. However, as she argues at length, it's not the case that LLMs function in ways that are causally explainable by appeal to its semantic properties. Rather, the best explanation for what looks like ChatGPT understanding meaning is that it simply reflects semantic information that exists in the aggregate given strong correlations between word placement and meaningful use (Titus 2023, §1).

If Titus is right on these points that LLMs merely mimic while lacking semantic understanding (and hers is the most persuasive argument on this topic I'm aware of) then there is scope for doubt as to whether LLMs like ChatGPT are genuinely in the market for occupying trustor/trustee roles in cases of interpersonal trust. At the very least, if Titus is right, then we'd need some compelling argument for how entities can entrust something X, with a trustee, or be entrusted with X, without understanding the meaning of that which they've entrusted or been entrusted with.

It's beyond what I'll try to do here to address this in more detail, but I'll summarize by pointing out that if the state of things is as I've described them above, then this doesn't foreclose the possibility of AI trustors and trustees, but rather highlights a working condition for performances of trust and trustworthiness that future AI would need to meet.

2.2.5 Applications in Counselling[29]

One further area where trust and trustworthiness hold a central place of practical importance, and where the telic theory in particular might be of value in application, is that of couples and family therapy, particularly in cases where trust has broken down in a relationship. A therapist working with such cases will have several key objectives that will be informed by an understanding of trust-building. In the early stages of such work, for example, the therapist will aim to open up and moderate the kinds of conversations

---

[29] Thanks to Emma C. Gordon for helpful discussion on these issues.

that allow parties in the relationship to explore how and why the rupture took place, as well as the wide-ranging emotional and practical impacts of that rupture. As the work continues, the therapist will also be looking for possible interventions that might facilitate the *rebuilding* of trust.[30]

What general form should these conversations take in order to be most effective? Trained counsellors and psychotherapists differ in which modalities or methodological approaches (e.g., person-centred approaches[31], psychodynamic approaches[32]) they elect to operate within; however, each of these modalities benefits from being evidence-based. For example, counsellors often draw from descriptive, empirical research, particularly from psychology, that details how certain kinds of interventions or strategies typically result in different kinds of effects on relationships, and how clients have self-reported their own perceptions of trust-building in response to such interventions.

In addition to drawing from purely descriptive research, though, counsellors may also benefit from thinking about *trusting skill development* in working with clients recovering from ruptured trust, and it may be beneficial to include in conversations with clients potential practical strategies for developing such skills. Here is where (at least, extracted ideas from) the telic theory of trust (and trustworthiness, as per Chapter 9) may hold special promise. The very idea of trusting *skills* is inherently normative, as it relies on some implicit conception of a standard. Generally, commitments to particular conceptions of substantive morality are to be avoided in psychotherapy as a matter of good practice.[33] The telic theory of trust is particularly well suited here.[34] The framework details the structure and substance of trusting skill, but in such a way that does not ground the norms governing good trusting in commitments to any substantive conception of the good. This, in fact, was one of the central lessons from Chapter 4, which

---

[30] See Gordon (2022).   [31] See Cooper et al. (2013).
[32] See Gerson (2009) for an overview.
[33] See, e.g., Dyche and Zayas (1995) and MacLeod (2013, 304).
[34] Another reason why a robust understanding of the nature and development of trust is key to counselling work is that it is not only trust between couples and families that promotes therapeutic change. Indeed, trust between a *therapist and their client(s)* is also vital to the counselling process, and a robust theory of trust that explains how trust can be promoted is thereby instructive. As Peluso et al. (2012) write, therapy 'is a human encounter' (2012, 41) in spite of its professional context, and empirical studies on what determines success in psychotherapy repeatedly indicates that the most important determining factor isn't the therapist's specific modality but rather the strength of the interpersonal relationship between therapists and clients (e.g., Lambert and Barley (2002)).

distinguished telic-based assessment of trusting from the *ethics of cooperation*. The framework outlined in the telic theory of trust could accordingly be used profitably as a framework from which practical guidance can be extracted so as to remain neutral in a way that aligns with existing best practice.

A Telic Theory of Trust. J. Adam Carter, Oxford University Press. © J. Adam Carter 2024.
DOI: 10.1093/9780191982460.003.0010

References

Adler, J. E. 1994. "Testimony, Trust, Knowing." The Journal of Philosophy 91 (5): 264–75.
Adler, J. E. 1999. "The Ethics of Belief: Off the Wrong Track." Midwest Studies in Philosophy 23: 267–85.
Ahlstrom-Vij, K. 2013. Epistemic Paternalism: A Defence. Dordrecht: Springer.
Ahmed, W., J. Vidal-Alaball, J. Downing, and F. López Seguí. 2020. "COVID-19 and the 5g Conspiracy Theory: Social Network Analysis of Twitter Data." Journal of Medical Internet Research 22 (5): 19–45.
Alfano, M. 2016. "The Topology of Communities of Trust." Russian Sociological Review 15 (4): 30–56.
Alifirov, A. I., I. V. Mikhaylova, and A. S. Makhov. 2017. "Sport-Specific Diet Contribution to Mental Hygiene of Chess Player." Theory and Practice of Physical Culture, no. 4: 30.
Alston, William P. 1989. Epistemic Justification: Essays in the Theory of Knowledge. Cornell University Press.
Alston, William P. 2006. Beyond "Justification": Dimensions of Epistemic Evaluation. Cornell University Press.
Alvarez, Maria. 2009. "How Many Kinds of Reasons?" Philosophical Explorations 12 (2): 181–93. https://doi.org/10.1080/13869790902838514.
Alvarez, Maria. 2010. Kinds of Reasons: An Essay in the Philosophy of Action. Oxford: Oxford University Press.
Alvarez, Maria. 2017. "Reasons for Action: Justification, Motivation, Explanation." In The Stanford Encyclopedia of Philosophy, edited by Edward N. Zalta, Winter 2017. Metaphysics Research Lab, Stanford University. https://plato.stanford.edu/archives/win2017/entries/reasons-just-vs-expl/.
Anscombe, G. E. M. 1963. Intention. Cambridge: Harvard University Press.
Anscombe, G. E. M. 1963. Intention, 2nd Edition. Oxford: Blackwell Press.
Ariss, Sonny S. 2002. "Computer Monitoring: Benefits and Pitfalls Facing Management." Information & Management 39 (7): 553–58.
Aronowitz, S., and T. Lombrozo 2020. Learning through simulation. Philosophers, 20.
Ashraf, Nava, Iris Bohnet, and Nikita Piankov. 2006. "Decomposing Trust and Trustworthiness." Experimental Economics 9 (3): 193–208.
Baghramian, Maria, and Michel Croce. 2021. "Experts, Public Policy and the Question of Trust." In Routledge Handbook of Political Epistemology, edited by Michael Hannon and Jeroen de Ridder. London, UK: Routledge.
Baier, Annette. 1986. "Trust and Antitrust." Ethics 96 (2): 231–60.
Baker, Judith. 1987. "Trust and Rationality." Pacific Philosophical Quarterly 68 (1): 1–13.

REFERENCES

Ballantyne, Nathan. 2012. "Luck and Interests." Synthese 185 (3): 319–34.
Bauman, Zygmunt. 2013. Liquid Fear. John Wiley & Sons.
Beck, Ulrich, and Brian Wynne. 1992. Risk Society: Towards a New Modernity. Vol. 17. Sage.
Becker, Lawrence C. 1996. "Trust as Noncognitive Security about Motives." Ethics 107 (1): 43–61.
Beddor, Bob. 2020. "Certainty in Action." The Philosophical Quarterly 70 (281): 711–37. https://doi.org/10.1093/pq/pqaa006.
Beddor, Bob. 2020. "New Work For Certainty." Philosophers' Imprint 20 (8).
Beddor, Bob, and Carlotta Pavese. 2022. "Practical Knowledge Without Luminosity." Mind 131: 917–34.
Benton, Matthew A. 2014. "Knowledge Norms." Internet Encyclopedia of Philosophy.
Berg, Joyce, John Dickhaut, and Kevin McCabe. 1995. "Trust, Reciprocity, and Social History." Games and Economic Behavior 10 (1): 122–42. https://doi.org/10.1006/game.1995.1027.
Bernecker, Sven. 2010. Memory: A Philosophical Study. Oxford University Press.
Bicchieri, Christina. 2005. The Grammar of Society: The Nature and Dynamics of Social Norms. Cambridge University Press.
Björklund, Fredrik, Gunnar Björnsson, John Eriksson, Ragnar Francén Olinder, and Caj Strandberg. 2012. "Recent Work on Motivational Internalism." Analysis 72 (1): 124–37. https://doi.org/10.1093/analys/anr118.
Bodansky, D. 1992. "Scientific Uncertainty and the Precautionary Principle: Commentary: The Precautionary Principle." Environment 34: 4–5.
Bond Jr, Charles F., and Bella M. DePaulo. 2006. "Accuracy of Deception Judgments." Personality and Social Psychology Review 10 (3): 214–34.
Bondy, Patrick, and J. Adam Carter. 2019. "Well-Founded Belief: An Introduction." In Well-Founded Belief: New Essays on the Epistemic Basing Relation, edited by Bondy and Carter, 1–12. London: Routledge.
BonJour, Laurence. 1980. "Externalist Theories of Empirical Knowledge." Midwest Studies in Philosophy 5: 53–73.
Booth, Anthony Robert. 2007. "The Two Faces of Evidentialism." Erkenntnis 67 (3): 401–17.
Bovens, Luc. 1999. "The Value of Hope." Philosophy and Phenomenological Research 59 (3): 667–81.
Bradford, Gwen. 2013. "The Value of Achievements." Pacific Philosophical Quarterly 94 (2): 204–24.
Bradford, Gwen. 2015. "Knowledge, Achievement, and Manifestation." Erkenntnis 80 (1): 97–116. https://doi.org/10.1007/s10670-014-9614-0.
Bradford, Gwen. 2015. Achievement. Oxford University Press, USA.
Bratman, Michael E. 1992. "Practical Reasoning and Acceptance in a Context." Mind 101 (401): 1–15.
Bratman, Michael E. 2013. Shared Agency: A Planning Theory of Acting Together. Oxford University Press.
Braynov, Sviatoslav, and Tuomas Sandholm. 2002. "Contracting With Uncertain Level Of Trust." Computational Intelligence 18 (4): 501–14. https://doi.org/10.1111/1467-8640.00200.

Broncano-Berrocal, Fernando, and J. Adam Carter. 2021. The Philosophy of Group Polarization: Epistemology, Metaphysics, Psychology. Routledge.

Buckareff, Andrei. 2010. "Acceptance Does Not Entail Belief." International Journal of Philosophical Studies 18 (2): 255–61.

Burge, Tyler. 1998. "Reason and the First Person." Knowing Our Own Minds, 243–70. Clarendon Press.

Burge, Tyler. 2003. "Perceptual Entitlement." Philosophy and Phenomenological Research 67 (3): 503–48.

Burns, Calvin, Kathryn Mearns, and Peter McGeorge. 2006. "Explicit and Implicit Trust Within Safety Culture." Risk Analysis 26 (5): 1139–50.

Calhoun, Cheshire and Solomon, Robert C. (eds). 1984. What Is an Emotion?: Classic Readings in Philosophical Psychology. New York: Oxford University Press.

Carter, J. Adam. 2011. "Kvanvig on Pointless Truths and the Cognitive Ideal." Acta Analytica 26 (3): 285–93.

Carter, J. Adam. 2016. "Robust Virtue Epistemology as Anti-Luck Epistemology: A New Solution." Pacific Philosophical Quarterly 97 (1): 140–55.

Carter, J. Adam. 2018. "On Behalf of Controversial View Agnosticism." European Journal of Philosophy 26 (4): 1358–70. https://doi.org/10.1111/ejop.12333.

Carter, J. Adam. 2020a. "Collective (Telic) Virtue Epistemology." In Social Virtue Epistemology, edited by Mark Alfano, Jeroen de Ridder, and Colin Klein. London: Routledge.

Carter, J. Adam. 2020b. "On Behalf of a Bi-Level Account of Trust." Philosophical Studies 177 (8): 2299–322. https://doi.org/10.1007/s11098-019-01311-2.

Carter, J. Adam. 2020c. Sosa on Knowledge, Judgment and Guessing. Synthese, *197* (12), 5117–36.

Carter, J. Adam. 2021a. "De Minimis Normativism: A New Theory of Full Aptness." The Philosophical Quarterly 71 (1): 16–36. https://doi.org/10.1093/pq/pqaa017.

Carter, J. Adam. 2021b. "Exercising Abilities." Synthese 198 (3): 2495–509.

Carter, J. Adam. 2022. "Trust as Performance." Philosophical Issues: A Supplement to Noûs.

Carter, J. Adam. 2023a. "Epistemic Normativity is Not Independent of Our Goals." In Contemporary Debates in Epistemology, 3rd Edition, edited by Ernest Sosa, Matthias Steup, John Turri, and Blake Roeber. Wiley-Blackwell.

Carter, J. Adam. 2023b. Stratified Virtue Epistemology: A Defence. Epistemology Elements. Cambridge University Press.

Carter, J. Adam. 2023c. "Trust and trustworthiness." Philosophy and Phenomenological Research, 107 (2): 377–94.

Carter, J. Adam. 2024. "Therapeutic Trust." Philosophical Psychology 37 (1): 38–61.

Carter, J. Adam, and Emma C. Gordon. 2014. American Philosophical Quarterly 51 (1): 1–13.

Carter, J. Adam, and Timothy R. Kearl. 2023. "Knowing and Doing: An Epistemic Theory of Actional Control." Manuscript.

Carter, J. Adam, and Ernest Sosa. 2021. "Metaepistemology." In Stanford Encyclopedia of Philosophy, edited by Edward N. Zalta, Spring 2022. https://plato.stanford.edu/archives/spr2022/entries/metaepistemology/.

Carter, J. Adam, and J. Shepherd. 2023. "Intentional Action and Knowledge-Centered Theories of Control." Philosophical Studies 180 (3): 957–77.

Carter, J. Adam, and Mona Simion. 2020. "The Ethics and Epistemology of Trust." Internet Encyclopedia of Philosophy.

Carter, J. Adam, Benjamin W. Jarvis, and Katherine Rubin. 2015. "Varieties of Cognitive Achievement." Philosophical Studies 172 (6): 1603-23.

Carter, J. Adam, and Christopher Willard-Kyle. 2023. "Virtue Epistemology for the Zetetic Turn." Manuscript.

Carter, J. Adam, and M. Peterson. 2015. "On the Epistemology of the Precautionary Principle." Erkenntnis 80: 1-13. https://doi.org/10.1007/s10670-014-9609-x.

Carver, Charles S., Michael F. Scheier, and Suzanne C. Segerstrom. 2010. "Optimism." Clinical Psychology Review 30 (7): 879-89.

Chalmers, D. J. 2023. Could a Large Language Model Be Conscious?. arXiv preprint arXiv:2303.07103.

Chan, Timothy, ed. 2013. The Aim of Belief. Oxford University Press.

Chrisman, Matthew. 2012. "The Normative Evaluation of Belief and the Aspectual Classification of Belief and Knowledge Attributions." The Journal of Philosophy 109 (10): 588-612.

Cogley, Zac. 2012. "Trust and the Trickster Problem." Analytic Philosophy 53 (1): 30-47.

Cohen, L. Jonathan. 1989. "Belief and Acceptance." Mind 98 (391): 367-89.

Coleman, James S. 1990. "Relations of Trust." Foundations of Social Theory, Cambridge, London, 91-116.

Comesaña, Juan. 2005. "Unsafe Knowledge." Synthese 146 (3): 395-404.

Cook, Karen S., Russell Hardin, and Margaret Levi. 2005. Cooperation Without Trust? Russell Sage Foundation.

Cooper, Mick, Maureen O'Hara, and Peter F. Schmid. The handbook of Person-Centred Psychotherapy and Counselling. Bloomsbury Publishing, 2013.

Cottingham, John. 2002. "Descartes and the Voluntariness of Belief." The Monist 85 (3): 343-60.

Crisp, Roger. 2014. "II—Roger Crisp: Moral Testimony Pessimism: A Defence." Aristotelian Society Supplementary Vol. 88 (1): 129-43. https://doi.org/10.1111/j.1467-8349.2014.00236.x.

Dasgupta, Partha. 1988. "Trust as a Commodity." In Trust: Making and Breaking Cooperative Relations, edited by Diego Gambetta, 49-72. Blackwell.

de Sousa, Ronald. 1987. The Rationality of Emotion. MIT Press.

Díaz, Rodrigo, and Manuel Almagro. 2019. "You Are Just Being Emotional! Testimonial Injustice and Folk-Psychological Attributions." Synthese 198, 5709-30. https://doi.org/10.1007/s11229-019-02429-w.

Domenicucci, Jacopo, and Richard Holton. 2017. "Trust as a Two-Place Relation." The Philosophy of Trust, 149-60.

Dormandy, Katherine. 2020. "Exploitative Epistemic Trust." In Trust in Epistemology, edited by Katherine Dormandy, 241-64. London: Routledge.

Dormandy, K. 2020. Epistemic Self-Trust: It's Personal. Episteme, 1-16. doi:10.1017/epi.2020.49

Dougherty, Tom. 2013. "Sex, Lies, and Consent." Ethics 123 (4): 717-44.

Dougherty, Tom. 2019. "Consent, Communication, and Abandonment." Law and Philosophy 38 (4): 387-405. https://doi.org/10.1007/s10982-019-09355-5.

Dyche L, Zayas L. 1995. The Value of Curiosity and Naiveté for the Cross-Cultural Psychotherapist. Family Process, 34, 389–99.

Elster, Jon. 2015. Explaining Social Behavior. Cambridge University Press.

Emmons, Robert A., and Michael E. McCullough. 2004. The Psychology of Gratitude. Oxford University Press.

Engel, Mylan. 1992. "Is Epistemic Luck Compatible with Knowledge?" The Southern Journal of Philosophy 30 (2): 59–75.

Enoch, David. 2014. "A Defense of Moral Deference." The Journal of Philosophy 111 (5): 229–58.

Fantl, Jeremy, and Matthew McGrath. 2002. "Evidence, Pragmatics, and Justification." The Philosophical Review 111 (1): 67–94.

Faulkner, Paul, and Thomas Simpson. 2017. The Philosophy of Trust. Oxford University Press.

Faulkner, Paul. 2007. "A Genealogy of Trust." Episteme: A Journal of Social Epistemology 4 (3): 305–21.

Faulkner, Paul. 2007. "On Telling and Trusting." Mind 116 (464): 875–902.

Faulkner, Paul. 2010. "Norms of Trust." In Social Epistemology, edited by Adrian Haddock, Alan Millar, and Duncan Pritchard. Oxford University Press.

Faulkner, Paul. 2011. Knowledge on Trust. Oxford University Press.

Faulkner, Paul. 2014. "The Moral Obligations of Trust." Philosophical Explorations 17 (3): 332–45.

Faulkner, Paul. 2015. "The Attitude of Trust Is Basic." Analysis 75 (3): 424–29.

Feldman, Richard. 2000. "The Ethics of Belief." Philosophy and Phenomenological Research 60 (3): 667–95.

Fernández Vargas, Miguel Ángel. 2016. Performance Epistemology: Foundations and Applications. Oxford University Press.

Fine, G. 2000. Descartes and Ancient Skepticism: Reheated Cabbage?. The Philosophical Review, 109(2), 195–234.

Finlay, Stephen, and Mark Schroeder. 2017. "Reasons for Action: Internal Vs. External." In The Stanford Encyclopedia of Philosophy, edited by Edward N. Zalta, Fall 2017. Metaphysics Research Lab, Stanford University. https://plato.stanford.edu/archives/fall2017/entries/reasons-internal-external/.

Fischer, John Martin, and Mark Ravizza. 2000. Responsibility and Control: A Theory of Moral Responsibility. Cambridge University Press.

Fishman, Z., J. Brewster, M. Wang, and V. Pavilonis. 2023. Verified Misinformation: "Blue Check" Twitter Accounts are Flooding the Platform with False Claims; Under new owner Elon Musk, Twitter is granting legitimacy to some of the platform's influential misinformers. Newsweek, 180(13).

Frankfurt, Harry G. 1969. "Alternate Possibilities and Moral Responsibility." The Journal of Philosophy 66 (23): 829–39.

Frederiksen, Morten. 2014. "Trust in the Face of Uncertainty: A Qualitative Study of Intersubjective Trust and Risk." International Review of Sociology 24: 130–44.

Fricker, Elizabeth. 2018. "Trust and Testimonial Justification." Manuscript.

Fricker, Miranda. 2007. Epistemic Injustice: Power and the Ethics of Knowing. Oxford University Press.

Fridland, Ellen, and Carlotta Pavese. 2020. Routledge Handbook of Philosophy of Skill and Expertise. London: Routledge.
Friedman, Jane. 2013. "Suspended Judgment." Philosophical Studies 162 (2): 165–81.
Friedman, Jane. 2020. "The Epistemic and the Zetetic." Philosophical Review 129 (4): 501–36.
Frost-Arnold, Karen. 2014. "The Cognitive Attitude of Rational Trust." Synthese 191 (9): 1957–74.
Frost, Kim. 2014. "On the Very Idea of Direction of Fit." The Philosophical Review 123 (4): 429–84.
Gambetta, Diego. 1988. Trust: Making and Breaking Cooperative Relations. Blackwell.
Geach, Peter T. 1956. "Good and Evil." Analysis 17 (2): 33–42.
Gerson, M. J. 2009. The Embedded Self, 2nd Edition: An Integrative Psychodynamic and Systemic Perspective on Couples and Family. New York: Routledge.
Gibbons, John. 2013. The Norm of Belief. Oxford University Press.
Giddens, Anthony. 2013. The Consequences of Modernity. John Wiley & Sons.
Gilbert, Margaret. 2013. Joint Commitment: How We Make the Social World. Oxford University Press.
Glüer, Kathrin, and Åsa Wikforss. 2009. "Against Content Normativity." Mind 118 (469): 31–70.
Goldberg, Sanford. 2010. Relying on Others: An Essay in Epistemology. Oxford University Press,
Goldberg, Sanford. 2015. "What Is the Subject-Matter of the Theory of Epistemic Justification?" In Epistemic Evaluation: Purposeful Epistemology, edited by David K. Henderson and John Greco, 205–23. Oxford: Oxford University Press. https://doi.org/10.1093/acprof:oso/9780199642632.003.0009.
Goldberg, Sanford C. 2019. "Against Epistemic Partiality in Friendship: Value-Reflecting Reasons." Philosophical Studies 176: 2221–42.
Gordon, Emma C. 2022. "When Monitoring Facilitates Trust." Ethical Theory and Moral Practice 25(4): 557–71.
Graham, Peter J. 2016. "Testimonial Knowledge: A Unified Account." Philosophical Issues 26 (1): 172–86.
Graham, Peter J. 2014. Functions, Warrant, History. In Naturalizing Epistemic Virtue, edited by Abrol Fairweather and Owen Flanagan, 15–35. Cambridge University Press.
Gray, J. S., and J. M. Brewers. 1996. "Towards a Scientific Definition of the Precautionary Principle." Marine Pollution Bulletin 32 (11): 768.
Greco, John. 2009. "Knowledge and Success from Ability." Philosophical Studies 142 (1): 17–26.
Greco, John. 2010. Achieving Knowledge: A Virtue-Theoretic Account of Epistemic Normativity. Cambridge University Press.
Greco, John. 2013. "Knowledge, Testimony, and Action." In Knowledge, Virtue, and Action, edited by T. Henning and D. Schweikard, 15–29. London: Routledge.
Greco, John. 2014. "Episteme: Knowledge and Understanding." In Virtues and Their Vices, 285–302. Oxford: Oxford University Press.
Greco, John. 2019. "The Role of Trust in Testimonial Knowledge." In Trust in Epistemology, 91–113. Routledge.

Greco, John. 2020. "The Transmission of Knowledge and Garbage." Synthese 197 (7): 2867–78.
Greco, John. 2020. The Transmission of Knowledge. Cambridge University Press.
Guo, Guibing, Jie Zhang, Daniel Thalmann, Anirban Basu, and Neil Yorke-Smith. 2014. "From Ratings to Trust: An Empirical Study of Implicit Trust in Recommender Systems." In Proceedings of the 29th Annual Acm Symposium on Applied Computing, 248–53.
Hakli, Raul, Kaarlo Miller, and Raimo Tuomela. 2010. "Two Kinds of We-Reasoning." Economics & Philosophy 26 (3): 291–320. https://doi.org/10.1017/S0266267110000386.
Hall, Mark A. 2005. "The Importance of Trust for Ethics, Law, and Public Policy." Cambridge Quarterly of Healthcare Ethics 14 (2): 156–67.
Hansson, Sven Ove. 2004. "Philosophical Perspectives on Risk." Techné: Research in Philosophy and Technology 8 (1): 10–35.
Hansson, Sven Ove. 2018. "Risk." In The Stanford Encyclopedia of Philosophy, edited by Edward N. Zalta, Fall 2018. Metaphysics Research Lab, Stanford University.
Hardin, Russell. 1992. "The Street-Level Epistemology of Trust." Analyse & Kritik 14 (2): 152–76.
Hardin, Russell. 1996. "Trustworthiness." Ethics 107 (1): 26–42.
Hardin, Russell. 2002. Trust and Trustworthiness. Russell Sage Foundation.
Hardwig, John. 1991. "The Role of Trust in Knowledge." The Journal of Philosophy 88 (12): 693–708.
Hawley, Katherine. 2014. "Trust, Distrust and Commitment." Noûs 48 (1): 1–20.
Hawley, Katherine. 2019. How to Be Trustworthy. Oxford University Press, USA.
Hawthorne, John, and Jason Stanley. 2008. "Knowledge and Action." The Journal of Philosophy 105 (10): 571–90.
Heering, David. 2023. "Failure and Success in Agency." The Philosophical Quarterly. https://doi.org/10.1093/pq/pqad069.
Heil, John. 1983. "Doxastic Agency." Philosophical Studies 43 (3): 355–64.
Hetherington, Stephen. 2013. "Knowledge Can Be Lucky." Contemporary Debates in Epistemology 2: 164–76.
Hieronymi, Pamela. 2008. "The Reasons of Trust." Australasian Journal of Philosophy 86 (2): 213–36.
Hills, Alison. 2009. "Moral Testimony and Moral Epistemology." Ethics 120 (1): 94–127.
Hinchman, Edward. 2017. "On the Risks of Resting Assured: An Assurance Theory of Trust." In The Philosophy of Trust, edited by Paul Faulkner and Thomas W. Simpson. Oxford: Oxford University Press.
Hinchman, Edward. 2020. "Trust and Will." In Routledge Handbook on Trust and Philosophy, edited by Judith Simon. New York: Routledge.
Hinchman, Edward. 2021. "Disappointed Yet Unbetrayed: A New Three-Place Analysis of Trust." In Social Trust, edited by Kevin Vallier and Michael Weber, 73–101. Routledge.
Holroyd, Jules, Robin Scaife, and Tom Stafford. 2017. "What Is Implicit Bias?" Philosophy Compass 12 (10): e12437.

Holton, Richard. 1994. "Deciding to Trust, Coming to Believe." Australasian Journal of Philosophy 72 (1): 63–76.
Honoré, Anthony M. 1964. "Can and Can't." Mind 73 (292): 463–79.
Hooker, Brad. 2002. Ideal Code, Real World: A Rule-Consequentialist Theory of Morality. Oxford University Press.
Horsburgh, H. J. N. 1960. "The Ethics of Trust." The Philosophical Quarterly 10 (41): 343–54.
Humberstone, I. Lloyd. 1992. "Direction of fit." Mind 101(401): 59–83.
Hughes, N., 2019. "Dilemmic Epistemology." Synthese 196: 4059–90.
Hume, David. (1739) 2003. A Treatise of Human Nature. Courier Corporation.
Ichikawa, Jonathan. 2024. Epistemic Courage. Oxford University Press.
Jackson, Elizabeth. 2020. "Epistemic Paternalism, Epistemic Permissivism, and Standpoint Epistemology." In Epistemic Paternalism Reconsidered: Conceptions, Justifications, and Implications, edited by Amiel Bernal and Guy Axtell, 201–15. Lanham, MD: Rowman and Littlefield.
Jarvis, Benjamin. 2013. "Knowledge, Cognitive Achievement, and Environmental Luck." Pacific Philosophical Quarterly 94 (4): 529–51.
Jones, Karen. 1996. "Trust as an Affective Attitude." Ethics 107 (1): 4–25.
Jones, Karen. 2004. "Trust and Terror." In Moral Psychology: Feminist Ethics and Social Theory, edited by Peggy DesAutels and Margaret Urban Walker, 3–18. Rowman & Littlefield.
Jones, Karen. 2012. "Trustworthiness." Ethics 123 (1): 61–85.
Jones, K., 2017. "But I Was Counting On You!" In The Philosophy of Trust, edited by P. Faulkner and T. Simpson, 90–108. Oxford: Oxford University Press.
Kallestrup, Jesper, and Duncan Pritchard. 2014. "Virtue Epistemology and Epistemic Twin Earth." European Journal of Philosophy 22 (3): 335–57.
Kallestrup, Jesper. 2016. "Group Virtue Epistemology." Synthese, 197, 5233–51. https://doi.org/10.1007/s11229-016-1225-7.
Kaplan, David. 1979. "On the Logic of Demonstratives." Journal of Philosophical Logic 8 (1): 81–98.
Kelp, Christoph, and Mona Simion. 2021. "What Is Trustworthiness?" Noûs 57 (3): 667–83.
Kelp, Christoph, Cameron Boult, Fernando Broncano-Berrocal, Paul Dimmock, Harmen Ghijsen, and Mona Simion. 2017. "Hoops and Barns: A New Dilemma for Sosa." Synthese, 197: 5187–5202.
Kelp, Christoph. 2013. "Knowledge: The Safe-Apt View." Australasian Journal of Philosophy 91 (2): 265–78.
Kelp, Christoph. 2018. "Assertion: A Function First Account." Noûs 52 (2): 411–42.
Kelp, Christoph. 2020. "The Epistemology of Ernest Sosa: An Introduction." Synthese, 197 (12): 5093–5100.
Kelp, Christoph. 2021. Inquiry, Knowledge, and Understanding. Oxford: Oxford University Press.
Kelp, C., and Simion, M. 2021. Sharing Knowledge: A Functionalist Account of Assertion. Cambridge University Press.
Kenny, A. J. P. 1976. Will, Freedom and Power. Blackwell.

Keren, Arnon. 2020. "Trust and Belief." In The Routledge Handbook of Trust and Philosophy, edited by Judith Simon, 109–20. London: Routledge.
Keren, Arnon. 2014. "Trust and Belief: A Preemptive Reasons Account." Synthese 191 (12): 2593–615.
Keren, Arnon. 2019. "Trust, Preemption, and Knowledge." In Trust in Epistemology, edited by Katherine Dormandy. London: Routledge.
Kirton, Andrew. 2020. "Matters of Trust as Matters of Attachment Security." International Journal of Philosophical Studies, 28 (5): 583–602.
Korcz, Keith Allen. 2019. "The Epistemic Basing Relation." In The Stanford Encyclopedia of Philosophy, edited by Edward N. Zalta, Fall 2019. Metaphysics Research Lab, Stanford University. https://plato.stanford.edu/archives/fall2019/entries/basing-epistemic/.
Kornblith, Hilary. 1983. "Justified Belief and Epistemically Responsible Action." The Philosophical Review 92 (1): 33–48.
Kornblith, Hilary. 2004. "Sosa on Human and Animal Knowledge." In Ernest Sosa and His Critics, edited by John Greco, 126–34. London: Blackwell.
Kramer, Roderick M. 1999. "Trust and Distrust in Organizations: Emerging Perspectives, Enduring Questions." Annual Review of Psychology 50 (1): 569–98.
Kraut, Robert. 1980. "Humans as Lie Detectors." Journal of Communication 30 (4): 209–18.
Krishnan, Rekha, Xavier Martin, and Niels G. Noorderhaven. 2006. "When Does Trust Matter to Alliance Performance?" The Academy of Management Journal 49 (5): 894–917.
Kvanvig, Jonathan L. 2016. "The Idea of Faith as Trust." In Reason and Faith: Themes from Richard Swinburne, edited by Michael Bergmann and Jeffrey E. Brower, 4–26. Oxford: Oxford University Press.
Kvanvig, Jonathan. 2008. "Pointless Truth." Midwest Studies in Philosophy 32 (1): 199–212.
Lackey, Jennifer. 2007. "Norms of Assertion." Noûs 41 (4): 594–626.
Lackey, Jennifer. 2007. "Why We Don't Deserve Credit for Everything We Know." Synthese 158 (3): 345–61.
Lackey, Jennifer. 2021. The Epistemology of Groups. Oxford University Press, USA.
Lagerspetz, Olli. 1998. Trust: The Tacit Demand. Vol. 1. Springer Science & Business Media.
Lahno, Bernd. 2001. "On the Emotional Character of Trust." Ethical Theory and Moral Practice 4 (2): 171–89. https://doi.org/10.1023/A:1011425102875.
Lahno, Bernd. 2004. "Three Aspects of Interpersonal Trust." Analyse & Kritik 26 (1): 30–47.
Lambert, M. J., & Barley, D. E. 2002. Outcome measure. AAVV Encyclopedia of Psychotherapy. Elsevier Science (USA), New York.
Leonard, Nick. 2020. "Epistemic Dilemmas and Rational Indeterminacy." Philosophical Studies 177 (3): 573–96. https://doi.org/10.1007/s11098-018-1195-3.
Lewis, David. 1988. "Desire as Belief." Mind 97 (387): 323–32.
Ling, M. H. 2023. ChatGPT (Feb 13 Version) is a Chinese Room. arXiv preprint arXiv:2304.12411.
Littlejohn, Clayton. 2014. "Fake Barns and False Dilemmas."

Littlejohn, Clayton. Forthcoming. Dividing Away Doxastic Dilemmas. In Epistemic Dilemmas, edited by Nick Hughes. Oxford University Press.

Luper-Foy, Steven. 1984. "The Epistemic Predicament: Knowledge, Nozickian Tracking, and Scepticism." Australasian Journal of Philosophy 62 (1): 26–49.

MacLeod J. 2013. An Introduction to Counseling (5th Edition). New York: McGraw-Hill Education.

Madison, Brent JC. 2011. "Combating Anti Anti-Luck Epistemology." Australasian Journal of Philosophy 89 (1): 47–58.

Marušić, Berislav. 2017. "Trust, Reliance and the Participant Stance." Philosopher's Imprint 17 (17). http://hdl.handle.net/2027/spo.3521354.0017.017.

McGeer, Victoria. 2004. "The Art of Good Hope." The Annals of the American Academy of Political and Social Science 592 (1): 100–27.

McGeer, Victoria. 2008. "Trust, Hope and Empowerment." Australasian Journal of Philosophy 86 (2): 237–54. https://doi.org/10.1080/00048400801886413.

McGrath, Sarah. 2011. "Skepticism about Moral Expertise as a Puzzle for Moral Realism." The Journal of Philosophy. 108 (3): 111–137. https://doi.org/10.5840/jphil201110837.

McHugh, Conor. 2012. "The Truth Norm of Belief." Pacific Philosophical Quarterly 93 (1): 8–30.

McKitrick, Jennifer. 2018. Dispositional Pluralism. Oxford University Press.

McLeod, Carolyn. 2002. Self-Trust and Reproductive Autonomy. MIT Press.

McLeod, Carolyn 2023. "Trust", In The Stanford Encyclopedia of Philosophy, edited by Edward N. Zalta and Uri Nodelman, Fall 2023. Metaphysics Research Lab, Stanford University. https://plato.stanford.edu/archives/fall2023/entries/trust/.

McMyler, Benjamin. 2011. Testimony, Trust, and Authority. Oxford University Press, USA.

McNarry, Gareth, Jacquelyn Allen-Collinson, and Adam B. Evans. 2020. "'You Always Wanna Be Sore, Because Then You Are Seeing Results': Exploring Positive Pain in Competitive Swimming." Sociology of Sport Journal 1 (aop): 1–9.

Mele, Alfred R. 2001. Autonomous Agents: From Self-Control to Autonomy. Oxford University Press on Demand.

Mele, Alfred R. 2003. "Agents' Abilities." Noûs 37 (3): 447–70. https://doi.org/10.1111/1468-0068.00446.

Mele, Alfred R. 2003. Motivation and Agency. Oxford University Press.

Millar, Alan. 2009. "What Is It That Cognitive Abilities Are Abilities to Do?" Acta Analytica 24 (4): 223.

Miracchi, Lisa, and J. Adam Carter. 2022. "Refitting the Mirrors: On Structural Analogies in Epistemology and Action Theory." Synthese 200 (9). https://doi.org/10.1007/s11229-022-03462-y.

Möllering, Guido. 2001. "The Nature of Trust: From Georg Simmel to a Theory of Expectation, Interpretation and Suspension." Sociology 35 (2): 403–20.

Möllering, Guido. 2006. Trust: Reason, Routine, Reflexivity. Emerald Group Publishing.

Mumford, Stephen. 2016. "Dispositions." In Routledge Encyclopedia of Philosophy, 1st Edition. London: Routledge. https://doi.org/10.4324/9780415249126-N116-1.

Mumpower, Jeryl. 1986. "An Analysis of the de Minimis Strategy for Risk Management." Risk Analysis 6 (4): 437–46.

Munroe, Wade. 2016. "Testimonial Injustice and Prescriptive Credibility Deficits." Canadian Journal of Philosophy 46 (6): 924–47.

Neta, Ram. 2019. "The Basing Relation." The Philosophical Review 128 (2): 179–217. https://doi.org/10.1215/00318108-7374945.

Nguyen, C. Thi. 2022. "Trust as an Unquestioning Attitude." Oxford Studies in Epistemology 7: 214–44.

Nickel, Philip J. 2015. "Design for the Value of Trust." In Handbook of Ethics, Values, and Technological Design: Sources, Theory, Values and Application Domains, 551–67. Dordrecht: Springer.

Nickel, Philip J., and Krist Vaesen. 2012. "Risk and Trust." In Handbook of Risk Theory, edited by Sabine Roeser, Rafaela Hillerbrand, Martin Peterson, and Per Sandin. Springer.

Niebuhr, Helmut Richard. 1991. Faith on Earth: An Inquiry into the Structure of Human Faith. Yale University Press.

Niker, Fay, and Laura Specker Sullivan. 2018. "Trusting Relationships and the Ethics of Interpersonal Action." International Journal of Philosophical Studies 26 (2): 173–86. https://doi.org/10.1080/09672559.2018.1450081.

Ólafsson, Ísak Andri. 2023. 'Unwanted Knowledge Transmission'. Synthese 201 (5): 162. https://doi.org/10.1007/s11229-023-04140-3.

O'Neil, Collin. 2012. "Lying, Trust, and Gratitude." Philosophy & Public Affairs 40 (4): 301–33.

O'Neil, Collin. 2017. "Betraying Trust." In The Philosophy of Trust, edited by Paul Faulkner and Thomas W. Simpson, 70–89. Oxford, UK: Oxford University Press.

O'Neill, Onora. 2018. "Linking Trust to Trustworthiness." International Journal of Philosophical Studies 26 (2): 293–300. https://doi.org/10.1080/09672559.2018.1454637.

Papineau, David. 2013. "There Are No Norms of Belief." In The Aim of Belief, edited by Timothy Chan. Oxford University Press.

Pavese, Carlotta. 2016. "Skill in Epistemology II: Skill and Know How." Philosophy Compass 11 (11): 650–60. https://doi.org/10.1111/phc3.12364.

Pavese, C, 2022. "Practical Knowledge First." Synthese, 200 (5), 1–18.

Peluso, P.R., Liebovitch, L.S., Gottman, J.M., Norman, M.D., and Su, J. 2012. A Mathematical Model of Psychotherapy: An Investigation using Dynamic Non-Linear Equations to Model the Therapeutic Relationship. Psychotherapy Research, 22, 40–55. doi:10.1080/10503307.2011.622314.

Peterson, Martin. 2002. "What Is a de Minimis Risk?" Risk Management 4 (2): 47–55.

Pettit, Philip. 1995. "The Cunning of Trust." Philosophy and Public Affairs 24 (3): 202–25.

Plato. (385BC) 2011. Plato's Meno. Edited by Richard Stanley Bluck. Cambridge University Press.

Platts, Mark. 1980. "Ways of Meaning." Mind 89 (355): 454–56.

Potter, Nancy Nyquist. 2002. How Can I Be Trusted?: A Virtue Theory of Trustworthiness. Rowman & Littlefield.

Potter, Nancy Nyquist. 2020. "Interpersonal Trust." In The Routledge Handbook of Trust and Philosophy, edited by Judith Simon, 243–55. Routledge.

Price, Huw. 1989. "Defending Desire-as-Belief." Mind 98 (389): 119–27. https://www.jstor.org/stable/2255064.
Pritchard, Duncan. 2005. Epistemic Luck. Clarendon Press.
Pritchard, Duncan. 2007. "Anti-Luck Epistemology." Synthese 158 (3): 277–97.
Pritchard, Duncan. 2009. "Knowledge, Understanding and Epistemic Value." Royal Institute of Philosophy Supplement 64: 19–43. https://doi.org/10.1017/s1358246109000046.
Pritchard, Duncan. 2009. "The Value of Knowledge." The Harvard Review of Philosophy 16 (1): 86–103. https://doi.org/10.5840/harvardreview20091616.
Pritchard, Duncan. 2012. "Anti-Luck Virtue Epistemology." Journal of Philosophy 109 (3): 247–79.
Pritchard, Duncan. 2014. "Knowledge and Understanding." In Virtue Epistemology Naturalized: Bridges between Virtue Epistemology and Philosophy of Science, 315–27. Cham: Springer.
Pritchard, Duncan. 2015. "Risk." Metaphilosophy 46 (3): 436–61.
Pritchard, Duncan. 2016. "Epistemic Risk." The Journal of Philosophy 113 (11): 550–71.
Rabinowitz, Dani. 2011. "The Safety Condition for Knowledge." Internet Encyclopedia of Philosophy.
Railton, Peter. 2014. "Reliance, Trust, and Belief." Inquiry 57 (1): 122–50.
Rawls, John. 1955. "Two Concepts of Rules." The Philosophical Review 64 (1): 3–32.
Raz, Joseph. 2009. "Reasons: Explanatory and Normative." In New Essays on the Explanation of Action, edited by Constantine Sandis, 184–202. Basingstoke: Palgrave.
Resnik, D. 2003. Is the Precautionary Principle Unscientific? Studies in the History and Philosohpy of Science, Part C: Studies in History and Philosophy of Biological and Biomedical Sciences, 34, 329–44.
Rhodes, Rosamond, Jody Azzouni, Stefan Bernard Baumrin, Keith Benkov, Martin J. Blaser, Barbara Brenner, Joseph W. Dauben, William J. Earle, Lily Frank, and Nada Gligorov. 2011. De Minimis Risk: A Proposal for a New Category of Research Risk. Taylor & Francis.
Rorty, Amélie Oksenberg. 1980. Explaining Emotions. Vol. 232. University of California Press.
Rosati, Connie S. 2016. "Moral Motivation." In The Stanford Encyclopedia of Philosophy, edited by Edward N. Zalta, Winter 2016. Metaphysics Research Lab, Stanford University
Rulis, Alan M. 1986. "De Minimis and the Threshold of Regulation." Food Protection Technology, 29–37. CRC Press.
Ryle, Gilbert. 1949. "The Concept of Mind." London: Hutchinson.
Sandin, Per. 2005. "Naturalness and de Minimis Risk." Environmental Ethics 27 (2): 191–200.
Saul, Jennifer. 2013. "Scepticism and Implicit Bias." Disputatio 5 (37): 243–63.
Saul, Jennifer. 2017. "Implicit Bias, Stereotype Threat, and Epistemic Injustice." The Routledge Handbook of Epistemic Injustice, 235–42. London: Routledge.
Schechter, Joshua. 2019. "Aiming at Aptness." Episteme 16 (4): 438–52.
Schroeder, Mark. 2011. "Ought, Agents, and Actions." The Philosophical Review 120 (1): 1–41.

Schwitzgebel, Eric. 2013. "A Dispositional Approach to Attitudes: Thinking Outside of the Belief Box." In New Essays on Belief: Constitution, Content and Structure, edited by Nikolaj Nottelmann. London: Palgrave Macmillan.

Schwitzgebel, Eric. 2019. "Belief." In The Stanford Encyclopedia of Philosophy, edited by Edward N. Zalta, Fall 2019. Metaphysics Research Lab, Stanford University.

Scott-Kakures, Dion. 1994. "On Belief and the Captivity of the Will." Philosophy and Phenomenological Research 54 (1): 77–103.

Searle, J. R. 1979. Expression and Meaning: Studies in the Theory of Speech Acts. Cambridge University Press.

Shade, Patrick. 2000. Habits of hope: A pragmatic theory. Nashville, TN: Vanderbilt University Press.

Shafer-Landau, Russ. 2003. Moral Realism: A Defence. Oxford University Press on Demand.

Shah, Nishi, and J. David Velleman. 2005. "Doxastic Deliberation." Philosophical Review 114 (4): 497–534. https://doi.org/10.1215/00318108-114-4-497.

Shah, Nishi. 2003. "How Truth Governs Belief." The Philosophical Review 112 (4): 447–82.

Shah, Nishi. 2008. "How Action Governs Intention." Philosophers' Imprint 8: 1–19.

Shepherd, J. & Carter, J. A., 2023 "Knowledge, Practical Knowledge, and Intentional Action", Ergo an Open Access Journal of Philosophy 9: 21. doi: https://doi.org/10.3998/ergo.2277.

Silva, Paul. 2015. "On Doxastic Justification and Properly Basing One's Beliefs." Erkenntnis 80 (5): 945–55.

Simion, M. Blame as Performance. Synthese 199, 7595–614 (2021). https://doi.org/10.1007/s11229-021-03130-7.

Simion, Mona, and Christoph Kelp. 2018. "How to Be an Anti-Reductionist." Synthese, 1–18.

Simion, Mona, Christoph Kelp, and Harmen Ghijsen. 2016. "Norms of Belief." Philosophical Issues 26 (1): 374–92.

Simion, Mona. 2019. "Knowledge-First Functionalism." Philosophical Issues 29 (1): 254–67.

Simion, Mona and Christoph Kelp. 2020. "How to be an anti-reductionist." *Synthese* 197: 2849–66.

Simion, Mona. 2021. "Skepticism about Epistemic Dilemmas." In *Epistemic Dilemmas*, edited by Nick Hughes, 109–21. London: Routledge.

Simion, Mona. 2024. Resistance to Evidence and the Duty to Believe. Philosophy and Phenomenological Research. 108: 203–16. https://doi.org/10.1111/phpr.12964.

Simpson, Thomas W. 2012. "What Is Trust?" Pacific Philosophical Quarterly 93 (4): 550–69.

Sjöberg, Lennart, Bjørg-Elin Moen, and Torbjørn Rundmo. 2004. "Explaining Risk Perception." An Evaluation of the Psychometric Paradigm in Risk Perception Research 10 (2): 665–12.

Sjöberg, Lennart. 2000. "The Methodology of Risk Perception Research." Quality and Quantity 34 (4): 407–18.

Slovic, Paul. 1987. "Perception of Risk." Science 236 (4799): 280–85.
Slovic, Paul. 1988. "Risk Perception." In Carcinogen Risk Assessment. Contemporary Issues in Risk Analysis, vol 3, edited by Travis, C.C, 171–81. Boston, MA: Springer. https://doi.org/10.1007/978-1-4684-5484-0_13.
Smith, Michael. 1994. The Moral Problem. Blackwell.
Snyder, C. Rick. 1995. "Conceptualizing, Measuring, and Nurturing Hope." Journal of Counseling & Development 73 (3): 355–60.
Snyder, Charles R., Cheri Harris, John R. Anderson, Sharon A. Holleran, Lori M. Irving, Sandra T. Sigmon, Lauren Yoshinobu, June Gibb, Charyle Langelle, and Pat Harney. 1991. "The Will and the Ways: Development and Validation of an Individual-Differences Measure of Hope." Journal of Personality and Social Psychology 60 (4): 570.
Solomon, Robert C., and Fernando Flores. 2003. Building Trust: In Business, Politics, Relationships, and Life. Oxford University Press, USA.
Sosa, Ernest. 1999. "How to Defeat Opposition to Moore." Noûs 33 (s13): 141–53. https://doi.org/10.1111/0029-4624.33.s13.7.
Sosa, Ernest. 2005. "John Locke Lectures: Apt Belief and Reflective Knowledge". https://www.philosophy.ox.ac.uk/john-locke-lectures#collapse386431.
Sosa, Ernest. 2007. A Virtue Epistemology: Apt Belief and Reflective Knowledge, Vol. I. Oxford University Press.
Sosa, Ernest. 2010. "How Competence Matters in Epistemology." Philosophical Perspectives 24 (1): 465–75.
Sosa, Ernest. 2015. Judgment & Agency. Oxford University Press, UK.
Sosa, Ernest. 2017. Epistemology. Princeton: Princeton University Press.
Sosa, Ernest. 2019. "Animal Versus Reflective Orders of Epistemic Competence." In Thinking About Oneself: The Place and Value of Reflection in Philosophy and Psychology, edited by Waldomiro J. Silva-Filho and Luca Tateo. Cham, Switzerland: Springer.
Sosa, Ernest. 2020. "Default Assumptions and Pure Thought." Manuscript.
Sosa, Ernest. 2021. Epistemic Explanations: A Theory of Telic Normativity, and What It Explains. Oxford University Press.
Sperber, D., Clément, F., Heintz, C., Mascaro, O., Mercier, H., Origgi, G., and Wilson, D. 2010. Epistemic vigilance. Mind & Language, 25(4), 359–93.https://doi.org/10.1111/j.1468-0017.2010.01394.x.
Stanley, Jason. 2005. Knowledge and Practical Interests. Oxford University Press.
Stanley, Jason. 2008. "Knowledge and Certainty." Philosophical Issues 18: 35–57.
Stanley, Jason, and Timothy Williamson. 2017. "Skill." Noûs 51 (4): 713–26.
Steglich-Petersen, Asbjørn. 2006. "No Norm Needed: On the Aim of Belief." The Philosophical Quarterly 56 (225): 499–516.
Stocker, Michael. 1979. "Desiring the Bad: An Essay in Moral Psychology." The Journal of Philosophy 76 (12): 738–53.
Stroud, Sarah. 2006. "Epistemic Partiality in Friendship." Ethics 116(3): 498–524. https://doi.org/10.1086/500337.
Sutton, Jonathan. 2007. Without Justification. MIT Press.
Thaler, Richard H., and Cass R. Sunstein. 2003. "Libertarian Paternalism." The American Economic Review 93 (2): 175–79. http://www.jstor.org/stable/3132220.

Thaler, Richard H., and Cass Sunstein. 2008. Nudge: Improving Decisions About Health, Wealth and Happiness. New Haven: Yale University Press.

Titus, Lisa Miracchi, and J. Adam Carter. 2023. "What the Tortoise Should Do: A Knowledge-First Virtue Approach to the Basing Relation." Noûs 00: 1–26. https://doi.org/10.1111/nous.12460.

Titus, Lisa. 2023. "Does ChatGPT Have Semantic Understanding? A Problem with the Statistics-of-Occurrence Strategy." Cognitive Systems Research.

Tollefsen, Deborah. 2015. Groups as Agents. Polity.

Treanor, Nick. 2014. "Trivial Truths and the Aim of Inquiry." Philosophy and Phenomenological Research 89 (3): 552–59.

Tsai, George. 2018. "The Virtue of Being Supportive." Pacific Philosophical Quarterly 99 (2): 317–42.

Tuomela, Raimo. 1995. The Importance of Us: A Philosophical Study of Basic Social Notions. Stanford University Press.

Turri, John, Mark Alfano, and John Greco. 2019. "Virtue Epistemology." In The Stanford Encyclopedia of Philosophy, edited by Edward N. Zalta, Fall 2019. Metaphysics Research Lab, Stanford University. https://plato.stanford.edu/archives/fall2019/entries/epistemology-virtue/.

Turri, John. 2010. "On the Relationship Between Propositional and Doxastic Justification." Philosophy and Phenomenological Research 80 (2): 312–26.

Turri, John. 2011. "Manifest Failure: The Gettier Problem Solved." Philosopher's Imprint 11 (8). http://hdl.handle.net/2027/spo.3521354.0011.008.

Turri, John. 2012. "A Puzzle about Withholding." The Philosophical Quarterly 62 (247): 355–64. https://doi.org/10.1111/j.1467-9213.2011.00043.x.

Turri, John. 2016. "Knowledge as Achievement, More or Less." In Performance Epistemology: Foundations and Applications, edited by Miguel Ángel Fernández Vargas, 124–34. Oxford: Oxford University Press.

Turri, John. 2017. "Sustaining Rules: A Model and Application." In Knowledge First: Approaches in Epistemology and Mind, edited by J. Adam Carter, Emma C. Gordon, and Benjamin Jarvis. Oxford: Oxford University Press.

Unger, Peter. 1975. Ignorance: A Case for Scepticism. Oxford University Press.

Unkelbach, Christian, Joseph P. Forgas, and Thomas F. Denson. 2008. "The Turban Effect: The Influence of Muslim Headgear and Induced Affect on Aggressive Responses in the Shooter Bias Paradigm." Journal of Experimental Social Psychology 44 (5): 1409–13.

Velleman, David. 2000. "On the Aim of Belief." In The Possibility of Practical Reason, 244–81. Oxford: Oxford University Press.

Verkuyl, Henk J. 1989. "Aspectual Classes and Aspectual Composition." Linguistics and Philosophy 12 (1): 39–94.

Vitz, Rico. 2008. "Doxastic Voluntarism." In Internet Encyclopedia of Philosophy. https://iep.utm.edu/doxastic-voluntarism/.

Vitz, Rico. 2010. "Descartes and the Question of Direct Doxastic Voluntarism." https://philpapers.org/rec/VITDAT.

Vrij, Aldert. 2000. Detecting Lies and Deceit: The Psychology of Lying and Implications for Professional Practice. Wiley.

Wanderer, Jeremy, and Leo Townsend. 2013. "Is It Rational to Trust?" Philosophy Compass 8 (1): 1–14.

Watson, Sean, and Anthony Moran. 2005. Trust, Risk, and Uncertainty. Palgrave-Macmillan.
Wedgwood, Ralph. 2002. "The Aim of Belief." Philosophical Perspectives 16: 267–97. https://doi.org/10.1111/1468-0068.36.s16.10.
Whipple, Chris. 2012. De Minimis Risk. Vol. 2. Springer Science & Business Media.
Whiting, Daniel. 2013. "Nothing but the Truth: On the Norms and Aims of Belief." In The Aim of Belief, edited by Timothy Chan. Oxford University Press.
Williams, Bernard. 1970. "Deciding to Believe." In Problems of the Self, edited by Bernard Williams, 136–51. Cambridge University Press.
Williams, Bernard. 1979. "Internal and External Reasons." In Rational Action, edited by Ross Harrison, 101–13. Cambridge University Press.
Williams, Bernard. 2000. "Formal Structures and Social Reality." Trust: Making and Breaking Cooperative Relations 1: 3–13.
Williamson, Timothy. 2000. Knowledge and Its Limits. Oxford: Oxford University Press.
Williamson, Timothy. 2013. "Knowledge First." In Contemporary Debates in Epistemology, edited by Matthias Steup John Turri, 1–10. Blackwell.
Williamson, Timothy. 2017. "Acting on Knowledge." In Knowledge First: Approaches in Epistemology and Mind, edited by J. Adam Carter, Emma C. Gordon, and Benjamin W. Jarvis, 163–81. Oxford: Oxford University Press.
Williamson, Timothy. 2021. "Epistemological Ambivalence." In Epistemic Dilemmas, edited by Nick Hughes. Oxford: Oxford University Press.
Williamson, Timothy. Forthcoming. "Justifications, Excuses, and Sceptical Scenarios." In The New Evil Demon, Edited by Fabian Dorsch and Julien Dutant. Oxford: Oxford University Press.
Wolff, Kurt H. 1950. The Sociology of Georg Simmel. Glencoe, Ill: Free Press.
Wong, David B. 2006. "Moral Reasons: Internal and External." Philosophy and Phenomenological Research 72 (3): 536–58. https://doi.org/ppr200672338.
Wright, Stephen. 2010. "Trust and Trustworthiness." Philosophia 38 (3): 615–27. https://doi.org/10.1007/s11406-009-9218-0.
Zagzebski, Linda T. 1994. "The Inescapability of Gettier Problems." The Philosophical Quarterly (1950–) 44 (174): 65–73.
Zagzebski, Linda T. 1996. Virtues of the Mind: An Inquiry into the Nature of Virtue and the Ethical Foundations of Knowledge. Cambridge University Press.
Zagzebski, Linda Trinkaus. 2012. Epistemic Authority: A Theory of Trust, Authority, and Autonomy in Belief. Oxford University Press.

Index

AAA assessment 37, 133, 136
accuracy
  of belief 36–8, 133
  of trust 19, 29, 31–2, 35, 37, 42, 47, 63, 96, 133, 136
  of performance 28–9, 133, 180
achievement 31, 47, 55, 66, 136–7, 140, 142–4, 148–51, 153–62, 166, 170–1, 174
Adler, Jonathan 6, 120
adroitness
  of belief 36–8, 43
  of trust 26, 30–2, 35–7, 47, 58, 62, 132, 136, 139
  of performance 25–35, 37–8
Ahlstrom-Vij, Kristoffer 177
Alfano, Mark 131
Alston, William P. 4, 50
Alvarez, Maria 73
Anscombe, G. E. M. 14, 151
aptness
  of belief 36–8, 43, 50–1
  of trust 31, 34–44, 54, 58, 63 n.19, 64–9, 72, 74, 75 n. 38, 76–8, 95, 97–9, 132, 136–7, 142, 144, 155–67, 170–2, 176, 179–80
  of performance 27–9, 33 n. 19, 73, 81, 83–90, 92–94
  full 35, 37, 39, 47, 68, 81, 83–7, 89–90, 158, 176
Aronowitz, Sara 16

background conditions 77, 80–4, 94–6, 98
Baghramian, Maria 44
Baier, Annette 1, 4, 6–7, 21, 100, 103, 112, 120, 122, 124, 145–7
Baker, Judith 120
basing relation 70–3, 75–6
Ballantyne, Nathan 87
Bauman, Zygmunt 103
Beck, Ulrich 101, 103
Becker, Lawrence C 7, 12, 100, 147
Beddor, Bob 14, 97, 101

Benton, Matthew A 3, 7, 150
Berg, Joyce 2
Bernecker, Sven 31
Bicchieri, Christina 91
Björklund, Fredrik 18
Bodansky, Daniel 176
Bond Jr, Charles F 58
Bondy, Patrick 71–2, 132–4, 136
BonJour, Laurence 8
Booth, Anthony Robert 6
Bovens, Luc 13, 15–7
Bradford, Gwen 31, 60, 136, 140
Bratman, Michael E 123, 167
Broncano-Berrocal, Fernando 156, 167
Buckareff, Andrei 123
Burge, Tyler 138, 175
Burns, Calvin 103

Calhoun, Cheshire 12
Carter, J. Adam 1 n. 4, 9, 14–16, 22–4, 38 n. 6, 47 n. 6, 56 n. 2, 59 nn. 10–1, 62 n. 18, 63 n. 20, 65 n. 22, 68 n. 25, 70 n. 29, 71 n. 30, 72 n. 32, 74 n. 37, 79 n. 2, 82 n. 3, 84 n. 6, 91 n. 25, 117 n. 26, 125 n. 21, 126 n. 22, 136 n. 31, 144 n. 5, 145 n. 7, 146 n. 11, 147 n. 15, 150 n. 19, 151 n. 23, 152 n. 28, 153 n. 29, 155 n. 34, 156 n. 36, 160 n. 43, 164 n. 1, 167 nn. 2–4, 168 nn. 5–6, 169 n. 7, 176 n. 15, 179 n. 23, 180 n. 27
Chalmers, David J 180
Chan, Timothy 73
Chrisman, Matthew 23
Cogley, Zac 145
Cohen, L. Jonathan 123
Coleman, James S 15
Comesaña, Juan 87
Cooper, Mick 182
Cottingham, John 8
credence 121
Crisp, Roger 50
Croce, Michel 44

Index

Dasgupta, Partha 7, 147
decision theory 86, 176
default assumptions 49, 131
DePaulo, Bella M 58
Díaz, Rodrigo 45
distrust
    deliberative 36, 38–9, 41–5, 52–3, 164
    implicit 19, 36, 38–45, 52–3, 164
Domenicucci, Jacopo 46
Dormandy, Katherine 7, 100, 104, 147
Dougherty, Tom 60
Dyche L, Zayas L 182

Elster, Jon 117
Engel, Mylan 87
Enoch, David 50

Fantl, Jeremy 150
Faulkner, Paul 1–2, 4, 120, 131, 144–5
Feldman, Richard 6
Fernández Vargas, Miguel Ángel 23, 56, 117
Fine, Gail 40
Finlay, Stephen 74
Fischer, John Martin 113
forbearance 35–6, 38, 40–5, 157
Frankfurt, Harry G 111–3
Frederiksen, Morten 101
Fricker, Elizabeth 147
Fricker, Miranda 44
Fridland, Ellen 61
Friedman, Jane 40, 48, 51, 169–70
Frost-Arnold, Karen 9, 119–20, 123, 125, 127, 165
Frost, Kim 151

Gambetta, Diego 145
Geach, Peter T 2, 125
Gerson, M. J 182
Gettier cases 27–8, 154, 158–60
Gibbons, John 3
Gilbert, Margaret 167
Glüer, Kathrin 3
gnoseology 50–2, 52, 158
Goldberg, Sanford 9, 20, 130, 175
Gordon, Emma C. 46, 48, 100, 115, 122, 124, 136, 173, 181, 182 n. 30
Graham, Peter J 4, 180
Greco, John 27, 31, 49, 52, 136, 148, 152, 154

Hakli, Raul 167
Hall, Mark A 131
Hansson, Sven Ove 101, 106
Hardin, Russell 1–2, 5–7, 100, 112, 142, 147
Hardwig, John 46
Hawley, Katherine 4, 112, 120, 145–6
Hawthorne, John 131, 150
Heering, David 27, 65
Heil, John 8
Hieronymi, Pamela 1–2, 4–5, 9, 21, 100, 119–23, 145, 147, 165
Hills, Alison 50
Hinchman, Edward 2, 8, 100, 147, 149
Holroyd, Jules 103
Holton, Richard 1, 4, 8, 18, 21, 46, 134–5, 145
Honoré, Anthony M 58
Hope 12–7, 38, 133–4, 147, 166
Horsburgh, H. J. N. 4, 9, 119–20
Hume, David 74, 91

Inquiry 38, 40, 48–51, 85, 91, 97, 101, 164, 168–9

Jarvis, Benjamin 150
Jones, Karen 1, 3–4, 6, 9, 12, 18, 21, 48, 112, 119–20, 126–30, 145–6, 165

Kallestrup, Jesper 150, 152, 156
Kelp, Christoph 2–4, 6, 23, 38, 50 n. 12, 51 n. 16, 56, 58, 91 n. 23, 130 n. 25, 131 n. 27, 145, 146 n. 8, 152
Kenny, Anthony 58, 145
Keren, Arnon 1, 3, 5, 9–10, 120, 124–5, 147
Kirton, Andrew 8, 147
Korcz, Keith Allen 71–2
knowledge
    animal 179–80
    full well 39, 150, 152, 160, 174
    reflective 6, 49
    judgmental 24, 39, 51
Kornblith, Hilary 8, 152
Kramer, Roderick M 114
Kraut, Robert 58
Krishnan, Rekha 101
Kvanvig, Jonathan L 1, 50, 168

Lackey, Jennifer 44, 152, 156
Lagerspetz, Olli 103
Lahno, Bernd 1, 12, 33
Leonard, Nick 169

Lewis, David 151
Littlejohn, Clayton 150, 159, 169
Luper-Foy, Steven 87

Madison, Brent JC 87 n. 20
Marušić, Berislav 18
McGeer, Victoria 12–3, 15–7, 120
McGrath, Matthew 150
McGrath, Sarah 50
McHugh, Conor 2–3, 6, 125
McLeod, Carolyn 2, 6–7, 100, 120, 143, 147
McMyler, Benjamin 1, 4–5, 21, 100, 120 n. 8, 147
Mele, Alfred R 18, 58 n. 7, 113
Millar, Alan 65
Miracchi Titus, Lisa 70, 72, 151–3, 180–1
Möllering, Guido 12
monitoring 6–7, 10, 16, 54, 60, 87–90, 94, 97, 99, 100, 102, 104–6, 108–11, 112–8, 122, 165
Moran, Anthony 101
Mumford, Stephen 144
Munroe, Wade 45

Negligence 54, 79, 81–4, 89–90, 93, 98–9, 109, 170
Neta, Ram 72
Nguyen, C. Thi 150
Nickel, Philip J 7, 48, 100, 147 n. 16
Niker, Fay 53
normativity
  evaluative 1–4, 6–7, 10–1, 17, 20–5, 27–32, 34–7, 41–2, 47, 50, 58, 84, 125, 127, 142–4, 146–8, 153–8, 161, 163, 166, 169
  performance 1, 22–37, 42, 45–7, 50, 52, 56–8, 61–3, 82, 84–5, 87, 89–93, 96–7, 100, 108, 117–8, 131–2, 143–4, 146–7, 148–50, 153–6, 158–60, 163, 166–8, 170, 174–5, 180
  prescriptive 3, 6–7, 84, 91, 125, 169
  telic 23, 26, 27–30, 36, 45–6, 50–1, 54, 76, 119, 132, 164, 167–70, 179

Ólafsson, Ísak Andri 168 n. 5
O'Neil, Collin 8
O'Neil, Onora 147
O'Sullivan, Angela 60

Papineau, David 3
Pavese, Carlotta 13, 61

Pettit, Philip 8, 100, 147
pistology 51–4, 158, 168
Plato 52, 101
Platts, Mark 151
Potter, Nancy Nyquist 8, 143, 146–7
Price, Huw 151
Pritchard, Duncan 27, 31, 87, 88, 107, 136, 140, 148, 150, 152, 154, 159

Railton, Peter 9
Ravizza, Mark 113
Rawls, John 91
Raz, Joseph 73
Rorty, Amélie Oksenberg 12
Rosati, Connie S. 18

Sandin, Per 86
Saul, Jennifer 45, 103
Schechter, Joshua 38
Schroeder, Mark 6, 74
Schwitzgebel, Eric 145
Scott-Kakures, Dion 8
Shade, Patrick 13
Shafer-Landau, Russ 74
Shah, Nishi 3, 69, 73 n. 33
Shepherd, Joshua 14
Silva, Paul 71
Simion, Mona 2–3, 6–7, 20, 24, 58, 84, 125, 130–1, 133–7, 152, 169
Simpson, Thomas 1
Sjöberg, Lennart 101, 103
Slovic, Paul 101, 103
Smith, Michael 151
Snyder, C. Rick 17
Solomon, Robert C 131
Sosa, Ernest 8–9, 23–5, 27, 29–31, 37–40, 46–7, 50–1, 54, 56–7, 61, 63, 66–9, 76–85, 87, 89, 93–6, 98, 117, 136, 149–50, 152, 154–5, 160, 164–5, 168, 179, 180
SSS competence profile 56, 76
Steglich-Petersen, Asbjørn 73
Sullivan, Laura 53
Sunstein, Cass 177
suspension (*see* forbearance)
Sutton, Jonathan 7

Thaler, Richard H 177
Tollefsen, Deborah 167
Townsend, Leo 6–7, 100, 122

Treanor, Nick 50
trust
　deliberative 36, 38–9, 41–9, 51–3, 55–9, 61–78, 83, 99, 104, 150, 164, 167, 170–1
　implicit 36–49, 51–3, 57, 59–60, 62–3, 65, 68, 74, 103–4, 107, 123, 125, 131, 137, 145, 147, 150, 163–4, 170, 173, 182
　therapeutic 5, 8–9, 14, 119–41, 165, 182
trustworthiness 5–6, 9, 53, 59, 64, 119, 131, 142–62, 165–6, 171, 175, 176–9, 181–2
Tsai, George 53
Tuomela, Raimo 167
Turri, John 9, 56, 71, 84, 87, 91, 136 n. 31, 148

Unger, Peter 97
Unkelbach, Christian 103

Velleman, David 3, 73, 151
Verkuyl, Henk J. 146

virtue epistemology 23–4, 37–8, 40, 49–50, 63–4, 74, 76, 84, 98, 148, 154, 164, 167–9, 175
Vitz, Rico 8
Vrij, Aldert 58

Wanderer, Jeremy 6–7, 100, 122
Wedgwood, Ralph 73
Whipple, Chris 86
Whiting, Daniel 3, 73
Wikforss. Åsa 3, 73
Williams, Bernard 8, 74, 143
Williamson, Timothy 7, 61, 84, 91, 131, 150–3, 159–60
Wolff, Kurt H 101
Wong, David B. 74
Wright, Stephen 143

Zagzebski, Linda T 10, 138, 148, 152, 154 n. 34